Personality Psychology

Insights, Issues, Case Histories and Applications

Joan B. Cannon

CENGAGE
Learning™

Australia • Brazil • Japan • Korea • Mexico • Singapore • Spain • United Kingdom • United States

CENGAGE
Learning™

Personality Psychology: Insights, Issues, Case Histories and Applications

Written and Edited by
Joan B. Cannon
Department of Psychology
University of Massachusetts-Lowell

Executive Editors:
Michele Baird

Maureen Staudt

Michael Stranz

Project Development Manager:
Linda deStefano

Senior Marketing Coordinators:
Sara Mercurio

Lindsay Shapiro

Production/Manufacturing Manager:
Donna M. Brown

PreMedia Services Supervisor:
Rebecca A. Walker

Rights & Permissions Specialist:
Kalina Hintz

Cover Image:
Getty Images*

© 2004 Cengage Learning

For product information and technology assistance, contact us at
Cengage Learning Customer & Sales Support, 1-800-354-9706

For permission to use material from this text or product,
submit all requests online at **cengage.com/permissions**
Further permissions questions can be emailed to
permissionrequest@cengage.com

ISBN-13: 978-0-759-33868-5

ISBN-10: 0-759-33868-X

Cengage Learning
5191 Natorp Boulevard
Mason, Ohio 45040
USA

Cengage Learning is a leading provider of customized learning solutions with office locations around the globe, including Singapore, the United Kingdom, Australia, Mexico, Brazil, and Japan. Locate your local office at:
international.cengage.com/region

Cengage Learning products are represented in Canada by Nelson Education, Ltd.

For your lifelong learning solutions, visit **custom.cengage.com**

Visit our corporate website at **cengage.com**

Printed in the United States of America

CREDITS

Chapter 1. 9: Freud, Sigmund, (1969). The Psychical Apparatus. An Outline of Psycholanalysis, 13-21. London: Hogarth Press.

Chapter 2. 13: Freud, Anna and Dorothy Burlingham. (1943). Survey of Psychological Reactions. War and Children, 1-8. Childreach.

Chapter 3. 21: Erikson, Erik. (1950). Eight Stages of Man. Childhood and Society, 219-234. New York: WW Norton & Co.

Chapter 4. 35: Cannon, Joan B. (1994). Psychoanalytic Psychology: An Overview. Survey of Social Psychology, 1905-1912. New York: Harcourt Brace.

Chapter 5. 43: Jung, Carl. (1971). Psychological Types. Psychological Types: A Revision of R.F.C. Hull of the Translation of H.G. Baynes, 510-523. Princeton, NJ: Princeton University Press.

Chapter 6. 49: Adler, Alfred. (1964). The Psychological Approach to the Investigation of the Style of Like. Social Interest: A Challenge to Mankind, 32-41. New York: Capricorn Books.

Chapter 7. 55: Sullivan, Harry S. (1953). Beginnings of the Self System. Interpersonal Theory of Psychiatry, 158-171. New York: WW Norton & Company, Inc.

Chapter 8. 67: Allport, Gordon. (1931). What is a Trait of Personality? Journal of Abnormal and Social Psychology, 25, 368-372. American Psychology Association (APA)

Chapter 9. 75: Maslow, Abraham. (1969). Existential Psychology – What's In it for Us? Existential Philosophy, 49-57. New York: McGraw Hill

Chapter 10. 81: Rogers, Carl and B.F. Skinner. (1956) Some Issues Concerning the Control of Human Behavior: A Symposium. Science, 124, 1057-1064. American Assoc. for the Advancement of Science.

Chapter 11. 91: Watson, John B. (1913). Psycholgoy As the Behaviorist Views It. Psychological Review, 20, 158-177, Public Domain

Chapter 12. 97: Skinner, B.F. (1987) Whatever Happened to Psychology as the Science of Behavior? American Psychologist, 42, 784-786, American Psychological Assoc.

Chapter 13. 105: Bandura, Albert, (1978). The Self System in Reciprocal Determinism. American Psychologist, 33, 344-458. American Psychology Association.

Chapter 14. 135: Freeman, Lucy. (1972). The Case of Anna O. The Story of Anna O., 187-202. New York: Walker and Company.

Chapter 15. 141: Fine, Reuben. (1973). Famous Freudian Case Histories. The Development of Freud's Thought, 117-141. New York: J. Aronson.

Chapter 16. 159: Gardiner, Muriel (Ed.) (1971). My Recollections of Sigmund Freud. The Wolf Man by the Wolf Man: The Double Story of Freud's Most Famous Case, 135-152. New York: Basic Books, Inc.

Chapter 17. 173: Jung, Carl. (1973) The Anxious Young Woman and the Retired Business Man. In Greenwalkd, Harold (ed.) Great Cases in Psychoanalysis, 155-174. New York: J. Aronson

Chapter 18. 187: Adler, Alfred, (1973). The Drive of Superiority. In Greenwald, Harold (Ed.), Great Cases in Psychoanalysis, 175-186. New York: J. Aronson

Chapter 19. 195: Sullivan, Harry Stack. (1959). The Inefficient. In Greenwald, Harodl (Ed.) Great Cases in Psychoanalysis, 201-208. New York: J. Aronson

Chapter 20. 203: Allport, Gordon. (2003) Letters from Jenny. In Hergenhahn, B.R. and M.H. Olson. (2003). An Introduction to Theories of Personality (6th e). Upper Saddle River, New Jersey: Prentice Hall/Pearson Education 218-220.

Chapter 21. 207: Murray, Henry. (1938) Explorations in Personality. Exploration in Personality. 531-545.

Chapter 22. 217: Rogers, Carl. (1959) The Angry Adolescent. In Greenwald, Harold (Ed.) Great Cases in Psychoanalysis, 209-216. New York: J. Aronson

Chapter 23. 223: Maslow, Abraham. (1970). Self-Actualizing People: A Study of Psychological Health. Motivation and Personality, 125-146. Upper Saddle River Pearson.

Chapter 24. 235: Watson, John B. and Rosalie Rayner. (1920) Conditioned Emotional Responses. Journal of Experimental Psychology, 3, 1-14 Public Domain

Chapter 25. 241: Skinner, B.F. (1953) Shaping and Maintain Operant Behavior. Science and Human Behavior, 91-93. Free Press/Simon & Schuster.

Chapter 26. 249: Bandura, A. Ross, D. and S. Ross. (1963) Initation of Filmed-Mediated Aggressice Models. Journal of Abnormal and Social Psyhcology, 66, 3-11 American Psychological Assoc.

Chapter 27. 269: Potkay, C.R. and Allen, B. P. (1986) A Personal Personality Theory. Personality Theory, Research, and Application, 1-4. Brooks/Cole

Chapter 28. 277: Bolt, M. (1993). Self Ratings Inventory. Instructor’s Manual to Myers’ (1993) Social Psychology (4th ed), p. 97. New York: McGraw Hill.

Chapter 29. 281: Miserandino, Mindy (1994). Beliefs about Freudian Principles. Teaching of Psychology, 21, (2), 93-95. Lawrence Erlbaum and Assoc.

Chapter 30. 285: Davidson, W. (1968). Measurement of Anal Characters. Teaching in Psychology, 14, (2), 101-103, Lawrence Erlbaum and Assoc.

Chapter 31. 289: Ochse, R. and Plug C. (1986). A Sense of Personal identity. Journal of Personality and Social Psychology, 50, 1240-1252. American Psychological Assoc.

Chapter 32. 295: Merrens, Matthew and Brannigan, Gary. (1992) early Recollections. Teaching of Psychology, 19, 40-42, Lawrence Erlbaum and Assoc

Chapter 33. 301: Dolnick, E. (1995). Health, July/August, Hotheads and Heart Attacks. Pp. 58-64 **301:** Dolnick, E. (1995). Hostility. Health, July/August, 58-64, CE Merrill Publishing Company

Chapter 34. 305: Weiner, B. (1992) Evolutionary Perspectives Questionnaire. Human Motivation: Metaphors, Theories and Research. Weiner, B. 5-5, Sage Publications

Chapter 35. 311: Polyson, J. (1985). Peak Experience Exercise. Teaching of Psychology, 12, 211-213. Lawrence Erlbaum

Chapter 37. 321: Merrens, M. Brannigan, G. (1998). Observing and Recording a Personality Behavior. Experiences in Personality, 157-160. New York: John Wiley and Sons

Chapter 38. 327: Rathus,S.D. (1973). A 30-Item Schedule for Assessing Assertive Behavior. Behavior Therapy, 4, 399-400, Association for the Advancement of Behavior Therapy

Chapter 39. 333: Scheier, M. and Carver, C. (1985). Life Orientation Test. Health Pscyhology, 4, 219-220. American Psychological Association

Section Opener 21. 207: Picture#8212;From Henry A. Murray, Thematic Apperception Test. Cambridge Univeristy Press. Copyright 1943 by the President of Fellows of Harvard by Henry A. Murray

 *Dedication*

*No person is ever entirely responsible for her
own creative works.*

**To my loving husband, parents and family
Catherine, Brian, Stas, and Matthew
Whose unique and wonderful personalities inspire me, and
Without whom the creation of this work would not have been realized.**

About the Author

Joan B. Cannon is Associate Professor of Psychology at the University of Massachusetts Lowell. She also serves as faculty advisor to *Psi Chi*, the National Honor Society in Psychology. Her research focuses on organizational change, role conflict, dual-career families, and personality. She is the author of dozens of articles, book chapters, and book, *Resources for Affirmative Action*, and currently is writing a book entitled *Three Force Movements in Personality Psychology*. Dr. Cannon is a recipient of the 1996 Haskell Award for Distinguished Teaching and 2003 University of Massachusetts Lowell Department of Psychology Distinguished Teaching Award. In her free time, she likes to read, write, and travel with her family. You may send comments about this book to her via e-mail at Joan_Cannon@uml.edu.

Contents

PART TWO   Case Histories, Research Studies, and Psychotherapies

PART THREE   Applications and Exercises in Personality

Preface

*P*ersonality Psychology: *Insights, Issues, Case Histories and Applications* is

based on my belief that a collection of original writings of the great masters in

personality and personality exercises developed by contemporary psychologists is an

extremely valuable tool for promoting a better understanding of the discipline.

After teaching personality psychology for three decades at the

undergraduate level, I have discovered that students come to a greater appreciation

of classical theories by examining the original manuscripts and case histories of

prominent theorists and a better integration of theory and practice by personally

engaging in an evaluative process of assessing aspects of their unique selves.

Clearly, this dual perspective enables students to further develop meaningful

insights into the field and bridge the gap between theory, research, and application.

This first edition of *Personality Psychology* is designed to expose students to

several key areas of personality, namely, theory, assessment, research, method of

personality change, and personal application. *Part One* provides a breadth of

exposure to classical articles in the field which illustrate the theoretical foundations

of personality from a psychoanalytic, neo-analytic, dispositional, humanistic, and

behavioral perspective. *Part Two* further examines these five major schools of

thought by presenting several famous case histories, relevant research studies, and

articles pertaining to various psychotherapies. These articles provide excellent insights into the nature of assessment, research, and methods of personality change. Finally, *Part Three* invites students to critically examine and assess some aspects of their own personalities from each of these viewpoints. These practical exercises in personality not only enable students to acquire first-hand personal insights as investigators, subjects, observers, and writers but, more importantly, familiarize themselves with the psychometric tools and techniques employed by personality psychologists. The selection of articles and exercises is based upon an extensive review of the literature, presentation of these original works and personality exercises in formal class settings, and student responses and evaluations of their relevance to the course.

Each part of this book begins with an introduction to the main topic under consideration and features distinct chapters reflecting the various schools of thought of personality. "Critical Thinking Questions" and "Suggested Readings" are included at the end of each section. These questions require students to critically evaluate issues and concerns exposed in the article itself, to speculate about the implications and applications of the findings, or, in some instances, to generate new ideas for future research. Finally, a list of suggested readings is included for students who wish to obtain more information on a particular topic and further explore the various aspects of personality.

Acknowledgments

I am especially indebted to Carolyn Siccama, Distance Learning Faculty Coordinator, University of Massachusetts Lowell, for inspiring me to create and develop this book of readings. It is because of her very special and influential personality that I endeavored to engage in this project at all. I would also like to thank Julie Howell, Bryant Chrzan, Donna Baum, Lori Peetz-Gud and their staff at Thomson Publishing for their help and guidance with the format of this book. Special thanks of appreciation are extended to Catherine Cannon-Francis and Stas Cannon for their critical review and assessment of the selections and application exercises contained in this book. Finally, it is important to acknowledge the many contributions of my family and undergraduate students in personality psychology who, through their unique personalities, provided invaluable insights and responses concerning the organization and content of this work.

Joan Bartczak Cannon

Part One

Theoretical Foundations of Personality: Insights and Issues

Part One
Theoretical Foundations of Personality: Insights and Issues

An introduction to a course such as personality psychology often includes a comprehensive consideration of the theoretical foundations and conceptualizations of its founders. Theory plays a very significant role in our understanding of the human personality and, as you will see, many unique and distinct ones exist in the field. In the following chapters, you will be presented with the original writings of several prominent theorists and exposed to their thoughts about personality formation. These perspectives cover **five major schools of thought**, namely, the **psychoanalytic model, neo-analytic model, dispositional model, humanistic model,** and **behavioral model.**

Selections in **Chapter One** reflect the psychoanalytic perspective of Sigmund Freud, Anna Freud, and Erik Erikson. In *An Outline of Psychoanalysis*, Sigmund Freud presents a concise summary of his theory of psychoanalysis and identifies three key components of personality structure: id, ego, and superego. Anna Freud and Dorothy Burlingham's treatise of *War and Children* illustrates the ravages of combat and its impact upon the lives and personalities of children. Here, they poignantly describe the

3

psychological reactions of children to war experiences, focusing upon their development of anxiety. Erik Erikson's *Eight Stages of Man* exemplifies his psychosocial perspective of human development and the unfolding of personality over the entire life span as an individual attempts to resolve eight major crises.

Chapter Two contains articles written by several illustrious revisionist theorists, who disassociated themselves from orthodox psychoanalysis and generated their own unique theories about personality. The section begins with the author's article, *Psychoanalytic Psychology*, which compares and contrasts the theory of Freud to those of several neo-analytic schools: Jung's Analytic Psychology, Adler's Individual Psychology, and Horney and Sullivan's Dynamic Cultural Schools of Psychoanalysis. In his manuscript, *Psychological Types,* Carl Jung describes his practical ideas about introversion-extroversion and four related styles of thinking. Alfred Adler's theoretical emphasis upon the relevance of an individual's style of life is shown in his article, *The Psychological Approach to the Investigation of the Style of Life.* Karen Horney's treatise on *The Basic Structure of Neurosis* considers the essential ingredients of anxiety and the protective measures an individual develops and uses to overcome it. Finally, Harry Stack Sullivan's *Beginnings of the Self System* emphasizes the significance of early relationships, especially between the mother and infant, and the development of good-me, bad-me, and not-me self personifications. Overall, each of these manuscripts further reveals the emergence of new ideas and theoretical orientations about human personality in the history of psychology.

The dispositional perspectives presented in **Chapter Three** demonstrate a major transition from a clinical setting to an academic or research one. Of significance is the fact that these personality theorists have elected to spend their entire professional careers focusing upon specific aspects of personality development. Gordon Allport's selection, *What is a Trait of Personality,* clearly demonstrates that he was most interested in a person's unique development of a trait structure. He elaborates on several characteristics of the trait in an effort to illustrate how it not only might be a source of personality but, more importantly, a cause of behavior.

Chapter Four presents a unique blend of theoretical perspectives that view personality from the individual's internal frame of reference. These theorists claim that "Beauty is in the eye of the beholder!" and it is an individual's perceptions, attitudes, and subjective experiences that are far more important than what is visible to the human eye. Carl Rogers' *Observations on the Organization of Personality* illustrates the derivation of his theoretical insights on personality emerging from the empathetic relationships established in the psychotherapeutic context. In *Existential Psychology-What's in it for Us,* Abraham Maslow traces the roots of humanism to European existential philosophy and shows how it applies to human personality. Carl Rogers and B. F. Skinner debate each other in *Some Issues Concerning the Control of Human Behavior: A Symposium.* Here, we witness two giants in their respective fields, humanism and behaviorism, confront each other on the topic of the prediction and control of human behavior.

Our final section, **Chapter Five**, contains key articles illustrating the theoretical tenets of behaviorism. Based upon a single set of learning principles, these prominent psychologists present their views which emphasize the role of respondent learning, instrumental learning, and observational learning in the formation of personality. In *Psychology as the Behaviorist Views It*, John B. Watson presents his case for an objective study of animal and human behavior. B. F. Skinner's article, ***Whatever Happened to Psychology as the Science of Behavior,*** identifies three villains that negated behaviorism from becoming a science; these are humanism, psychotherapy, and cognitive psychology. Finally, Albert Bandura's manuscript, ***The Self System in Reciprocal Determinism***, effectively shows how the establishment of an individual's self system is contingent upon the interrelationship between the person, his behavior, and the environment.

Chapter One
Psychoanalytic Perspectives

"The core of our being...is formed by the obscure id, which has no direct communication with the external world and is accessible even to our own knowledge through the medium of another agency...The ego, driven by the id, confined by the super-ego, repulsed by reality, struggles to master its economic task of bringing about harmony among the forces and influences working in and upon it; and we can understand how it is that so often we cannot suppress a cry: 'Life is not easy!'"

Sigmund Freud

The Psychical Apparatus
Sigmund Freud

In your exploration of the world of psychology, you will discover many different definitions of the term, "personality." Some psychologists define it as the totality of your identity and behavior; in other words, it is the summation of who you are and what you do. As you will see, there are also several different approaches to investigating the complex field of personality. Some prominent psychologists examine intrapsychic events and covert behavior, while others emphasize overt behavior and environmental influences. It is your task to decide which, if any, theoretical model supplies the most comprehensive definition of all. As part of your inquiry, you should also ask yourself which definition and perspective enables you to better describe, understand, predict and control human behavior.

Sigmund Freud's (1856-1939) psychoanalytic theory of personality represents one of the first attempts to describe the hidden structures of personality. An Austrian neurologist, he received his M.D. in 1881 from the University of Vienna. Through his medical practice, he became intrigued with aberrations of the mind and began to study his patients' disorders by employing his theory and therapy of psychoanalysis. The evolution of his ideas and development of his model spanned a lifetime. Essentially, Freud discovered that an individual's past experiences and unconscious motivations were crucial determinants of his personality. He likened personality to an iceberg, with only the tip surfacing the water and representing conscious behavior. To him, the most significant piece of the iceberg was that which was submerged---the unconscious. It represented the greatest region of the mind, which was the storehouse of hidden thoughts, fantasies, dreams, wish-fulfillments and early experiences. He visualized personality as the consequence of the interaction of the three personality structures, namely, the id, ego, and superego.

This selection, "The Psychical Apparatus," is part of Freud's manuscript, An Outline of Psycho-Analysis. Originally published in 1940, here he describes mental life, characteristics of personality and briefly defines the id, ego, and superego as key components of personality. In it, Freud states that we do not really know what the apparatus of personality is, but can make a prediction through our observations of people. What do you think?

*   *   *

* Freud, Sigmund. (1969). The Psychical Apparatus. *An Outline of Psychoanalysis,* 13-21. London: Hogarth Press. Reprinted by permission.

Psycho-analysis makes a basic assumption, the discussion of which is reserved to philosophical thought but the justification for which lies in the results. We know only two kinds of things about what we call our psyche (or mental life), firstly, its bodily organ and scene of action, the brain (or nervous system) and, on the other hand, our acts of consciousness, which are immediate data and cannot be further explained by any sort of description. Everything that lies between is unknown to us, and the data do not include any direct relation between these two terminal points of our knowledge. If it existed, it would at the most afford an exact localization of the processes of consciousness and would give us no help towards understanding them.

Our two hypotheses start out from these ends or beginnings of our knowledge. The first is concerned with localization. We assume that mental life is the function of an apparatus to which we ascribe the characteristics of being extended in space and of being made up of several portions---which we imagine, that is, as resembling a telescope or microscope or something of the kind. Notwithstanding some earlier attempts in the same direction, the consistent working-out of a conception such as this is a scientific novelty.

We have arrived at our knowledge of this psychical apparatus by studying the individual development of human beings. To the oldest of these psychical provinces or agencies we give the name of *id*. It contains everything that is inherited, that is present at birth, that is laid down in the constitution---above all, therefore, the instincts, which originate from the somatic organization and which find a first psychical expression here (in the id) in forms unknown to us.

Under the influence of the real external world around us, one portion of the id has undergone a special development. From what was originally a cortical layer, equipped with the organs for receiving stimuli and with arrangements for acting as a protective shield against stimuli, a special organization has arisen which henceforward acts as an intermediary between the id and the external world. To this region of our mind we have given the name of *ego*.

Here are the principal characteristics of the ego. In consequence of the pre-established connection between sense perception and muscular action, the ego has voluntary movement at its command. It has the task of self-preservation. As regards *external* events, it performs that task by becoming aware of stimuli, by storing up experiences about them (in the memory), by avoiding excessively strong stimuli (through flight), by dealing with moderate stimuli (through adaptation) and finally by learning to bring about expedient changes in the external world to its own advantage (through activity). As regards *internal* events, in relation to the id, it performs the task by gaining control over the demands of the instincts, by deciding whether they are to be allowed satisfaction, by postponing that satisfaction to times and circumstances favourable in the external world or by suppressing their excitations entirely. It is guided in its activity by consideration of the tensions produced by stimuli, whether these tensions are present in it or introduced into it. The raising of these tensions is in general felt as *unpleasure* and their lowering as *pleasure*. It is probably, however, that what is felt as pleasure or unpleasure is not the absolute height of this tension but something in the rhythm of the changes in them. The ego strives after pleasure and seeks to avoid unpleasure. An increase in unpleasure that is expected and foreseen is met by a *signal of anxiety*; the occasion of such an increase, whether it threatens from without or within, is known as a *danger*. From time to time the ego gives up its connection with the external world and withdraws into the state of sleep, in which it makes far-reaching changes in its organization. It is to be inferred from the state of sleep that this organization consists in a particular distribution of mental energy.

The long period of childhood, during which the growing human being lives in dependence on his parents, leaves behind it as a precipitate the formation in his ego of a special agency in which this parental influence is prolonged. It has received the name of *super-ego*. In so far as this super-ego is differentiated from the ego or is opposed to it, it constitutes a third power which the ego must take into account.

An action by the ego is as it should be if it satisfies simultaneously the demands of the id, of the super-ego and of reality---that is to say, if it is able to reconcile their demands with one another. The details of the relation between the ego and the super-ego become completely intelligible when they are traced back to the child's attitude to its parents. This parental influence of course includes in its operation not only the personalities of the actual parents but also the family, racial and national traditions handed on through them, as well as the demands of the immediate *social milieu* which they represent. In the same way, the super-ego, in the course of an individual's development, receives contributions from later successors and substitutes of his parents, such as teachers and models in public life of admired social ideals. It will be observed that, for all their fundamental difference, the id and the super-ego have one thing in common: they both represent the influences of the past---the id, the influence of heredity, the super-ego the influence, essentially, of what is take over from other people---whereas the ego is principally determined by the individual's own experience, that is, by accidental and contemporary events.

This general schematic picture of a psychical apparatus may be supposed to apply as well to the higher animals which resemble man mentally. A super-ego must be presumed to be present wherever, as is the case with man, there is a long period of dependence in childhood. A distinction between ego and id is an unavoidable assumption. Animal psychology has not yet taken in hand the interesting problem which is here presented.

Survey of Psychological Reactions[*]
Anna Freud and Dorothy Burlingham

The effects of war on human beings, particularly children, are devastating. The historical literature on World War II, Korean War, Gulf War and recent War on Iraq bears testimony to the development of psychological conflict and post-traumatic syndrome not only in those who militarily participate in war, but also in those who, directly or indirectly, experience it.. During World War II, European children were unusually traumatized partly because they experienced nightly air raids. Between the years of 1942 to 1945, psychoanalysts Anna Freud and Dorothy T. Burlingham dedicated themselves to working with children at the Hampstead War Nursery in London. This residential center for 80 children was established upon the belief that young children would suffer serious long-range consequences if essential human needs went unmet. Hence, a program was created to provide food, medical care, nurturance, and educational opportunities.

Anna Freud (1895-1982), the daughter of psychoanalyst Sigmund Freud, became a pioneer in the field of child analysis. Of all of Freud's six children, she was the only one to follow in his footsteps and apply his work to the psychological development of young children. During her lifetime, she wrote, lectured, and worked closely with the Foster Parents Plan for War Children, Inc. Her "Kinderseminar" series was a significant influence on psychoanalyst Erik Erikson, whom she persuaded to join the Freudian ranks. She is most famous for her book, Ego Mechanisms of Defense. Her research at the nursery, later known as the Hampstead Child Therapy Clinic, with Burlingham, resulted in the publication of three books.

The significance of this selection, War and Children (Medical War Books, 1943), rests in the fact that it is the first psychological study to examine and discuss the effects of war on children. Not only does it provide keen insights on the effects of war but, more importantly, implications for other contemporary contexts. Today, many individuals, including young children, live in a constant state of fear and threat given the Terror Attack of September 11th. Others experience life in war-like communities all over the world where violence and the sound of some enemy permeates the streets. Many of these fears and anxieties are not very different from those observed by Freud and Burlingham many years ago.

*   *   *

[*] **Freud, Anna and Dorothy Burlingham. (1943). Survey of Psychological Reactions.** *War and Children, 1-8.* **Childreach. Reprinted by permission.**

All our bigger children have had their fair share of war experiences. All of them have witnessed the air raids either in London or in the provinces. A large percentage of them have seen their houses destroyed or damaged. All of them have seen their family life dissolved, whether by separation from or by death of the father. All of them are separated from their mothers and have entered community life at an age which is not usually considered ripe for it. The questions arise which part these experiences play in the psychological life of the individual child, how far the child acquires understanding of what is going on around it, how it reacts emotionally, how far its anxiety is aroused, and what normal or abnormal outlets it will find to deal with these experiences which are thrust on it.

It can be safely said that all the children who were over two years at the time of the London *"blitz"* have acquired knowledge of the significance of air raids. They all recognize the noise of flying aeroplanes; they distinguish vaguely between the sounds of falling bombs and anti-aircraft guns. They realize that the house will fall down when bombed and that people are often killed or get hurt in falling houses. They know that fires can be started by incendiaries and that roads are often blocked as a result of bombing. They fully understand the significance of taking shelter. Some children who have lived in deep shelters will even judge the safety of a shelter according to its depth under the earth. The necessity to make them familiar with their gas masks may give them some ideas about a gas attack, though we have never met a child for whom this particular danger had any real meaning.

The children seem to have no difficulty in understanding what it means when their fathers join the Forces. We even overhear talk among the children where they compare their fathers' military ranks and duties. A child, for instance, with its father in the navy or air force, will be offended if somebody by mistake refers to the father as being "in the army." As far as the reasoning processes of the child are concerned, the absence of their father seems to be accounted for in this manner.

Children are similarly ready to take in knowledge about the various occupations of their mothers, though the constant change of occupation makes this slightly more difficult. Mothers of three-year-olds will change backwards and forwards between the occupations of railway porter, factory worker, bus conductor, milk cart drivers, etc. They will visit their children in their varying uniforms and will proudly tell them about their new war work until the children are completely confused. Though the children seem proud of their fathers' uniforms, they often seem to resent and feel very much estranged when their mothers appear in such unexpected guises.

It is still more difficult for all children to get any understanding of the reason why they are being evacuated and cannot stay in the place where their mothers are. In the case of our children, as in the case of many others, this is further aggravated by the fact that they actually did live in London with their mothers during the worst dangers and were sent to the country afterwards when London seemed quite peaceful. They reason with some justification that they can live wherever their mothers do and that if "home" is as much in danger as all that, their mothers should not be there either. This, of course, concerns the bigger children of five or more.

The understanding of catastrophes, like the death of father, has little to do with reasoning. In these cases children meet the usual psychological difficulties of grasping the significance of death at such an early age. Their attitude to the happening is completely a matter of emotion.

We may, of course, be often wrong in assuming that children "understand" the happenings around them. In talking, they only use the proper words for them but without the meaning attached. Words like "army," "navy," "air force," may mean to them strange countries to which their fathers have gone. America, for the children, the place where all the good things, especially the parcels come from, was discovered the other day to mean to one child at least "a merry car." The word "bombing" is often used indiscriminately for all manners of destruction of unwanted objects. "London" is the word used for the children's former homes, irrespective of the fact whether the child now lives in Essex or still in Hampstead.

Several of our children in Wedderburn Road used to say in talking: "When I was still in London..."

And one boy of four once explained in a London shop, to the shop assistant's great astonishment: "I used to live in London, but London is all bombed and gone, and all the houses have fallen down."

He was unable to realize the fact that the comparatively unbombed street in which he now lived with us was still the same city. "Home" is the place to which all children are determined to return, irrespective of the fact that in most cases they are aware of its destruction. "War," above everything else, signifies the period of time for which children have to be separated from their parents.

A striking example of such "misunderstanding" was Pamela, a girl of four and a half years, who as we thought, had perfectly grasped the meaning of evacuation. She was a thrice bombed child, lived in Wedderburn Road and like all others wanted for the opening of our country house. We had carefully explained to all the children that they were being transferred to the country and the reason for it.

But when at last, after weeks of expectation---because the lease of the country house did not materialize---she stood in our front hall, all dressed and ready, waiting for the American ambulance car to take her out, she exclaimed joyfully, "The war is over and we are going to the country. It has lasted a long time!"

The longing for the Country House, which had been the centre of interest for the Nursery children for some weeks, had suddenly got confused in her mind with the more general longing for the end of the war, which would as all the children firmly believed, take them all back to their former homes and to their parents.

Reaction To Destruction

In this war, more than in former ones, children are frequently to be found directly on the scenes of battle. Though, here in England, they are spared the actual horror of seeing people fight around them, they are not spared sights of destruction, death, and injury from air raids. Even when removed from the places of the worst danger there is no certainty, as some of our cases show, that they will not meet new bombing incidents at places to which they were sent for safety. General sympathy has been aroused by the idea that little children, all innocently, should thus come into close contact with the horrors of the war. It is this situation which led many people to expect that children would receive traumatic shocks from air raids and would develop abnormal reactions very similar to the traumatic or war neuroses of soldiers in the last war.

We can only describe our observation on the basis of our own case material, which excludes children who have received severe bodily injuries in air raids though, as mentioned before, it does not exclude children who have been bombed repeatedly and partly buried in debris. So far as we can notice, there were no signs of traumatic shock to be observed in these children. If these bombing incidents occur when small children are in the care either of their own mothers or a familiar mother substitute, they do not seem to be particularly affected by them. Their experience remains an accident, in line with other accidents of childhood. This observation is borne out by the reports of nurses or social workers in London County Council Rest Centres where children used to arrive, usually in the middle of the night, straight from their bombed houses. They also found that children who arrived together with their own families showed little excitement and no undue disturbance. They slept and ate normally and played with whatever toys they had rescued or which might be provided. It is a widely different matter when children, during an experience of this kind, are separated from or even lose their parents.

It is a common misunderstanding of the child's nature which leads people to suppose that children will be saddened by the sight of destruction and aggression. Children between the ages of one and two years, when put together in a play-pen will bite each other, pull each other's hair and steal each other's toys without regard for the other child's unhappiness. They are passing through a stage of development where destruction and aggression play one of the leading parts. If we observe young children at play, we notice that they will destroy their toys, pull off the arm and legs of their dolls or soldiers, puncture their balls, smash whatever is breakable, and will only mind the result because complete destruction of the toy blocks further play. The more their strength and independence are growing the more they will have to be watched so as not to create too much damage, not to hurt each other or those weaker than themselves. We often say, half jokingly, that there is continual war raging in a nursery. We mean by this, that at this time of life destructive and aggressive impulses are still at work in children in a manner in which they only recur in grown-up life when they are let loose for the purpose of war.

It is one of the recognized arms of education to deal with the aggressiveness of the child's nature, i.e., in the course of the first four or five years to change the child's own attitude towards these impulses in himself. The wish to hurt people and later, the wish to destroy objects undergo all sorts of changes. They are usually first restricted, then suppressed by commands and prohibitions; a little later they are repressed, which means that they disappear from the child's consciousness. The child does not dare any more to have knowledge of these wishes. There is always the danger that they might return from the unconscious, therefore, all sorts of protections are built up against them---the cruel child develops pity, the destructive child will become hesitant and over careful. If education is handled intelligently the main part of these aggressive impulses will be directed away from their primitive aim of doing harm to somebody or something, and will be used to fight the difficulties of the outer world---to accomplish tasks of all kinds, to measure one's strength in competition and to use it generally to "do good" instead of "being bad" as the original impulse demanded.

In light of these considerations, it is easier to determine what the present war conditions, with their incidents of wholesale destruction may do to a child. Instead of turning away from them instinctive horror, as people seem to expect, the child may turn towards them with primitive excitement. The real danger is not that the child, caught up all innocently in the whirlpool of the war, will be shocked into illness. The danger lies in the fact that the destruction raging in the outer world may meet the very real aggressiveness which rages in the inside of the child. At the age when education should start to deal with these impulses confirmation should not be given from the outside world that the same impulses are uppermost in other people. Children will play joyfully on bombed sites and around bomb centers, they will play with blasted bits of furniture and throw bricks from crumbled walls at each other. But it becomes impossible to educate them towards a repression of, a reaction against destruction while they are doing so. After their first years of life they fight against their own wishes to do away with people of whom they are jealous, who disturb or disappoint them, or who offend their childish feelings in some other way. It must be very difficult for them to accomplish this task of fighting their own death wishes when, at the same time, people are killed and hurt every day around them. Children have to be safeguarded against the primitive horrors of the war, not because horrors and atrocities are so strange to them, but because we want them at this decisive stage of their development to overcome and estrange themselves from the primitive and atrocious wishes of their own infantile nature.

Five Types of Air Raid Anxiety

What is true about the child's attitude to destruction applies in a certain measure to the subject of anxiety. Children are, of course, afraid of air raids, but their fear is neither as universal nor as overwhelming as has been expected. An explanation is required as to why it is present in some cases, absent in others, comparatively mild in most and rather violent in certain types of children.

It will be easier to answer these practical questions if we draw on our theoretical knowledge about the motives for fear and anxiety reactions in human beings. We have learned that there are three main reasons for the development of fear reactions.

An individual is afraid quite naturally and sensibly when there is some real danger present in the outside world which threatens either his safety or his whole existence. His fear will be all the greater the more he knows about the seriousness of the danger. His fear will urge him to adopt precautionary measures. Under its influence he will either fight it or if that is impossible, try to escape from it. Only when the danger is of overwhelming extent and suddenness will he be shocked and paralysed into inaction. This so-called "real anxiety" plays its part in the way in which children are afraid of air raids. They fear them as far as they can understand what is happening. As described above they have, in spite of their youth, acquired a certain degree of knowledge of this new danger. But it would be a mistake to over-rate this understanding, and consequently, to over-rate the amount or the permanency of this real fear of air raids. Knowledge and reason only play a limited part in a child's life. Its interest quickly turns away from the real things in the outer world, especially when they are unpleasant, and reverts back to its own childish interests, to its toys, its games and to its phantasies. The danger in the outer world which it recognizes at one moment and to which it answers with its fear, is put aside in another moment. Precautions are not kept up, and the fear gives way to an attitude of utter disregard.

There is the observation made by one of our colleagues during a day-light air raid in a surface shelter into which a mother had shepherded her little son of school age. For a while they both listened to the dropping of the bombs, then the boy lost interest and became engrossed in a story book which he had brought with him. The mother tried to interrupt his reading several times with anxious exclamations.

He always returned to his book after a second, until she at last said to in angry and scolding tone: "Drop your book and attend to the air raid."

We made exactly the same observations in the Children's Centre at the time of the December, March, and May raids. When our unexploded bomb lay in a neighboring garden, the children began by being mildly interested and afraid. They learned to keep away from glass windows and to avoid the entrance into the garden. By keeping up continual talk about the possible explosion we could have frightened them into continuation of that attitude. Whenever we let the subject alone their interest flagged. They forgot about the menace from the glass whenever they returned to their accustomed games, when the threat from outside lasted more than a week they began to get cross with it and denied its presence.

In spite of the bomb still being unremoved, they suddenly declared, "The bomb is gone and we shall go into the garden!"

There is nothing outstanding in this behavior of children towards the presence of real danger and real fear. It is only one example of the way in which, at this age, they deal with the facts of reality whenever they become unpleasant. They drop their contact with reality, they deny the facts; get rid of their fear in this manner and return, apparently undisturbed, to the pursuits and interests of their own childish world.

The second reason for anxiety can best be understood by reverting to the child's attitude towards destruction and aggression which we have described before.

After the first years of life the individual learns to criticize and overcome in himself certain instinctive wishes, or rather he learns to refuse them conscious expression. He learns that it is bad to kill, to hurt and to destroy, and would like to believe that he has no further wish to do any of these things. But he can only keep up this attitude when the people in the outer world do likewise. When he sees killing and destruction going on outside it arouses his fear that the impulses which he has only a short while ago buried in himself will be awakened again.

We have described above how the small child in whom these inhibitions against aggression have not yet been established is free of the abhorrence of air raids. The slightly older child who has just been through this fight with itself will, on the other hand, be particularly sensitive to their menace. When it has only just learned to curb its own aggressive impulses, it will have real outbreaks of anxiety when bombs come down and do damage around it.

This type of anxiety is of a completely different nature. There is no education without fear. Children are afraid of disobeying the commands and prohibitions of their elders either because they fear punishments or because they fear losing their parents' love whenever they are naughty. This fear of authority develops a little later into a fear of the child's own conscience. We regard it as progress in the child's education when commands and prohibitions from outside become more and more unnecessary, and the child knows what to do and what not to do under the direction of his own conscience. At the time when this nucleus of inner ideas which we call conscience, is formed, it turns back continually to the figures of the outside world on the one hand, to the imaginations of his own phantasy on the other, and borrows strength from both to reinforce the inner commandments.

The child of four or five who is afraid in the evening before sleep because it thinks it has done wrong, or thought forbidden thoughts, will not only have a 'bad conscience' or be afraid what father and mother would say if they knew about its wickedness. It will also be afraid of ghosts and bogeymen as reinforcements of the real parent figures and of the inner voice.

Children have a large list of dangers which serve as convenient symbols for their conscience---they are afraid of policemen who will come and arrest them, gypsies and robbers who will steal them, chimney sweeps or coal carriers who will put them in their bags, dustmen who will put them in their bins, lions and tigers who will come and eat them, earthquakes which will shake their houses, and thunderstorms which will threaten them. When they receive religious teaching they may leave all else aside and be afraid of the devil and of hell. There are many children who cannot go to sleep in the evening because they are afraid that God will look in on them and punish them for their sins. There are others who receive no religious teaching who transfer the same fear to the moon. They cannot fall asleep if the moon looks at them through the window; there are even children who cannot fall asleep because their fears are busy with expectations of the end of the world.

For children in this stage of development of their inner conscience air raids are simply a new symbol for old fears. They are as afraid of sirens and of bombs as they are afraid of thunder and lightning. Hitler and German planes take the place of the devil, of the lions again in the morning.

In the Children's Centre, for instance, Charlie, four and a half years old, called from his bed in the evening that the shelter was not safe enough, and that the house would fall down on him. He would certainly have called out in the same way in peace time to say that he had a fear of earthquakes or of thunderstorms. Roger, four years old, demanded that his mother come every evening and stand arched over his bed until he fell asleep. It is well known that there are many children of that same age, who, at all times, refuse to go to sleep unless their mothers stand by to hold their hands and safeguard them against forbidden actions. There is another boy of the same age whom the nursery superintendent has to assure with endless repetitions that if she leaves him at night he will surely find her and the tigers.

This fear also only disguises itself as a fear of air attack at night. When we inquire into it more closely we realize that he is afraid that he has done wrong somehow, and that for punishment his teacher and protector will be spirited away at night. We can convince ourselves of the truth of this explanation when we have the chance to remove these children from the danger and put them in surroundings where there is no talk of air raids. They will slowly revert to their former forms of anxiety. We shall know that peace has returned when nothings is left for the children to be afraid of except their own former ghosts and bogeymen.

Eight Stages of Man [*]

Erik H. Erikson

The last of our Freudians, Erik Homburg Erikson, was not a contemporary colleague of Sigmund Freud, but rather an associate of Anna Freud who successfully persuaded him to join the ranks of classical psychoanalysis. His professional career in psychology began after Freud's death in 1939 and concluded with his own death in 1994. Of all of Freud's colleagues, Erikson never departed ways from the master, himself. He claimed, "I am first and foremost a Freudian!" Indeed, this is seen in the fact that he considered himself to be a loyal disciple to the end, merely extending the stages of development to cover the entire life span and emphasizing the significant role played by social and cultural factors.

Accordingly, Erikson's psychosocial theory of development goes far beyond the territory examined by Freud. While Freud emphasized the significance of psychosexual development and the establishment of personality by age seven, Erikson extended this personality foundation to include three additional stages and significant psychosocial crises in life. For him, personality covered the entire span of one's life; that is, from infancy to old age.

The entire field of developmental psychology---as well as personality psychology---was profoundly influenced by Erikson's theoretical perspective of the eight stages of life. He is credited with having invented what is known today as "life-span developmental psychology," a psychology that examines the development of people from birth to death. Erikson's most profound contribution to the field is his belief and insistence that human development is a continuing process.

*   *   *

[*] Erikson, Erik. (1950). Eight Stages of Man. *Childhood and Society*, 219-234. New York: W. W. Norton & Company, Inc. Reprinted by permission.

I Trust vs. Basic Mistrust

The first demonstration of social trust in the baby is the ease of his feeding, the dept of his sleep, the relaxation of his bowels. The experience of a mutual regulation of his increasingly receptive capacities with the material techniques of provision gradually helps him to balance the discomfort caused by the immaturity of homeostasis with which he was born. In his gradually increasing waking hours he finds that more and more adventures of the senses arouse a feeling of familiarity, of having coincided with a feeling of inner goodness. Forms of comfort, and people associated with them, become as familiar as the gnawing discomfort of the bowels. The infant's first social achievement, then, is his willingness to let the mother out of sight without undue anxiety or rage, because she has become an inner certainty as well as an outer predictability. Such consistency, continuity, and sameness of experience provide a rudimentary sense of ego identity which depends, I think, on the recognition that there is an inner population of remembered and anticipated sensations and images which are firmly correlated with the outer population of familiar and predictable things and people. Smiling crowns this development.

The constant tasting and testing of the relationship between inside and outside meets its crucial test during the rages of the biting stage, when the teeth cause pain from within and when outer friends either prove of no avail or withdraw from the only action which promises relief of biting. I would assume that this experience of an urge turning upon the self has much to do with the masochistic tendency of finding cruel and cold comfort in hurting oneself whenever an object has eluded one's grasp.

Out of this, therefore, comes that primary sense of badness, that original sense of evil and malevolence which signifies the potential loss of all that is good because we could not help destroying it inside, thus driving it away outside. This feeling persists in a universal homesickness, a nostalgia for familiar images undamaged by change. Tribes dealing with one segment of nature develop a collective magic which seems to treat the Supernatural Providers of food and fortune as if they were angry and must be appeased by prayer and self-torture. Primitive religions, the most primitive layer in all religions, and the religious layer in each individual, abound with efforts at atonement, which try to make up for vague deeds against a maternal matrix and try to restore faith in the goodness of one's striving and in the kindness of the powers of the universe.

The general state of trust implies not only that one has learned to rely on the sameness and continuity of the outer providers, but also that one may trust oneself and the capacity of one's own organs to cope with urges, and that one is able to consider oneself trustworthy enough so that the providers will not need to be on guard lest they be nipped.

In psychopathology the absence of basic trust can best be studied in infantile schizophrenia, while weakness of such trust is apparent in adult personalities of schizoid and depressive character. The reestablishment of a state of trust has been found to be the basic requirement for therapy in these cases. For no matter what conditions may have caused a psychotic break, the bizarreness and withdrawal in the behavior of many very sick individuals hides an attempt to reconquer social mutuality by a testing of the borderlines between senses and physical reality, between words and social meanings.

Psychoanalysis assumes the early process of differentiation between inside and outside to be the organ of the mechanisms of projection and introjection which remain some of our deepest and most dangerous defense mechanisms. In introjection we feel and act as if an outer goodness had become an inner certainty. In projection, we experience an inner harm as an outer one we endow significant people with the evil which actually is in us. These two mechanisms, then, projection and introjection, are assumed to be modeled after whatever goes on in infants when they would like to externalize pain and internalize pleasure, an intent which must yield to the testimony of the maturing senses and ultimately of reason. These mechanisms are, more or less normally, reinstated in acute crises of love, trust, and faith in the adult. Where they persist, they mark the "psychotic character."

The firm establishment of enduring patterns for the solution of the nuclear conflict of basic trust versus basic mistrust in mere existence is the first task of the ego, and thus first of all a task for maternal care. But let it be said here that the amount of trust derived from earliest infantile experience does not seem to depend on absolute quantities of food or demonstrations of love, but rather on the quality of the maternal relationship. Mothers, I think, increase a sense of trust in their children by that kind of administration which in its quality combines sensitive care of the baby's individual needs and a firm sense of personal trustworthiness within the trusted framework of their culture's life-style. This forms the basis in the child for a sense of identity which will later combine a sense of being "all right," or being oneself, and of becoming what other people trust one will become...

2 Autonomy vs. Shame and Doubt

Anal-muscular maturation sets the stage for experimentation with two simultaneous sets of social modalities "holding on" and "letting go." As is the case with all of these modalities, their basic conflicts can lead in the end to either hostile or benign expectations and attitudes. Thus, "to hold" can become a destructive and cruel retaining or restraining, and it can become a pattern of care to have and to hold. To let go, too, can turn into an inimical letting loose of destructive forces, or it can become a relaxed "to let pass" and "to let be." Culturally speaking, these attitudes are neither good nor bad; their value depends on whether their hostile implications are turned against enemy, or fellow man---or the self.

The latter danger is the one best known to us for it denied the gradual and well-guided experience of the autonomy of free choice (or if, indeed, weakened by an initial loss of trust) the child will turn against himself all his urge to discriminate and to manipulate. He will overmanipulate himself; he will develop a precocious conscience. Instead of taking possession of things in order to test them by purposeful repetition, he will become obsessed by his own repetitiveness. By such obsessiveness, of course, he then learns to repossess the environment and to gain power by stubborn and minute control, where he could not find large-scale mutual regulation. Such hollow victory is the infantile model for a compulsion neurosis. It is also the infantile source of later attempts in adult life to govern by the letter, rather than by the spirit.

Outer control at this stage, therefore, must be firmly reassuring. The infant must come to feel that the basic faith in existence, which is the lasting treasure saved from the rages of the oral stage, will not be jeopardized by this about face of his, this sudden violent wish to have a choice, to appropriate demandingly, and to eliminate stubbornly. Firmness must protect him against the potential anarchy of his as yet untrained sense of discrimination, his inability to hold on and to let go with discretion. As his environment encourages him to "stand on his own feet," it must protect him against meaningless and arbitrary experiences of shame and of early doubt.

Shame is an emotional insufficiently studied, because in our civilization it is so early and easily absorbed by guilt. Shame supposes that one is completely exposed and conscious of being looked at in one world, self-conscious. One is visible and not ready to be visible, which is why we dream of shame as a situation in which we are stared at in a condition of incomplete dress, in night attire, "with one's pants down." Shame is early expressed in an impulse to bury one's face, or to sink, right then and there, into the ground. But this, I think, is essentially rage turned against the self. He who is ashamed would like to force the world not to look at him, not to notice his exposure. He would like to destroy the eyes of the world. Instead he must wish for his own invisibility. This potentiality is abundantly used in the educational method of "shaming" used so exclusively by some primitive peoples; its destructiveness is balanced in some civilizations by devices for "saving face." Visual shame precedes auditory guilt, which is a sense of badness to be had all by oneself when nobody watches and when everything is quiet---except the voice of the superego. Such shaming exploits an increasing sense of being small, which can develop only as the child stands up and as his awareness permits him to note the relative measures of size and power.

Doubt is the brother of shame. Where shame is dependent on the consciousness of being upright and exposed, doubt, so clinical observation leads me to observe, has much to do with a consciousness of having a front and a back---and especially a "behind." For this reverse area of the body, with its aggressive and libidinal focus in the sphincters and in the buttocks cannot be seen by the child, and yet it can be dominated by the will of others. The "behind" is thus the individual's dark continent, an area of the body which can be magically dominated and effectively invaded by those who would attack one's power of autonomy and who would designate as evil those products of the bowels which were felt to be all right when they were being passed. This basic sense of doubt in whatever one has left behind forms a substratum for later and more verbal forms of compulsive doubting, this finds its adult expression in paranoiac fears concerning hidden persecutors and secret persecutions threatening from behind and from within the behind.

3 Initiative vs. Guilt

The ambulatory stage and that of infantile genitality add to the inventory of basic social modalities that of "making," first in the sense of "being on the make." There is no simpler, stronger word to match the social modalities previously enumerated. The word suggests pleasure in attack and conquest in the boy, the emphasis remains on phallic-intrusive modes, in the girl it turns to modes of "catching" in more aggressive forms of snatching and "bitchy" possessiveness, or in the milder form of making oneself attractive and endearing.

The danger of this stage is a sense of guilt over the goals contemplated and the acts initiated in one's exuberant enjoyment of new locomotor and mental power acts of aggressive manipulation and coercion which go far beyond the executive capacity of organism and mind and therefore call for an energetic halt on one's contemplated initiative. While autonomy concentrates on keeping potential rivals out, and is therefore more an expression of jealous rage most often directed against encroachments by younger siblings, initiative brings with it anticipatory rivalry with those who have been there first and may, therefore, occupy with their superior equipment the field toward which one's initiative is directed. Jealousy and rivalry, those often embittered and yet essentially futile attempts at demarcating a sphere of unquestioned privilege, now come to a climax in a final context for a favored position with the mother, the inevitable failure leads to resignation, guilt, and anxiety. The child indulges in fantasies of being a giant and a tiger, but in his dreams he runs in terror for dear life. This, then, is the stage of the "castration complex," the fear of losing the (now energetically eroticized) genitals as a punishment for the fantasies attached to their excitements.

Infantile sexuality and incest taboo, castration complex and superego, all unite here to bring about that specifically human crisis during which the child must turn from an exclusive, pregenital attachment to his parents to the slow process of becoming a parent, a carrier of tradition. Here the most fateful split and transformation in the emotional powerhouse occurs, a split between potential human glory and potential total destruction. For here the child becomes forever divided in himself. The instinct fragments which before had enhanced the growth of this infantile body and mind now become divided into an infantile set which perpetuates the exuberance of growth potentials, and a parental set which supports and increases self-observation, self-guidance, and self-punishment.

Naturally, the parental set is at first infantile in nature. The fact that human conscience remains partially infantile throughout life is the core of human tragedy. For the superego of the child can be primitive, cruel, and uncompromising, as may be observed in instances where children overcontrol and oveconstrict themselves to the point of self-obliteration, where they develop an over-obedience more literal than the one the parent has wished to exact, or where they develop deep regressions and lasting resentments because the parents themselves do not seem to live up to the new conscience which they have installed in the child. One of the deepest conflicts in fact is the hate for a parent who served as the model and the executor of the superego, but who (in some form) was found trying to get away with the very transgressions which the child can no longer tolerate in himself. The suspiciousness and evasiveness which is thus mixed in with the all-or-nothing quality of the superego, this organ of tradition, makes moral (in the sense of moralistic) man a great potential danger to his own ego---and to that of his fellow men.

The problem, again, is one of mutual regulation. Where the child, now so ready to overmanipulate himself, can gradually develop a sense of paternal responsibility, where he can gain some insight into the institutions, functions, and roles which will permit his responsible participation, he will find pleasurable accomplishment in wielding tools and weapons, in manipulating meaningful toys--- and in caring for younger children.

4 Industry vs. Inferiority

Before the child, psychologically already a rudimentary parent, can become a biological parent, he must begin to be a worker and potential provider. With the oncoming latency period,[1] the normally advanced child forgets, or rather sublimates, the necessity to "make" people by direct attack or to become papa and mama in a hurry; he now learns to win recognition by producing things. He has mastered the ambulatory field and the organ modes. He has experienced a sense of finality regarding the fact that there is no workable future within the womb of his family, and thus becomes ready to apply himself to given skills and tasks, which go far beyond the mere playful expression of his organ modes or the pleasure in the function of his limbs. He develops industry---i.e., he adjusts himself to the inorganic laws of the tool world. He can become an eager and absorbed unit of a productive situation. To bring a productive situation to completion is an aim which gradually supersedes the whims and wishes of his autonomous organism. His ego boundaries include his tools and skills; the work principle teaches him the pleasure of work completion by steady attention and persevering diligence.

His danger, at this stage, lies in a sense of inadequacy and inferiority. If he despairs of his tools and skills or of his status among his tool partners, his ego boundaries suffer, and he abandons hope for the ability to identify early with others who apply themselves to the same general section of the tool world. To lose the hope of such "industrial" association leads back to the more isolated, less tool-conscious "anatomical" rivalry of the Oedipal time.[2] The child despairs of his equipment in the tool world and in anatomy, and considers himself doomed to mediocrity or mutilation. It is as this point that wider society becomes significant in its ways of admitting the child to an understanding of meaningful roles in its total economy. Many a child's development is disrupted when family life may not have prepared him for school life, or when school life may fail to sustain the promises of earlier stages.

5 Identity vs. Role Diffusion

With the establishment of a good relationship to the world of skills and tools, and with the advent of sexual maturity, childhood proper comes to an end. Youth begins. But in puberty and adolescence all sameness and continuities relied on earlier are questioned again, because of a rapidity of body growth which equals that of early childhood and because of the entirely new addition of physical genital maturity. The growing and developing youths, faced with this physiological revolution within them, are now primarily concerned with what they appear to be in the eyes of others as compared with what they feel they are, and with the question of how to connect the roles and skills cultivated earlier with the occupational prototypes of the day. In their search for a new sense of continuity and sameness, adolescents have to refight many of the battles of earlier years, even though to do so they must artificially appoint perfectly well-meaning people to play the roles of enemies, and they are ever ready to install lasting idols and ideals as guardians of a final identity; here puberty rites "confirm" the inner design for life.

The integration now taking place in the form of ego identity is more than the sum of the childhood identifications. It is the accrued experience of the ego's ability to integrate these identifications with the vicissitudes of the libido, with the aptitudes developed out of endowment, and with the opportunities offered in social roles. The sense of ego identity, then, is the accrued confidence that the inner sameness and continuity are matched by the sameness and continuity of one's meaning for others, as evidenced in the tangible promise of a "career."

The danger of this stage is role diffusion. Where this is based on a strong previous doubt as to one's sexual identity, delinquent and outright psychotic incidents are not uncommon. If diagnosed and treated correctly, these incidents do not have the same fatal significance which they have at other ages. It is primarily the inability to settle on an occupational identity which disturbs young people. To keep themselves together they temporarily overidentify, to the point of apparent complete loss of identity, with the heroes of cliques and crowds. This initiates the stage of "falling in love," which is by no means entirely, or even primarily, a sexual matter---except where the mores demand it. To a considerable extent adolescent love is an attempt to arrive at a definition of one's identity by projecting one's diffused ego images on one another and by seeing them thus reflected and gradually clarified. This is why many a youth would rather converse, and settle matters of mutual identification, than embrace.

Puberty rites and confirmations help to integrate and to affirm the new identity.

6 Intimacy vs. Isolation

It is only as young people emerge from their identity struggles that their egos can master the sixth stage, that of intimacy. What we have said about genitality now gradually comes into play. Body and ego must now be masters of the organ mode and of the nuclear conflicts, in order to be able to face the fear of ego loss in situations which call for self-abandon in orgasms and sexual unions, in close friendships and in physical combat, in experiences of inspiration by teachers and of initiation from the recesses of the self. The avoidance of such experiences because of a fear of ego loss may lead to a deep sense of isolation and consequent self-absorption.

Thus, then, may be the place to complete our discussion of genitality.

For a basic orientation in the matter, I shall quote what has come to me as Freud's shortest saying. It has often been claimed, and bad habits of conversation seem to sustain the claim, that psychoanalysis as a treatment attempts to convince the patient that before God and man he has only one obligation to have good orgasms, with a fitting "object," and that regularly. This, of course, is not true. Freud was once asked what he thought a normal person should be able to do well. The questioner probably expected a complicated answer. But Freud, in the curt way of his old days, is reported to have said "Lieben and arbeiten" (to love and to work). It pays to ponder on this simple formula; it gets deeper as you think about it. For when Freud said "love" he meant genital love, and genital love, when he said love and work, he meant a general work-productiveness which would not preoccupy the individual to the extent that he loses his right or capacity to be genital and a loving being. Thus we may ponder, but we cannot improve on the formula which includes the doctor's prescription for human dignity---and for democratic living.

Genitality, then, consists in the unobstructed capacity to develop an orgastic potency so free of pregenital interferences that genital libido (not just the sex products discharged in Kinsey's "outlets") is expressed in heterosexual mutuality, with full sensitivity of both penis and vagina, and with a convulsion-like discharge of tension from the whole body. This is a rather concrete way of saying something about a process which we really do not understand. To put it more situationally the total fact of finding, via the climactic turmoil of the orgasm, a supreme experience of the mutual regulation of two beings in some way breaks the point oft the hostilities and potential rages caused by the oppositeness of male and female, of fact and fancy, of love and hate. Satisfactory sex relations thus make sex less obsessive, overcompensation less necessary, sadistic controls superfluous.

The kind of mutuality in orgasm which psychoanalysis has in mind[3] is apparently easily obtained in classes and cultures which happen to make a leisurely institution of it. In more complex societies this mutuality is interfered with by so many factors of health, of tradition, of opportunity, and of temperament, that the proper formulation of sexual health would be rather this. A human being should be potentially able to accomplish mutuality of genital orgasm, but he should also be so constituted as to bear frustration in the matter without undue regression wherever considerations of reality and loyal call for it.

In order to be of lasting social significance, the utopia of genitality should include:
1. mutuality of orgasm
2. with a loved partner
3. of the other sex
4. with whom one is able and willing to share a mutual trust
5. and with whom one is able and willing to regulate the cycles of

a. work
b. procreation
c. recreation
6. so as to secure to the offspring, too, a satisfactory development.

It is apparent that such utopian accomplishment on a large scale cannot be an individual or, indeed, a therapeutic task. Nor is it a purely sexual matter by any means.

7 Generativity vs. Stagnation

The discussion of intimacy versus isolation has already included a further nuclear conflict which, therefore, requires only a short explicit formulation. I mean generativity versus stagnation. I apologize for creating a new and not even pleasant term. Yet neither creativity nor productivity nor any other fashionable term seems to me to convey what must be conveyed---namely, that the ability to lose oneself in the meeting of bodies and minds leads to a gradual expansion of ego interests and of libidinal cathexis over that which has been thus generated and accepted as a responsibility. Generativity is primarily the interest in establishing and guiding the next generation or whatever in a given case becomes the absorbing object of a parental kind of responsibility. Where this enrichment fails, a regression from generativity to an obsessive need for pseudo intimacy, punctuated by moments of mutual repulsion, takes place, often with a pervading sense (and objective evidence) of individual stagnation and interpersonal impoverishment.

8 Ego Integrity vs. Despair

Only he who is in some way has taken care of things and people and has adapted himself to the triumphs and disappointments adherent to being, by necessity, the originator of others and the generator of things and ideas---only he may gradually grow the fruit of these seven stages. I know no better word for it than ego integrity. Lacking a clear definition, I shall point to a few constituents of this state of mind. It is the ego's accrued assurance of its proclivity for order and meaning. It is a post-narcissistic love of the human ego---not of the self---as an experience which conveys some world order and spiritual sense, no matter how dearly paid for. It is the acceptance of one's one and only life cycle as something that had to be and that, by necessity, permitted of no substitutions; it thus means a new, a different love of one's parents. It is a comradeship with the ordering ways of distant times and different pursuits, as expressed in the sample products and sayings of such times and pursuits. Although aware of the relativity of all the various lifestyles which have given meaning to human striving, the possessor of integrity is ready to defend the dignity of his own life style against all physical and economic threats. For he knows that an individual life is the accidental coincidence of but one life cycle with but one segment of history, and that for him all human integrity stands on falls with the one style of integrity of which he partakes. The style of integrity developed by his culture on civilization thus becomes the "patrimony of his soul," the seal of his moral paternity of himself"[4]...Before this final solution, death loses its sting.

The lack or loss of this accrued ego integration is signified by fear of death; the one and only life cycle is not accepted as the ultimate of life. Despair expresses the feeling that the time is short, too short for the attempt to start another life and to try out alternate roads to integrity. Disgust hides despair.

Each individual, to become a mature adult, must to a sufficient degree develop all the ego qualities mentioned, so that a wise Indian, a true gentleman, and a mature peasant share and recognize in one another the final stage of integrity. But each cultural entity, to develop the particular style of integrity suggested by its historical place, utilizes a particular combination of these conflicts, along with specific provocations and prohibitions, of infantile sexuality. Infantile conflicts become creative only if sustained by the firm support of cultural institutions and of the special leader---classes representing them. In order to approach or experience integrity, the individual must know how to be a follower or image bearer in religion and in politics, in the economic order and in technology, in aristocratic living and in the arts and sciences. Ego integrity, therefore, implies an emotional integration which permits participating by followership as well as acceptance of the responsibility of leadership.

Webster's dictionary is kind enough to help us complete this outline in a circular fashion. Trust (the first of our ego values) is here defined as "the assured reliance on another's integrity," the last of our values. I suspect that Webster had business in mind rather than babies, credit rather than faith. But the formulation stands. And it seems possible to further paraphrase the relation of adult integrity and infantile trust by saying that healthy children will not fear life if their parents have integrity enough not to fear death.

In order to indicate the whole conceptual area which is awaiting systematic treatment, I shall conclude this chapter with a diagram.[5] In this, as in the diagram of pregenital zones and modes, the diagonal represents the sequence of enduring solutions, each of which is based on the integration of the earlier ones. At any given stage of the life cycle the solution of one more nuclear conflict adds a new ego quality, a new criterion of increasing strength. The criteria proposed in this chart are to be treated in analogy to the criteria for health and illness in general---i.e., by ascertaining whether or not there is "a prevailing subjective sense of" the criterion in question, and whether or not "objective evidence of the dominance of" the criterion can be established by indirect examination (by means of depth psychology). Above the diagonal there is space for a future elaboration of the precursors of each of these solutions, all of which begin with the beginning, below the diagonal there is space for the designation of the derivatives of these solutions in the maturing and the mature personality.

Oral Sensory	Trust Vs. Mistrust							
Muscular-Anal		Autonomy Vs. Shame, Doubt						
Locomotor Genital			Initiative Vs. Guilt					
Latency				Industry Vs. Inferiority				
Puberty & Adolescence					Identity Vs. Role Diffusion			
Young Adulthood						Intimacy Vs. Isolation		
Adulthood							Generativity vs. Stagnation	
Maturity								Integrity vs. Despair

[1] At the end of the phallic period, around age 7, Freud described children as entering a "latency period" until the beginning of puberty a few years later. During this period issues of sexual development are temporarily set aside while the child learns important skills for later life.

[2] Part of the story of the Oedipal crisis told by Freud consists of the young boy comparing the size of his genitals with that of his father's, and feeling thoroughly inferior as a result.

[3] The reference here is to Alfred Kinsey, one of the first modern sex researchers. Kinsey focused closely on the nature and meaning of literal sex acts and "outlets," a term and approach Erikson obviously found limited and even distasteful as the ideal outcome of a sexual relationship.

[4] Erikson seemed to take this advice to heart. He never knew his father and in midlife abandoned his stepfather's name and took instead the name Erikson, as a way of claiming his own moral paternity of himself.

[5] The meaning of this diagram, reproduced in many textbooks, is not made entirely clear by Erikson. But Franz and White (1985) "fill in" the rows and columns associated with identity and intimacy, showing the heuristic power of Erikson's theory even as they seek to offer their own revision of it.

Chapter Two
Neo-analytic Perspectives

"If we look at a pine tree growing in the valley we will notice that it grows differently from one on top of a mountain....It is much the same way with human beings. We see the 'style of life' under certain conditions of environment and it is our task to analyze its exact relation to the existing circumstances...."

Alfred Adler

Psychoanalytic Psychology: An Overview [*]

Joan B. Cannon

Type of Psychology: Origin and definition of psychology
Fields of Study: Psychodynamic and Neo-Analytic models, psychodynamic therapies

Psychoanalytic and neo-analytic schools of thought provide explanations of human and neurotic behavior. Each of their models contributes to the understanding of personality development and psychological conflict by presenting unique theoretical conceptualizations, assessment techniques, research methodologies, and psychotherapeutic strategies for personality change.

Principal Terms

ANALYTIC PSYCHOLOGY: A school of psychology founded by Carl Jung which views the human mind as the result of prior experiences and the preparation of future goal; it deemphasizes the role of sexuality in psychological disorders.

DYNAMIC CULTURAL SCHOOLS OF PSYCHOANALYSIS: Two branches of psychoanalysis, represented in the schools of Karen Horney and Harry Stack Sullivan, both emphasizing cultural, environmental and social factors.

INDIVIDUAL PSYCHOLOGY: A school of psychology founded by Alfred Adler which stresses the unity of the person and his or her striving for superiority in order to compensate for feelings of inferiority

NEOANALYTIC PSYCHOLOGY: Schools of that extended and revised the ideas proposed by Freud; included are the theories of Adler, Jung, Horney, Sullivan and Erikson.

---

[*] Cannon, Joan B. (1994). Psychoanalytic Psychology: An Overview. *Survey of Social Psychology*, 1905-1912. New York: Harcourt Brace. Reprinted by permission.

PSYCHOANALYTIC PSYCHOLOGY: A school of psychology founded by Sigmund Freud, which provides a theory concerning mental disorders, a procedure for examining mental processes and the therapeutic technique of psychoanalysis.

PSYCHOSOCIAL THEORY OF PSYCHOLOGY: An eight-stage model of human growth and psychosocial development proposed by Erik H. Erikson, emphasizing the role played by social and cultural forces.

*　　*　　*

Overview

One grand theory in psychology that dramatically revolutionized the way in which personality and its formation were viewed is psychoanalysis. Orthodox psychoanalysis and later versions of this model offer several unique perspectives of personality development, assessment, and change.

The genius of Sigmund Freud (1856-1939), the founder of psychoanalysis, is revealed in the magnitude of his achievements and the monumental scope of his works. Over the course of his lifetime, Freud developed a theory of personality and psychopathology, a method for probing the realm of the unconscious mind, and a therapy for dealing with personality disorders. He posited that an individual is motivated by unconscious forces that are instinctual in nature. The two major instinctual forces are the life instincts, or Eros, and the death instinct, or Thanatos. Their source is biological tension whose aim is tension reduction through a variety of objects. Freud viewed personality as a closed system composed of three structures of personality: the id, ego, and superego. The irrational id consists of the biological drives and libido, or psychic energy. It operates according to the pleasure principle, which seeks the immediate gratification of needs. The rational ego serves as the executive component of personality and the mediator between the demands of the id, superego and environment. Governed by the reality principle, it seeks to postpone the gratification of needs. The superego, or moral arm of personality, consists of conscience (internalized values) and ego ideal (that which the person aspires to be).

According to Freud, the origins of personality are embedded in the first seven years of life. Personality develops through a sequence of psychosexual stages which focus upon an area of the body (erogenous zone) that gives pleasure to the individual. These are the oral, anal, phallic, latency and genital stages. The frustration or overindulgence of needs contributes to a fixation, or arrest in development at a particular stage.

Clinically speaking, Freud also developed a therapy for treating individuals experiencing personality disturbances. Psychoanalysis has shown how physical disorders have psychological roots, how unbearable anxiety generates conflict, and how problems in adulthood result from early childhood experiences. In therapy, Freud surmounted his challenge to reveal the hidden nature of the unconscious by exposing the resistances and transferences of his patients. His method for probing a patient's unconscious thoughts, motives and feelings was based upon the use of many clinical techniques. Free association, dream interpretation, analyses of slips of the tongue, misplaced objects and humor enabled him to discover the contents of an individual's unconscious mind and open the doors to a new and grand psychology or personality.

Erik Erikson's (1902-1994) theory of psychosocial development occupies a position between orthodox psychoanalysis and neoanalytic schools of thought. His theory builds upon the basic concepts and tenets of Freudian psychology by illustrating the influential role of social and cultural forces in personality development. Erikson's observations of infants and investigations of the parent-child relationship in various societies contributed to his development of the model of eight stages of human development. He proposes that personality unfolds over the entire life cycle according to a predetermined or epigenetic plan. As an individual moves through this series of stages, he or she encounters periods of vulnerability that require him or her to resolve crises of a social nature and develop new abilities and patterns of behavior. Erikson's eight psychosocial stages not only parallel Freud's psychosexual ones but, more importantly, have contributed immensely to contemporary thought in developmental psychology.

Several other schools of thought arose in opposition to Freudian orthodoxy. Among the proponents of these new psychoanalytic models were Carl Gustav Jung (1875-1961), Alfred Adler (1870-1937), Karen Horney (1885-1952) and Harry Stack Sullivan (1892-1949). These theorists advocated revised versions of Freud's psychoanalytic model and became known as the neo-analysts.

Jung's Analytical Psychology stresses the complex interaction of opposing forces within the total personality (psyche) and the manner in which these inner conflicts influence development. Personality is driven by general life process energy called libido. It operates according to the principle of opposites; for example, a contrast between conscious and unconscious. An individual's behavior is seen as a means to some end, whose goal is to create a balance between these polar opposites through a process of self-realization. Personality is composed of several regions, including the ego (a unifying force at the center of consciousness), the personal unconscious (experiences blocked from consciousness), and the collective unconscious (inherited predispositions of ancestral experiences). The major focus of Jung's theory is the collective unconscious, with its archetypes (primordial thoughts and images), persona (public self), anima/animus (feminine and masculine components), shadow (repulsive side of the personality), and self (an archetype reflecting a person's striving for personality integration. Jung further proposed two psychological attitudes that the personality could use in relating to the world: introversion and extroversion. He also identified four functions of thought: sensing, thinking, feeling, and intuiting. Eight different personality types emerge when one combines these attitudes and functions. Like Freud, Jung proposed developmental stages: childhood, young adulthood, and middle age. Through the process of individuation, a person seeks to create an inner harmony that results in self-realization. In conjunction with dream analysis, Jung used painting therapy and a word association test to disclose underlying conflicts in patients. Therapy helped patients to reconcile the conflicting sides of their personalities and experience self-realization.

The Individual Psychology of Adler illustrates the significance of social variables in personality development and the uniqueness of the individual. Adler proposed that an individual seeks to compensate for inborn feelings of inferiority by striving for superiority. It is a person's life-style that helps him achieve future goals, ideals and superiority. Adler extended this theme of perfection to society by using the concept of social interest to depict the human tendency to create a productive society. He maintained that early childhood experiences play a crucial role in the development of a person's unique life-style. An individual lacking in social interest develops a mistaken life-style (for example, an inferiority complex). Physical inferiority as well as spoiling or pampering and neglecting children contributes to the development of faulty life-styles. Adler examined dreams, birth order, and first memories to trace the origins of life-styles and goals. These data were used in psychotherapy to help the person create a new social-interest-oriented life style.

Horney's Social and Cultural Psychoanalysis considers the influence of social and cultural forces upon the development and maintenance of neurosis. Her theory focuses upon disturbed human relationships, especially between parents and children.

She discussed several negative factors, such as parental indifference, erratic behavior, and unkept promises, which contributed to basic anxiety in children. This basic anxiety led to certain defenses or neurotic needs. Horney proposed ten neurotic needs that are used to reestablish safety. She further summarized these needs into three categories that depicted the individual's adjustment to others: moving towards people (compliant person), moving against people (aggressive person), and moving away from people (detached person). Horney believed that neurosis occurs when an individual lives according to his or her ideal rather than real self. She also wrote a number of articles on feminine psychology that stressed the importance of cultural rather than biological factors in personality formation. Like Freud, she used the techniques of transference, dream analysis, and free association in her psychotherapy; however, the goal of therapy was to help an individual overcome his or her idealized neurotic self and become more real as he or she experienced self-realization.

Sullivan's Interpersonal Theory examines personality from the perspective of the interpersonal relationships that have influenced it, especially the mother-infant relationship. Sullivan believed that this relationship contributed to an individual's development of a "good me," "bad me," or "not me" personification of self. He also proposed six stages of development: infancy, childhood, juvenile epoch, preadolescence, early adolescence and late adolescence. These stages illustrate an individual's experiences and need for intimacy with significant others. Overall, his theory emphasizes the importance of interpersonal relations, the appraisals of others toward an individual, and the need to achieve interpersonal security and avoid anxiety.

Applications

Psychoanalytic psychology and its later versions have been used to explain normal and abnormal personality development. Regardless of their perspectives, psychologists in all these schools of thought have relieved upon the case study method to communicate their theoretical insights and discoveries.

The theoretical roots of orthodox psychoanalysis may be traced to the famous Case of "Anna O., "a patient under the care of Josef Breuer, Freud's friend and colleague. Fascinated with the hysterical symptoms of this young girl and with Breuer's success in using catharsis (the talking cure) with her, Freud asked Breuer to collaborate on a work entitled *Studien uber Hysterie* (1895; *Studies in Hysteria*, 1950) and discuss his findings. It was the world's first book on psychoanalysis, containing information on the unconscious, defenses, sexual causes of neurosis, resistance and transference. Freud's own self-analysis and analyses of family members and other patients further contributed to the changing nature of his theory. Among his great case histories are "Dora" (hysteria), "Little Hans" (phobia), the "Rat Man" (obsessional neurosis), the "Schreiber" case (paranoia) and the "Wolf Man" (infantile neurosis). His method of treatment, psychoanalysis, is also well documented in contemporary cases such as the one described in the book *Sybil* (1974).

In his classic work, *Childhood and Society* (1950), Erikson discussed the applicability of the clinical method of psychoanalysis and the case history technique to normal development in children. His case analyses of the Sioux and Yurok Indians and his observations of children led to the creation of a psychosocial theory of development that emphasized the significant role played by one's culture. Moreover, Erikson's psychohistorical accounts, *Young Man Luther: A Study in Psychoanalysis and History* (1958) and *Gandhi's Truth on the Origins of Militant Nonviolence* (1969) illustrated the application of clinical analyses to historical and biographical research so prominent today.

The founders of other psychoanalytic schools of thought have similarly shown that their theories can best be understood in the context of the therapeutic situation and in the writings of case histories. Harold Greenwald's *Great Cases in Psychoanalysis (1959)* is an excellent source of original case histories written by Freud, Jung, Adler, Horney and Sullivan. Jung's case of "The Anxious Young Woman and the Retired Business Man" clarifies the differences and similarities between his theory and Freud's psychoanalytic model. In "Drive for Superiority," Adler uses material from several cases to illustrate the themes of life-style, feelings of inferiority and striving for superiority. Horney's case of "The Ever Tired

Editor" portrays her use of the character analysis method; that is, she concentrates upon the way in which a patient characteristically functions. Sullivan's case of "The Inefficient Wife" shed some light on the manner in which professional advice may be given to another (student) practitioner. In retrospect, all these prominent theorists have exposed their independent schools of thought through case histories. Even today, this method continues to be used to explain human behavior and to enhance understanding of personality functioning.

Context

Historically, the evolution of psychoanalytic psychology originated with Freud's clinical observations of the work conducted by the famous French neurologist, Jean Martin Charcot, and his collaborations on the treatment of hysteria neurosis with Breuer. The publication of *Studies in Hysteria* (1895) marked the birth of psychoanalysis since it illustrated a theory of hysteria, a therapy of catharsis, and an analysis of unconscious motivation. Between 1900 and 1920, Freud made innumerable contributions to the field. His major clinical discoveries were contained in his publications *Die Traumdeutung* (1900; *The Interpretation of Dreams*, 1913), and *Drei Abhandlungen zur Sexualtheorie* (1905; *Three Contributions to the Sexual Theory*, 1910; also translated as *Three Essays on the Theory of Sexuality* in 1949) as well as in various papers on therapy, case histories, and applications to everyday life. During this time, Freud began his international correspondence with people such as Jung. He also invited a select group of individuals to his home for evening discussions; these meetings were known as the Psychological Wednesday Society. Eventually, these meetings led to the establishment of the Vienna Psychoanalytic Society, with Adler as its president, and the First International Psychoanalytic Congress, with Jung as its president. In 1909, Freud, Jung and others were invited by President G. Stanley Hall of Clark University to come to the United States to deliver a series of introductory lectures on psychoanalysis. This momentous occasion acknowledged Freud's achievements and gave him international recognition. In subsequent years, Freud reformulated his theory and demonstrated how psychoanalysis could be applied to larger social issues.

Trained in psychoanalysis by Anna Freud, Erikson followed in Freud's footsteps by supporting and extending his psychosexual theory of development with eight stages of psychosocial identity. Among the members of the original psychoanalytic group, Adler was the first to defect from the Freudian school in 1911. Protesting Freud's Oedipus complex, Adler founded his own Individual Psychology. Two years later (in 1913), Jung parted company with Freud to established his Analytic Psychology. He objected to Freud's belief that all human behavior stems from sex. With Horney's publications *New Ways in Psychoanalysis* (1939) and *Our Inner Conflicts: A Constructive Theory of Neurosis* (1945), it became quite clear that her ideas remotely resembled Freud's. Objecting to a number of Freud's major tenets, she attributed the development of neurosis and the psychology of being feminine to social, cultural, and interpersonal influences. Similarly,

Sullivan extended psychoanalytic psychology to interpersonal phenomena, arguing that the foundations of human nature and development are not biological but rather cultural and social.

The accomplishments of Freud and his followers are truly remarkable. The creative genius of each theorist spans a lifetime of effort and work. The magnitude of their achievements is shown in their efforts to provide new perspectives on personality development and psychopathology, theories of motivation, psychotherapeutic methods of treatment, and methods for describing the nature of human behavior. Clearly, these independent schools of thought have had a profound influence not only upon the field of psychology, but also upon art, religion, anthropology, sociology, and literature. Undoubtedly, they will continue to serve as the cornerstone of personality theory and provide the foundation for new and challenging theories of tomorrow---theories that seek to discover the true nature of what it means to be human.

Bibliography

Adler, Alfred. *Social Interest, A Challenge to Mankind.* New York: Capricorn Books, 1964. An excellent summary of Adler's theories of human nature and social education, incorporating his ideas on life style, inferiority/superiority complex, neurosis, childhood memories, and social feelings. Also contains a chapter on the consultant and patient relationship, and a questionnaire for understanding and treating difficult children.

Erikson, Erik Homburger. *Identity, Youth and Crisis.* New York: W. W. Norton, 1968. An impressive summation of Erikson's theories of human nature and development and the importance of societal forces. Erikson discusses his clinical observations, the life cycle and the formation of identity, and case histories to illustrate identity confusion and other relevant issues. This book carries forward concepts expressed in *Childhood and Society* (1963).

Freud, Sigmund. *A General Introduction to Psychoanalysis.* New York: W. W. Norton, 1977. An easy-to-read account of Freud's complete theory of psychoanalysis. Freud presents twenty-eight lectures to reveal major aspects of his theory, essential details in his method of psychoanalysis, and the results of his work. He also examines the psychology of errors, dream analysis technique, and general theory of neurosis.

Greenwald, Harold (Ed.). *Great Cases in Psychoanalysis.* New York: Ballantine, 1959. An outstanding source of case histories written by the theorists themselves. Greenwald uses these case histories to portray the historical context of the psychoanalytic movement. These original case studies provide insight into therapeutic methods used by these great analysts as well as their assessments. Included are Freud, Adler, Jung, Horney and Sullivan.

Horney, Karen. *The Neurotic Personality of Our Time.* New York: W. W. Norton, 1937. This classic work contains Horney's portrayal of the neurotic personality and the relevance of cultural forces in the etiology of psychological disturbances. This post-Freudian document examines Horney's theoretical conceptualizations, including basic anxiety, neurotic trends, methods of adjustment, and the role played by culture.

Sullivan, Harry Stack. *The Interpersonal Theory of Psychiatry.* New York: W. W. Norton, 1953. A classic work on human development from an interpersonal perspective. Sullivan provides a comprehensive overview of his theory by describing his key concepts and developmental stages. He further illustrates the application of his theory by focusing upon inappropriate interpersonal relationships.

Joan Bartczak Cannon

Cross-References

Analytical Psychology: Carl G. Jung, 240; Case-Study Methodologies, 481; Dream Analysis, 830; Ego Defense Mechanisms, 860; Ego Psychology: Erik Erikson, 867; Individual Psychology: Alfred Adler, 1275; Psychoanalysis: Classical versus Modern, 1898; Psychoanalytic Psychology and Personality: Sigmund Freud, 1912; Psychology of Women: Karen Horney, 1950; Psychosexual Development, 1969; Psychotherapeutic Effectiveness, 1989; Social Psychological Models: Erich Fromm, 2318; Social Psychological Models: Karen Horney, 2324.

Psychological Types
Carl Gustav Jung[*]

One mark of Freud's stature in the history of psychology is evidenced in the number of his followers---and former adherents---who became leading figures in their own right. Perhaps, the most distinguished among the group is Carl Gustave Jung, who began his career in psychoanalysis as Freud's anointed "crown prince." It was Freud's intention to have Jung succeed him as president of the International Psychoanalytic Association and carry the psychoanalytic movement forward into the future. For many years, these two gentlemen engaged in an intense correspondence and even traveled to the United States together in 1909 to attend the Twentieth Anniversary Celebration of Clark University in Worcester, Massachusetts.

When the relationship ended in 1913, the split between the two gentlemen was strong and bitter. Jung opposed Freud's emphasis upon the role of sexuality and de-emphasis upon the constructive role played by the unconscious. On a more personal level, he may have been annoyed by Freud's dominating role as his intellectual father and sought a need to achieve more independence. For Freud, these defections were devastating, especially Jung's disassociation from the psychoanalytic camp. After all, he had lost his heir apparent to a new school of thought called Analytic Psychology. Jung formulated ideas, about a "collective unconscious," "shadows," "archetypes," and an "oceanic feeling" of being one with the universe. These ideas were loathed by the atheistic Freud.

In the following selection Jung presents his theoretical conceptualization of introversion and extraversion and four related styles of thinking. Even today, these ideas are applied in the field and used in various research including the Big Five factors of personality. But Jung's conception is unique and somewhat different from the personality styles labeled as extraversion and introversion today. His introvert represents an individual who has turned into himself and away from the world and, his extravert is an individual who is entirely dependent on others for his intellectual and emotional life. In fact, a widely used personality test, the Myers-Briggs Type Indicator (Myers & McCaulley, 1985) was designed to classify people in Jungian terms. You might be classified as dominated by sensation, thinking, feeling, or intuition.

* * *

---

[*] **Jung, Carl. (1971). Psychological Types.** *Psychological Types: A Revision of R.F.C. Hull of the Translation by H.G. Baynes,* **510-523. Princeton, New Jersey: Princeton University Press. Reprinted by permission.**

From *Psychological Types,* translated by R. Hull and H. Baynes (Princeton, NJ: Princeton University Press, 1971, pp. 510-523).

We shall discover, after a time, that in spite of the great variety of conscious motives and tendencies, certain groups of individuals can be distinguished who are characterized by a striking conformity of motivation. For example, we shall come upon individuals who in all their judgments, perceptions, feelings, affects, and actions feel external factors to be the predominant motivating force, or who at least give weight to them no matter whether causal or final motives are in question. I will give some examples of what I mean. St. Augustine "I would not believe the Gospel if the authority of the Catholic Church did not compel it." A dutiful daughter "I could not allow myself to think anything that would be displeasing to my father." On man finds a piece of modern music beautiful. Another marries in order to please his parents but very much against his own interests. There are people who contrive to make themselves ridiculous in order to amuse others, they even prefer to make butts of themselves rather than remain unnoticed. These are not a few who in everything they do or don't do have but one motive in mind what will others think of them. "One need not be ashamed of a thing if nobody knows about it." There are some who can find happiness only when it excites the envy of others, some who make trouble for themselves in order to enjoy the sympathy of their friends.

Such examples could be multiplied indefinitely. They point to a psychological peculiarity that can be sharply distinguished from another attitude which, by contrast, is motivated chiefly by internal or subjective factors. A person of this type might say "I know I could give my father the greatest pleasure if I did so and so, but I don't happen to think that way." Or "I see that the weather has turned out bad, but in spite of it I shall carry out my plan." This type does not travel for pleasure but to execute a preconceived idea. Or "My book is probably incomprehensible, but it is perfectly clear to me." Or, going to the other extreme, "Everybody thinks I could do something, but I know perfectly well I can do nothing." Such a man can be so ashamed of himself that he literally dares not meet people. There are some who feel happy only when they are quite sure nobody knows about it, and to them a thing is disagreeable just because it is pleasing to everyone else. They seek the good where no one would think of finding it. At every step the sanction of the subject must be obtained, and without it nothing can be undertaken or carried out. Such a person would have replied to St. Augustine "I would believe the Gospel if the authority of the Catholic Church did *not* compel it." Always he has to prove that everything he does rests on his own decisions and convictions, and never because he is influenced by anyone, or desires to please or conciliate some person or opinion.

44

This attitude characterizes a group of individuals whose motivations are derived chiefly from the subject, from inner necessity. There is, finally, a third group, and here it is hard to say whether the motivation comes chiefly from within or without. This group is the most numerous and includes the less differentiated normal man, who is considered normal either because he allows himself no excesses or because he has no need of them. The normal man is, by definition, influenced as much from within as from without. He constitutes the extensive middle group, on one side of which are those whose motivations are determined mainly by the external object, and, on the other, those who motivations are determined from within. I call the first group *extraverted*, and the second group *introverted.* The terms scarcely require elucidation, as they explain themselves from what has already been said.

Although there are doubtless individuals whose types can be recognized at first glance, this is by no means always the case. As a rule, only careful observation and weighing of the evidence permit a sure classification. However, simple and clear, the fundamental principle of the two opposing attitudes may be, in actual reality they are complicated and hard to make out, because every individual is an exception to the rule. Hence one can never give a description of a type, no matter how complete, that would apply to more than one individual, despite the fact that in some ways, it aptly characterizes thousand of others. Conformity is one side of a man, uniqueness is the other. Classification does not explain the individual psyche. Nevertheless, an understanding of psychological types opens the way to a better understanding of human psychology in general.

Type differentiation often begins very early, so early that in some cases, one must speak of it as innate. The earliest sign of extraversion in a child is his quick adaptation to the environment, and the extraordinary attention he gives to objects and especially to the effect he has on them. Fear of objects is minimal, he lives and moves among them with confidence. His apprehension is quick but imprecise. He appears to develop more rapidly than the introverted child, since he is less reflective and usually without fear. He feels no barrier between himself and objects, and can therefore, play with them freely and learn through them. He likes to carry his enterprises to the extreme and exposes himself to risks. Everything unknown is alluring.

To reverse the picture, one of the earliest signs of introversion in a child is a reflective, thoughtful manner, marked shyness, and even fear of unknown objects. Very early there appears a tendency to assert himself over familiar objects, and attempts are made to master them. Everything unknown is regarded with mistrust; outside influences are usually met with violent resistance. The child wants his own way, and under no circumstances will he submit to an alien rule he cannot understand. When he asks questions, it is not from curiosity or a desire to create a sensation, but because he wants names, meanings, explanations to give him subjective protection against the object. I have seen an introverted child who made his first attempts to walk only after he had learned the names of all the objects in the room he might touch. Thus very early in an introverted child the characteristic defensive attitude can be noted which the adult introvert display towards the object, just as in an extravert child one can very early observe a marked assurance and initiative, a happy trustfulness in his dealing with objects. This is indeed the basic feature of the extraverted attitude psychic life is, as it were, enacted outside the individual in objects and objective relationships. In extreme cases there is even a sort of blindness for his own individuality. The introvert, on the contrary, always acts as though the object possessed a superior power over him against which he has to defend himself. His real world is the inner one.

Sad though it is, the two types are inclined to speak very badly of one another. This fact will immediately strike anyone who investigates the problem. And the reason is that the psychic values have a diametrically opposite localization for the two types. The introvert sees everything that is in any way valuable for him in the subject, the extravert sees it in the object. This dependence on the object seems to the introvert a mark of the greatest inferiority, while to the extravert the preoccupation with the subject seems nothing but infantile autoeroticism. So it is not surprising that the two types often come into conflict. This does not, however, prevent most men from marrying women of the opposite type. Such marriages are very valuable as psychological symbiosis so long as the partners do not attempt a mutual "psychological" understanding. But this phase of understanding belongs to the normal development of every marriage provided the partners have the necessary leisure or the necessary urge to development---though even if both these are present real courage is needed to risk a rupture of the marital peace. In favorable circumstances this phase enters automatically into the lives of both types, for the reason that each type is an example of one-sided development. The one develops only external relations and neglects the inner, the other develops inwardly but remains outwardly at a standstill. In time the need arises for the individual to develop what has been neglected. The development takes the form of a differentiation of certain functions, to which I must now turn in view of their importance for the type problem.

The conscious psyche is an apparatus for adaptation and orientation, and consists of a number of different psychic functions. Among these we can distinguish from basic ones: *sensation, thinking, feeling, intuition.* Under *sensation* I include all perceptions by means of the sense organs, by *thinking* I mean the function of intellectual cognition and the forming of logical conclusions, *feeling* is a function of subjective valuation, *intuition* I take as perception by way of the unconscious, or perception of unconscious contents.

So far as my experience goes, these four basic functions seem to me sufficient to express and represent the various modes of conscious orientation. For complete orientation, all four functions should contribute equally: *thinking* should facilitate cognition and judgment, *feeling* should tell us how and to what extent a thing is important or unimportant to us, *sensation* should convey concrete reality to us through seeing, hearing, tasting, etc., and *intuition* should enable us to divine the hidden possibilities in the background, since these too belong to the complete picture of a given situation.

In reality, however, these basic functions are seldom or never uniformly differentiated and equally at our disposal. As a rule one or the other function occupies the foreground, while the rest remain undifferentiated in the background. Thus, there are many people who restrict themselves to the simple perception of concrete reality, without thinking about it or taking feeling values into account. They bother just as little about the possibilities hidden in a situation. I describe such people as *sensation types*. Others are exclusively oriented by what they think, and simply cannot adapt to a situation which they are unable to understand intellectually. I call such people *thinking types*. Others, again, are guided in everything entirely by feeling. They merely ask themselves whether a thing is pleasant or unpleasant, and orient themselves by then feeling impressions. These are the *feeling types*. Finally, the *intuitives*, concern themselves neither with ideas nor with feeling reactions, not yet with the reality of things, but surrender themselves wholly to the lure of possibilities, and abandon every situation in which no further possibilities can be scented.

Each of these types represents a different kind of one-sidedness, but one which is linked up with and complicated in a peculiar way by the introverted or extraverted attitude. It was because of this complication that I had to mention these function-types, and this brings us back to the question of the one-sidedness of the introverted and extraverted attitudes. This one-sidedness would lead to a complete loss of psychic balance if it were not compensated by an unconscious counterposition. Investigation of the unconscious has shown, for example, that alongside or behind the introvert's conscious attitude there is an unconscious extraverted attitude which automatically compensates his conscious one-sidedness.

* * *

The alteration of the conscious attitude is no light matter, because any habitual attitude is essentially a more or less conscious ideal, sanctified by custom and historical tradition, and founded on the bedrock of one's innate temperament. The conscious attitude is always in the nature of a *Weltanschauung*, if it is not explicitly a religion. It is this that makes the type problem so important. The opposition between the types is not merely an external conflict between men; it is the source of endless inner conflicts, the cause not only of external disputes and dislikes, but of nervous ills and psychic suffering. It is this fact, too, that obliges us physicians constantly to widen our medical horizon and to include within it not only general psychological standpoints but also questions concerning one's views of life and the world.

* * *

Recapitulating, I would like to stress that each of the two *general attitudes, introversion and extraversion,* manifests itself in a special way in an individual through the predominance of one of the four basic functions. Strictly speaking, there are no introverts and extraverts pure and simple, but only introverted and extraverted function-types, such as thinking types, sensation types, etc. There are thus at least eight clearly distinguishable types. Obviously, one could increase this number at will if each of the functions were split into three subgroups, which would not be impossible empirically. One could, for example, easily divide thinking into its three well-known forms, intuitive and speculative, logical and mathematical, empirical and positivist, the last being mainly dependent on sense perception. Similar subgroups could be made of the other functions, as in the case of intuition, which has an intellectual as well as an emotional and sensory aspect. In this way a large number of types could be established, each new division becoming increasingly subtle.

For the sake of completeness, I must add that I do not regard the classification of types according to introversion and extraversion and the four basic functions as the only possible one. Any other psychological criterion could serve just as well as a classifier, although, in my view, no other possesses so great a practical significance.

The Psychological Approach To The Investigation of the Style of Life[*]
Alfred Adler

We will summarily reject no method and no way of discovering the attitude of the individual to the question of life and of finding out the meaning which life wants to disclose to us. The individual's interpretation of the meaning of life is a trivial matter, for it is ultimately the plumb-line of his thinking, feeling, and acting. The real meaning of life, however, is shown in the opposition that meets the individual who acts wrongly. The task of instruction, education, and healing is to bridge the distance between the real meaning of life and the erroneous action of the individual. Our knowledge of man as an individual has existed from time immemorial. To give only a single instance, the historical and personal narratives of ancient peoples---the Bible, Homer, Plutarch, and all the Greek and Roman poets, sagas, fairy-tales, fables, and myths---show a brilliant understanding of the human personality. Until more recent times it was chiefly the poets who best succeeded in getting the clue to a person's style of life. Their ability to show the individual living, acting, and dying as an *indivisible* whole in closest connection with the problems of his environment rouses our admiration to the highest pitch. There can be no doubt that there were also unknown men of the people who were in advance of others in their knowledge of human nature and who passed on their experiences to their descendants. Plainly, both these men and the great geniuses in the knowledge of humanity were distinguished by their more profound insight into the connection of the mainsprings of human action with one another. This talent could only have sprung from their sympathetic bond with the community and from their interest in mankind. Their wider experience, their better knowledge, their more profound insight, came as the reward of their social feeling. There was one feature of their work that could not be missed: that was their ability to describe the myriad, incalculable expressive movements of the individual in such a way that others were able to comprehend them without needing to have recourse to weighing and

[*] Adler, Alfred. (1964). The Psychological Approach to the Investigation of the Style of Life. *Social Interest: A Challenge to Mankind*, 32-41. New York: Capricorn Books. Reprinted by permission.

measuring This power was due to their gift of divination. Only by guessing did they come to see what lies behind and between the expressive movements, names, and the individual's law of movement. Many people call this gift "intuition," and believe that it is the special possession only of the loftiest spirits. As a matter of fact, it is the most universal of all human gifts. Every one makes use of it constantly in the chaos of life, before the abysmal uncertainty of the future.

Since all our problems, the least as well as the greatest, are always new and always modified, we would constantly be involved in fresh mistakes if we were forced to solve them by one single method---for instance, by "conditioned reflexes." This perpetual variety in our problems imposes on us ever fresh demands, and forces us to test anew any mode of conduct, we may have adopted hitherto. Even in a game of cards "conditioned reflexes" are not much use. Correct guessing is the first step towards the mastery of our problems. But this correct guessing is the specially distinctive mark of the man who is a partner, a fellow man, and is interested in the successful solution of all human problems. Peculiar to him is the view into the future of all human happenings, and this attracts him whether he is examining human history in general or the fortunes of a single individual.

Psychology remained a harmless art until philosophy took charge of it. A scientific knowledge of human nature has its roots in psychology and in the anthropology of the philosophers. In the manifold attempts to bring all human events under a comprehensive, universal law the individual man could not be disregarded. The knowledge of the unity of all the individual's expressive forms became an irrefutable truth. The transference to human nature of the laws governing every event resulted in the adoption of varied points of view, and the unfathomable, unknown regulating force was sought for by Kant, Schelling, Hegel, Schopenhauer, Hartmann, Nietzsche, and others in some unconscious motive power that was called either moral law, will, will to power, or the 'unconscious.' Along with the transference of general laws to human activity introspection came into vogue. By this human beings were to be able to predicate something about psychical events and the processes connected with them. This method did not remain long in use. It fell rightly into discredit because there could be no assurance of obtaining objective reports from any one.

In an age of technical development, the experimental method was extensively used. With the help of apparatus and carefully selected questions, tests were arranged that were mean to throw light on the functions of the senses, on the intelligence, character, and personality. By this method, knowledge of the continuity of the personality was lost, or could only be restored by guessing. The doctrine of heredity which later on came to the fore gave up the whole attempt and contented itself with showing that the main thing was the possession of capacities and not the use made of them. The theory of the influence of the endocrine glands also pointed in the same direction, and concentrated on special cases of feelings of inferiority, and their compensation in the event of organic inferiority.

Psychology underwent a renaissance with the advent of psycho-analysis. This resurrected the omnipotent Ruler of human destiny in the form of the sexual libido and conscientiously depicted in the unconscious the pains of hell, and original sin in the 'sense of guilt.' Heaven was left out of account, but this omission, was afterwards rectified by the creation of the 'ideal-ego,' which found support in Individual Psychology's 'ideal' goal of perfection. Still, it was a notable attempt to read between the lines of consciousness—a step forward towards the re-discovery of the style of life—of the individual's line of movement—and of the meaning of life, although the author of psycho-analysis, reveling in sexual metaphors, did not perceive this goal that hovers before humanity. Besides, psychoanalysis, was far too encumbered by the world of spoiled children, and the result was that it always saw in this type, the permanent pattern of the psychical structure, and the deeper layers of the mental life as a part of human evolution remained hidden from it. Its transitory success was due to the predisposition of the immense number of pampered persons who willingly accepted the views of psycho-analysis as rules universally applicable, and who were thereby confirmed in their own style of life. The psycho-analytic technique was directed, with great energy and patience, towards showing that expressive gestures and symptoms were connected with the sexual libido, and making human activity appears to be dependent on an inherent sadistic impulse. Individual Psychology was the first to make it sufficiently clear that these latter phenomena were artificially produced by the resentment of spoiled children. Still there is here also an approach to the recognition of the evolutionary impulse—a tentative adjustment to it. The effort is, however, unsuccessful; in the usual pessimistic fashion the idea of the death-wish is taken as the goal of fulfillment. But this is not an active adaptation; it is simply the expectation of a lingering death founded on the somewhat doubtful second basic law of physics.

Individual Psychology stands firmly on the ground of evolution[1] and in the light of evolution regards all human striving as a struggle for perfection. The craving for life, material and spiritual, is irrevocable bound up with this struggle. So far, therefore, as our knowledge goes, every psychical expressive form presents itself as a movement that leads from a minus to a plus situation. Each individual adopts for himself at the beginning of his life, a law of movement, with comparative freedom to utilize for this his innate capacities and defects, as well as the first impressions of his environment. This law of movement is for each individual different in tempo, rhythm, and direction. The individual, perpetually comparing himself with the unattainable ideal of perfection, is always possessed and spurred on by a feeling of inferiority. We may deduce from this that every human law of movement is faulty when regarded *sub specie aeternitatis*, and seen from an imagined standpoint of absolute correctness.

Each cultural epoch forms this ideal for itself from its wealth of ideas and emotions. Thus in our day it is always to the past alone that we turn to find in the setting-up of this ideal the transient level of man's mental power, and we have the right to admire most profoundly this power that for countless ages has conceived a reliable ideal of human social life. Surely the commands, "Thou shalt not kill" and "Love they neighbor," can hardly every disappear from knowledge and feeling as the supreme court of appeal. These and other norms of human social life, which are undoubtedly the products of evolution and are as native to humanity as breathing, and the upright gait, can be embodied in the conception of an ideal human community, regarded here as the impulse and the goal of evolution. They supply Individual Psychology with the plumb-line, by which alone the right and wrong of all the other goals and modes of movement opposed to evolution are to be valued. It is as this point that Individual Psychology becomes a "psychology of values," just as medical science, the promoter of evolution by its researches and discoveries, is a "science of values."

The sense of inferiority, the struggle to overcome, and social feeling—the foundations upon which the researches of Individual Psychology are based—are therefore essential in considering either the individual or the mass. The truth they represent may be evaded or put into different words; they may be misunderstood and attempts may be made to split hairs about them, but they can never be obliterated. In the right estimate, of any personality these factors must be taken into account, and the state of the feeling of inferiority, of the struggle to overcome, and of the social feeling must be ascertained.

But just as other civilizations under the pressure of evolution drew different conclusions and followed wrong courses, so does every single individual. It is the child's work to create, in the stream of development, the mental structure of a style of life and the appropriate emotions associated with it. The child's emotional, and as yet barely grasped capacity of action, serves him as a standard of his creative power in an environment that is by no means neutral, and provides a very indifferent preparatory school for life. Building on a subjective impression, and guided often by successes or defeats that supply insufficient criteria, the child forms for himself a path, a goal, and a vision of a height lying in the future. All the methods of Individual Psychology that are meant to lead to an understanding of the personality take into account the meaning of the individual about his goal of superiority, the strength of his feeling of inferiority, and the degree of his social feeling. A closer scrutiny of the relation of these factors to one another will make it clear that they all contribute to the nature and extent of the social feeling. The examination proceeds in a way similar to that of experimental psychology, or to that of functional tests in medical cases. The only difference is that it is life itself that sets the test, and this shows how strong the bond is between the individual and the problems in life. That is to say, the individual as a complete being cannot be dragged out of his connection with life—perhaps it would be better to say, with the community. His attitude to the community is first revealed by his style of life. For that reason, experimental tests, which at the best deal only with partial aspects of the individual's life can tell us nothing abut his character or even about his future achievements in the community. And even the *Gestalpsychologie* needs to be supplemented by Individual Psychology in order to be able to form any conclusion regarding the attitude of the individual in the life-process.

The technique of Individual Psychology employed for the discovery of the style of life must therefore in the first place presuppose knowledge of the problems of life and their demands on the individual. It will be evident that their solution presumes a certain degree of social feeling, a close union with life as a whole, and an ability to cooperate and mix with other persons. If this ability is lacking there can be noticed an acute feelings of inferiority in its innumerable variations together with its consequences. This in the main will take the form of evasiveness and the 'hesitant attitude.' The interrelated bodily and mental phenomena that make their appearance with it I have called an 'inferiority complex.' The unresting struggle for superiority endeavors to mask this complex by a 'superiority complex,' which, ignoring social feeling, always aims at the glitter of personal conquest. Once all the phenomena occurring in a case of failure are clearly understood, the reasons for the inadequate preparation are to be sought for in early childhood. By this means we succeed in obtaining a faithful picture of the homogeneous style of life, and at the same time in estimating the extent of the divergence from social feeling in the case of a failure. This is always seen to be a lack of ability to get into contact with other people. It follows from this that the task of the educationist, the teacher, the physician, the pastor is to increase the social feeling and thereby strengthen the courage of the individual. He does this by convincing him of the real causes of failure, by disclosing is wrong meaning---the mistaken significance he has foisted on life---and thus giving him a clearer view of the meaning that life has ordained for humanity.

This task can only be accomplished if a thorough-going knowledge of the problems of life is available, and if the too slight tincture of social feeling both in the inferiority and superiority complexes, as well as in all kinds of human errors is understood. There is likewise require in the consultant a wide experience regarding those circumstances and situations which are likely to hinder the development of social feeling in childhood. Up till now my own experience has taught me that the most trustworthy approaches to the exploration of the personality are to be found in a comprehensive understanding of the earliest childhood memories, of the place of the child in the family sequence, and of any childish errors; in day and night dreams, and in the nature of the exogenous factor that causes the illness. All the results of such an investigation---and along with these the attitude to the doctor has also to be included---have to be assessed with great caution, and the conclusion drawn from them has constantly to be tested for its harmony with other facts that have been established.

---

[1] Of *Studie uber Minderwertigkeit von Organen.* (Hirzel, Leipzig, 2nd edition).

Beginnings of the Self System
Harry Stack Sullivan

Three Aspects of Interpersonal Cooperation

We have got our human animal as far, in the process of becoming a person, as the latter part of infancy, and we find him being subjected more and more to the social responsibilities of the parent. As the infant comes to be recognized as educable, capable of learning, the mothering one modifies more and more the exhibition of tenderness, or the giving of tenderness, to the infant. This earlier feeling that the infant must have unqualified cooperation is now modified to the feeling that the infant should be learning certain things, and this implies a restriction, on the part of the mothering one, of her tender cooperation under certain circumstances.

Successful training of the functional activity of the anal zone, of interaction accentuates a new aspect of tenderness---namely, the additive role of tenderness as a sequel to what the mothering one regards as good behavior. Now this is, in effect--- however it may be prehended by the infant---a reward, which, once the approved social ritual connected with defecating has worked out well, is added to the satisfaction of the anal zone. Here is tenderness taking on the attribute of a reward for having learned something, or for behaving right.

Thus the mother, or the parent responsible for acculturation or socialization, now adds tenderness to her increasingly neutral behavior in a way that can be called rewarding. I think that very, very often the parent does this with no thought of rewarding the infant. Very often the rewarding tenderness merely arises from the pleasure of the mothering one in the skill which the infant has learned---the success which has attended a venture on the toilet chair, or something of that kind. But since tenderness in general is becoming more restricted by the parental necessity to train, these incidents of straightforward tenderness, following the satisfaction of a need like that to defecate, are really an addition---a case of getting something extra for good behavior---and this is, in its generic pattern, a reward. This type of

* Sullivan, Harry S. (1953). Beginnings of the Self System. *Interpersonal Theory of Psychiatry*, 158-171. New York: W.W. Norton & Company, Inc. Reprinted by permission.

learning can take place when the training procedure has been well adjusted to the learning capacity of the infant. The friendly response, the pleasure which the mother takes in something having worked out well, comes more and more to be something special in the very last months of infancy, whereas earlier, tenderness was universal when the mothering one was around, if she was a comfortable mothering one. Thus, to a certain extent, this type of learning can be called learning under the influence of reward---the reward being nothing more or less than tender behavior on the part of the acculturating or socializing mothering one.

Training in the functional activity of the oral-manual behavior---that is, conveying things by the hand to the mouth and so on---begins to accentuate the differentiation of anxiety-colored situations in contrast to approved situations. The training in this particular field is probably, in almost all cases, the area in which *grades of anxiety* first become of great importance in learning; as I have already stressed, behavior of a certain unsatisfactory type provokes increasing anxiety, and the infant learns to keep a distance from, or to veer away from, activities which are attended by increasing anxiety, just a the amoebae avoid high temperatures.

This is the great way of learning in infancy, and later in childhood---by the grading of anxiety, so that the infant learns to chart his course by mild forbidding gestures, or by mild states of worry, concern, or disapproval mixed with some degree of anxiety on the part of the mothering one. The infant, plays, one might say, the old game of getting hotter or colder, in charting a selection of behavioral units which are not attended by an increase in anxiety. Anxiety in its most severe form is a rare experience after infancy, in the more fortunate courses of personality development, and anxiety as it is a function in chronologically adult life, in a highly civilized community confronted by no particular crisis, is never very severe for most people. And yet it is necessary to appreciate that it is anxiety which is responsible for a great part of the inadequate, inefficient, unduly rigid, or otherwise unfortunate performances of people; that anxiety is responsible in a basic sense for a great deal of what comes to a psychiatrist for attention. Only when this is understood, can one realize that this business of whether one is getting more or less anxious is in a large sense the basic influence which determines interpersonal relations---that is, it is not the motor, it does not call interpersonal relations into being, but it more or less directs the course of their development. And even in late infancy, there is a good deal of learning by the anxiety gradient, particularly where there is a mothering one who is untroubled, but still intensely interested in producing the right kind of child; and this learning is apt to first manifest itself when the baby is discouraged from putting the wrong things in the mouth, and the like. This kind of learning applies over a vast area of behavior. But, in this discussion, I am looking for where things are apt to start.

Training of the manual-exploratory function---which I have discussed in connection with the infant's getting his hands near the anus, or into the feces, or, perhaps, his contact with the external genitals---almost always begins the discrimination of situations which are marked by what we shall later discuss as *uncanny emotion.* This uncanny feeling can be described as the abrupt super-vention of *severe anxiety,* with the arrest of anything like the learning process, and with only gradual informative recall of the noted circumstances which preceded the extremely unpleasant incident.

Early in infancy, when situations approach the 'all-or-nothing' character, the induction of anxiety is apt to be the sudden translation fro a condition of moderate euphoria to one of very severe anxiety. And this severe anxiety, as I have said before, has a little bit the effect of a blow on the head, in that later one is not clear at all as to just what was going on at the time anxiety became intense. The educative effect is not by any means as simple and useful as is the educative effect in the other two situations which we have discussed, because the sudden occurrence of severe anxiety practically prohibits ay clear prehension, or understanding of the immediate situation. It does no, however, preclude recall, and as recall develops sufficiently so that one recalls what was about to occur when severe anxiety intervened---in other words, when one has a sense of what one's action was addressed to at the time when everything was disorganized by severe anxiety---then there come to be in all of us certain areas of 'uncanny taboo,' which I think is a perfectly good way of characterizing those things which one stops doing, once one has caught himself doing them. This type of training is much less immediately useful, and, shall I say, is productive of much less healthy acquaintance with reality, than are the other two.

Good-Me, Bad-Me, and Not-Me

Now here I have set up three aspects of interpersonal cooperation which are necessary for the infant's survival, and which dictate learning. That is, these aspects of interpersonal cooperation require acculturation or socialization of the infant. Infants are customarily exposed to all of these before the era of infancy is finished. From experience of these three sorts---with rewards, with the anxiety gradient, and with practically obliterative sudden severe anxiety---there comes an initial personification of three phases of what presently will be *me*, that which is invariably connected with the sentience of *my body*---and you will remember that *my body* as an organization of experiences has come to be distinguished from everything else by its self-sentient character. These beginning personifications of three different kinds, which have in common elements of the prehended body, are organized in about mid-infancy---I can't say exactly when. I have already spoken of the infant's very early double personification of the actual mothering one as the good mother and the bad mother. Now, at this time, the beginning personifications of *me* are *good-me*, *bad-me*, and *not-me*. So far as I can see, in practically every instance of being trained for life, in this or another culture, it is rather inevitable that there shall be this tripartite cleavage in personifications, which have as their central tie--- the thing that binds them ultimately into one, that always keeps them in very close relation---their relatedness to the growing conception of "my body."

Good-me is the beginning personification which organizes experience in which satisfactions have been enhanced by rewarding increments of tenderness, which come to the infant because the mothering one is pleased with eh way things are going; therefore, and to that extent, she is free, and moves toward expressing tender appreciation of the infant. Good-me, as it ultimately develops, is the ordinary topic of discussion about "I."

Bad-me, on the other hand, is the beginning personification which organizes experience in which increasing degrees of anxiety are associated with behavior involving the mothering one in the more-or-less clearly prehended interpersonal setting. That is to say, bad-me is based on the increasing gradient of anxiety and that, in turn, is dependent, at this stage of life, on the observation, if misinterpretation, of the infant's behavior by someone who can induce anxiety.[1] The frequent coincidence of certain behavior on the part of the infant with increasing tenseness and increasingly evident forbidding on the part of the mother is the source of the type of experience which is organized as a rudimentary personification to which we may apply the term bad-me.

So far, the two personifications I have mentioned may sound like sort of laboring of reality. However, these personifications are part of the communicated thinking of the child, a year or so later, and therefore it is not an unwarranted use of inference to presume that they exist at this earlier stage. When we come to the third of these beginning personifications, *not-me,* we are in a different field—one which we know about only through certain very special circumstances. And these special circumstances are not outside the experience of any of us. The personification of not-me is most conspicuously encountered by most of us in an occasional dream while we are asleep, but it is very emphatically encountered by people who are having a severe schizophrenic episode, in aspects that are to them most spectacularly real. As a matter of fact, it is always manifest—not every minute, but every day, in every life—in certain peculiar absences of phenomena where there should be phenomena; and in a good many people—I know not what proportion—it is very striking in its indirect manifestations (dissociated behavior), in which people do, and say things of which they do not and could not have knowledge, things which may be quite meaningful to other people but are unknown to them. The special circumstances which we encounter in grave mental disorders may be, so far as you know, outside your experience; by they were not once upon a time. It is from the evidence of these special circumstances—including both those encountered in everybody and those encountered in grave disturbances of personality, all of which we shall presently touch upon—that I choose to set up this third beginning personification which is tangled up with the growing acquaintance of "my body," the personification of *not-me.* This is a very gradually evolving personification of an always relatively primitive character—that is, organized in unusually simple signs in the parataxic mode of experience, and made up of poorly grasped aspects of living which will presently be regarded as 'dreadful,' and which still later will be differentiated into incidents which are attended by awe, horror, loathing, or dread.

This rudimentary personification of not-me evolves very gradually, since it comes from the experience of intense anxiety—a very poor method of education. Such a complex and relatively inefficient method of getting acquainted with reality would naturally lead to relatively slow evolution of an organization of experiences; furthermore, these experiences are largely truncated, so that what they are really about is not clearly known. Thus organizations of these experiences which, when observed, have led to intense forbidding gestures on the part of the mother, and induced intense anxiety in the infants---are not nearly as clear and useful guides to anything as the other two types of organizations have been. Because experiences marked by uncanny emotion, which are organized in the personification of not-me, cannot be clearly connected with cause and effect---cannot be dealt with in all the impressive ways by which we explain our referential processes later—they persist throughout life as relatively primitive, unelaborated, parataxic symbols. Now that does not mean that the not-me component in adults is infantile, but it does mean that the not-me component is, in all essential respects, practically beyond discussion in communicative terms. Not-me is part of the very 'private mode' of living. But, as I have said, it manifests itself at various times in the life of everyone after childhood---or of nearly everyone. I can't swear to the statistics---by the eruption of certain exceedingly unpleasant emotions in what are called nightmares.

These three rudimentary personifications of *me* are, I believe, just as distinct as the two personifications of the objectively same mother were earlier. But while the personifications of me are getting under way, there is some change going on with respect to the personification of mother. In the latter part of infancy, there is some evidence that the rudimentary personality, as it were, is already fusing the previously disparate personifications of the good and the bad mother; and within a year and a half after the end of infancy we find evidence of this duplex personification of the mothering one as the good mother and the bad mother clearly manifested only in relatively obscure mental processes, such as these dreamings while asleep. But, as I have suggested, when we come to consider the question of the peculiarly inefficient and inappropriate interpersonal relations which constitute problems of mental disorder, there again we discover that the trend in organizing experience which began with this duplex affair has not in any sense utterly disappeared.

The Dynamism of the Self-System

From the essential desirability of being good-me, and from the increasing ability to be warned by slight increase of anxiety---that is, slight diminutions in euphoria---in situations involving the increasingly significant other person, there comes into being the start of an exceedingly important, as it were, secondary dynamism, which is purely the product of interpersonal experience arising from anxiety encountered in the pursuit of the satisfaction of general and zonal needs. This secondary dynamism I call the *self-system.* As a dynamism it is secondary in that it does not have any particular zones of interaction, any particular physiological apparatus, behind it; but it literally uses all zones of interaction and all physiological apparatus which is integrative and meaningful from the interpersonal standpoint. And we ordinarily find its ramifications spreading throughout interpersonal relations in every area where there is any chance that anxiety may be encountered.

The essential desirability of being good-me is just another way of commenting on the essential undesirability of being anxious. Since the beginning personification of good-me is based on experience in which satisfactions are enhanced by tenderness, then naturally there is an essential desirability of living good-me. And since sensory and other abilities of the infant are well matured by now---perhaps even space perception, one of the slowest to come along, is a little in evidence---it is only natural that along with this essential desirability there goes increasing ability to be warned by slight forbidding---in other words, by slight anxiety. Both these situations, for the purpose now under discussion, are situations involving another person---the mothering one, or the congeries of mothering ones--- and she is becoming increasingly significant because, as I have already said, the manifestation of tender cooperation by her is now complicated by her attempting to teach, to socialize the infant; and this makes the relationship more complex, so that it requires better, more effective differentiation by the infant of forbidding gestures, and so on. For all these reasons, there comes into being in late infancy an organization of experience which will ultimately be of nothing less than stupendous importance in personality, and which comes entirely from the interpersonal relations in which the infant is now involved---and these interpersonal relations have their motives (or their motors, to use a less troublesome word) in the infant's general and zonal needs for satisfaction. But out of the social responsibility of the mothering one, which gets involved in the satisfaction of the infant's needs, there comes the organization in the infant of what might be said to be a dynamism directed at how to live with this significant other person. The self-system thus is an organization of educative experience called into being by the necessity to avoid or to minimize incidents of anxiety. The functional activity of the self-system, I am now speaking of it from the general standpoint of a dynamism---is primarily directed to avoiding and minimizing this disjunctive tension of anxiety, and thus indirectly to protecting the infant from this evil eventuality in connection with the pursuit of satisfactions---the relief of general or of zonal tensions.

Thus we may expect, at least until well along in life, that the components of the self-system will exist and manifest functional activity in relation to every general need that a person has, and to every zonal need that the excess supply of energy to the various zones of interaction gives rise to. How conspicuous the 'sector' of the self-system connected with any particular general need or zonal need will be, or how frequent its manifestations, is purely a function of the past experience of the person concerned.

I have said that the self-system begins in the organizing of experience with the mothering one's forbidding gestures, and that these forbidding gestures are refinements in the personification of the bad mother; this might seem to suggest that the self-system comes into being by the *incorporation* or *introjection* of the bad mother, or simply by the introjection of the mother. These terms, incorporation or introjection, have been used in this way, not in speaking of the self-system, but in speaking of the psychoanalytic superego, which is quite different from my conception of the self-system. But, if I have been at all adequate in discussing even what I have presented thus far, it will be clear that the use of such terms in connection with the development of the self-system is a rather reckless oversimplification, if not also a great magic verbal gesture the meaning of which cannot be made explicit. I have said that the self-system comes into being because the pursuit of general and zonal needs for satisfaction is increasingly interfered with by the good offices of the mothering one in attempting to train the young. And so the self-system, far from being anything like a function or an identity with the mothering one, is an organization of experience for avoiding increasing degrees of anxiety which are connected with the educative process. But these degrees of anxiety cannot conceivably, in late infancy (and the situation is similar in most instances at any time in life), mean to the infant what the mothering one, the socializing person, believes she means, or what she actually represents, from the standpoint of the culture being inculcated in the infant. This idea that one can, in some way, take in another person to become a part of one's personality is one of the evils that comes from overlooking the fact that between a doubtless real 'external object' and a doubtless real 'my mind' there is a group of processes---the act of perceiving, understanding, and what not---which is intercalated, which is highly subject to past experience and increasingly subject to foresight of the neighboring future. Therefore, it would in fact be one of the great miracles of all time if our perception of another person were, in any greatly significant number of respects, accurate or exact. Thus I take some pains at this point to urge you to keep your mind free from the notion that I am dealing with something like the taking over of standards of value and the like from another person. Instead, I am talking about the organization of experience connected with relatively successful education in becoming a human being, which begins to be manifest late in infancy.

When I talk about the self-system, I want it clearly understood that I am talking about a *dynamism* which comes to be enormously important in understanding interpersonal relations. This dynamism is an explanatory conception; it is not a thing, a region, or what not, such as superego, egos, ids, and so on. Among the things this conception explains is something that can be described as a quasi-entity, the personification of the self. The personification of the self is what you are talking about when you talk about yourself as "I, and what you are often, if not invariably, referring to when you talk about "me" and "my." But I would like to make it forever clear that *the relation of personifications to that which is personified is always complex and sometimes multiple; and that personifications are not adequate descriptions of that which is personified.* In my effort to make that clear, I have gradually been compelled, in my teaching, to push the beginnings things further and further back in the history of the development of the person, to try to reach the point where the critical deviations from convenient ideas become more apparent. Thus I am now discussing the beginning of the terrifically important self-dynamism as the time when ---far from there being a personification of good-me and bad-me, and the much more rudimentary personification of not-me. These rudimentary personifications constitute anything but a personification of the self such as you all believe you manifest, and which you believe serves its purpose, when you talk about yourself one to another in adult life.

Of the Self-System

The origin of the self-system can be said to rest on the irrational character of culture or, more specifically, society. Were it not for the fact that a great many prescribed ways of doing things have to be lived up to, in order that one shall maintain workable, profitable, satisfactory relations with his fellows; or, were the prescriptions for the types of behavior in carrying on relations with one's fellows perfectly rational---then, for all I know, there would not be evolved, in the course of becoming a person, anything like the sort of self-system that we always encounter. If the cultural prescriptions which characterize any particular society were better adapted to human life, the notions that have grown up about incorporating or introjecting a punitive, critical person would not have arisen.

But even at that, I believe that a human being without a self-system is beyond imagination. It is highly probable that the type of education which we have discussed, even probably the inclusion of certain uncanny experience that tends to organize in the personification of not-me, would be inevitable in the process of the human animal's becoming a human being. I say this because the enormous capacity of the human animal which underlies human personality is bound to lead to exceedingly intricate specializations---differentiations of living, function, and one thing and another; to maintain a workable, profitable, appropriate, and adequate type of relationship among the great numbers of people that can become involved in a growing society, the young have to be taught a vast amount before they begin to be significantly involved in society outside the home group. Therefore, the special secondary elaboration of the sundry types of learning---which I call the self-system-- would, I believe, be ubiquitous aspect of all really human beings in any case. But in an ideal culture, which has never been approximated and at the present moment looks as if it never will be, the proper function of the self-system would be conspicuously different from its actual function in the denizens of our civilization. In our civilization, no parental group actually reflects the essence of the social organization for which the young are being trained in living; and after childhood, when the family influence in acculturation and socialization begins to be attenuated and augmented by other influences, the discrete excerpts, you might say, of the culture which each family has produced as its children come into collision with other discrete excerpts of the culture---all of them more or less belonging to the same cultural system, but having very different accents and importances mixed up in them. As a result of this, the self-system in its actual functioning in life in civilized societies, as they now exist, is often very unfortunate. But do no overlook the fact that the self-system comes into being because of, and can be said to have as its goal, the securing of necessary satisfaction without incurring much anxiety. And however unfortunate the manifestations of the self-system in many contexts may seem, always keep in mind that, if one had no protection against very severe anxiety, one would do practically nothing---or, if one still had to do something, it would take an intolerably long time to get it done.

So, you see, however truly the self-system is the principal stumbling block to favorable changes in personality---a point which I shall develop later on---that does not alter the fact that it is also the principal influence that stands in the way of unfavorable changes in personality. And while the psychiatrist is skillful, in large measure, in his ability to formulate the self-system of another person with whom he is integrated, and to, shall I say, "intuit" the self-system aspects of his patient which tend to perpetuate the type of morbid living that the patient is showing, that still, in no sense, makes the self-system something merely to be regretted. In any event, it is always before us, whether we regret or praise it. This idea of the self-system is simply tremendously important in understanding the vicissitudes of interpersonal relations from here on. If we understand how the self-system begins, then perhaps we will be able to follow even the most difficult idea connected with its function.

The self-system is a product of educative experience, part of which is of the character of reward, and a very important part of which has the graded anxiety element that we have spoken of. But quite early in life, anxiety is also a very conspicuous aspect of the self-dynamism *function.* This is another way of saying that experience functions in both recall and foresight. Since troublesome experience, organized in the self-system, has been experience connected with grades of anxiety, it is not astounding that this element of recall, functioning on a broad scale, makes the intervention of the self-dynamism in living tantamount to the warning, or foresight, of anxiety. And warning of anxiety means noticeable anxiety, really a warning that anxiety will get worse.

There are two things which I would like to mention briefly at this point. One is the infant's discovery of the unobtainable, his discovery of situations in which he is powerless, regardless of all the cooperation of the mothering one. The infant's crying for the full moon is an illustration of this. Now even before the end of infancy, it is observable that these unattainable objects gradually come to be treated *as if* they did not exist; that is, they do not call out the expression of zonal needs. This is possible the simplest example of a very important process manifested in living which I call *selective inattention.*

The other thing I would like to mention is this: Where the parental influence is peculiarly incongruous to the actual possibilities and needs of the infant---before speech has become anything except a source of marvel in the family, before it has any communicative function whatever, before alleged words have any meaning--- there can be inculcated in this growing personification of bad-me and not-me disastrous distortions which will manifest themselves, barring very fortunate experience, in the whole subsequent development of personality. I shall soon discuss some typical distortions, one of the most vicious of which occurs in late infancy as the outcome of the mothering one's conviction that infants have *wills* which have to be guided, governed, broken, or shaped. And when, finally, we come to discuss concepts of mental disorders we will have to pick up the manifestations of a few particularly typical distortions, in each subsequent stage from the time that they first occur.

[1] Incidentally, for all I know, anybody can induce anxiety in an infant, but there is no use cluttering up our thought by considering that, because frequency of events is of very considerable significance in all learning processes; and at this stage of life, when the infant is perhaps nine or ten months old, it is likely to be the mother who is frequently involved in interpersonal situations with the infant.

Chapter Three
Dispositional Perspectives

"Thought…is an integral part of personality. One might say…that the life of feeling and emotion is the warp and that higher mental processes are the wool of the fabric."

Gordon Allport

What Is A Trait of Personality?[*]
Gordon W. Allport

What Sigmund Freud is to psychoanalysis, Gordon Allport is---almost---to trait theory. In this selection," What is a Trait of Personality," Allport offers one of the earliest psychological definitions of a personality trait. This article was presented at a conference held in 1929, when the modern field of personality psychology was just beginning to be established in the field. Allport's essential contribution was to take the study of normal variations in personality out of the exclusive hands of novelists, dramatists, theologians, and philosophers and to begin to transform it into a scientific discipline.

Based on the age of this article, it is astonishing to see how many contemporary issues Allport anticipates and how convincingly he addresses them. Some of these issues include the person-situation debate, whether a trait is a cause or simply a synopsis of behavior and the distinction between the idiographic (single case) and nomothetic (group) approaches. As you will see, Allport focuses on how traits are structured within a single individual. Even today, Allport is still given credit for this article's contribution to the current field of personality psychology.

At the heart of all investigation of personality lies the puzzling problem of the nature of the unit or element which is the carrier of the distinctive behavior of a man. Reflexes and habits are too specific in reference, and connote constancy rather than consistency in behavior; attitudes are all defined, and as employed by various writers refer to determining tendencies that range in inclusiveness from the *Aufgabe* to the *Weltanschauungs,*[1] *dispositions* and *tendencies* are even less definitive. But *traits*, although appropriated by all manner of writers for all manner of purposes, may still be salvaged, I think, and limited in their reference to a certain

[*] Allport, Gordon. (1931). What is a Trait of Personality? *Journal of Abnormal and Social Psychology,* 25, 368-372, American Psychological Association (APA). Reprinted by permission.

definite conception of a generalized response-unit in which resides the distinctive quality of behavior that reflects personality. Foes as well as friends of the doctrine of traits will gain from a more consistent use of the term.

The doctrine itself has never been explicitly stated. It is my purpose with the aid of eight criteria to define *trait*, and to state the logic and some of the evidence for the admission of this concept to good standing in psychology.

1. A trait has more than nominal existence. A trait may be said to have the same kind of existence that a habit of a complex order has. Habits of a complex, or higher, order have long been accepted as household facts in psychology. There is no reason to believe that the mechanism which produces such habits (integration, *Gestaltung,* or whatever it may be) stops short of producing the more generalized habits which are here called traits of personality.

2. A trait is more generalized than a habit. Within a personality there are, of course, many independent habits; but there is also so much integration, organization, and coherence among habits that we have no choice but to recognize great systems of interdependent habits. If the habit of brushing one's teeth can be shown, statistically or genetically, to be unrelated to the habit of dominating a tradesman, there can be no question of a common trait involving both these habits but if the habit of dominating a tradesman can be shown, statistically or genetically, to be related to the habit of bluffing one's way past guards, there is the presumption that a common trait of personality exists which includes these two habits. Traits may conceivably embrace anywhere from two habits to a legion of habits. In this way, there may be said to be major, widely extensified traits and minor, less generalized traits in a given personality.

3. A trait is dynamic, or at least determinative. It is not the stimulus that is the crucial determinant in behavior that expresses personality; it is the trait itself that is decisive. Once formed a trait seems to have the capacity of directing responses to stimuli into characteristic channels. This emphasis upon the dynamic nature of traits, ascribing to them a capacity for guiding the specific response is variously recognized by many writers. The principle is nothing more than that which has been subscribed to in various connections by Woodworth, Prince, Sherrington, Coghill, Kurt Lewin, Troland, Lloyd Morgan, Thurstone, Bentley, Stern, and others.[2] From this general point of view traits might be called "derived drives" or "derived motives." Whatever they are called they may be regarded as playing a motivating role in each act, thus endowing the separate adjustments of the individual to specific stimuli with that adverbial quality that is the very essence of personality.

* * *

4. The existence of a trait may be established empirically or statistically. In order to know that a person has a *habit* it is necessary to have evidence of repeated reactions of a constant type. Similarly in order to know that an individual has a trait it is necessary to have evidence of repeated reactions which, though not necessarily constant in type, seem none the less to be consistently a function of the same underlying determinant. If this evidence is gathered casually by mere observation of the subject or through the reading of a case history or biography, it may be called *empirical* evidence.

More exactly, of course, the existence of a trait may be established with the aid of statistical techniques that determine the degree of coherence among the separate responses. Although this employment of statistical aid is highly desirable, it is not necessary to wait for such evidence before speaking of traits, any more than it would be necessary to refrain from speaking of the habit of biting fingernails until the exact frequency of the occurrence is known. Statistical methods are at present better suited to intellective than to conative functions, and it is with the latter that we are chiefly concerned in our studies of personality. [3]

5. Traits are only relatively independent of each other. The investigative desires, of course, to discover what the fundamental traits of personality are, that is to say, what broad trends in behavior do exist independently of one another. Actually with the test methods and correlational procedures in use, completely independent variation is seldom found. In one study expansion correlated with extroversion to the extent of +.39, ascendance with conservatism, +.32, and humor with insight, +.83, and so on. This overlap may be due to several factors, the most obvious being the tendency of the organism to react in an integrated fashion, so that when concrete acts are observed or tested they reflect not only the trait under examination, but also simultaneously other traits; several traits may thus converge into a final common path. It seems safe, therefore, to predict that traits can never be completely isolated for study, since they never show more than a relative independence of one another.

In the instance just cited, it is doubtful whether humor and insight (provided their close relationship is verified in subsequent studies) represent distinct traits. In the future perhaps it may be possible to agree upon a certain magnitude of correlation below which it will be acceptable to speak of *separate* traits, and above which *one* trait only will be recognized. If one trait only is indicated it will presumably represent a broadly generalized disposition. For example, if humor and insight cannot be established as independent traits, it will be necessary to recognize a more inclusive trait, and name it perhaps "sense of proportion."

6. A trait of personality, psychologically considered, is not the same as moral quality. A trait of personality may or may not coincide with some well-defined, conventional, social concept. Extroversion, ascendance, social participation, and insight are free from preconceived moral significance, large because each is a word newly coined or adapted to fit a psychological discovery. It would be ideal if we could in this way find our traits first and then name them. But honesty, loyalty, neatness, and tact, though encrusted with social significance, may likewise represent true traits of personality. The danger is that in devising scales for their measurement we may be bound by the conventional meanings, and thus be led away from the precise integration as it exists in a given individual. Where possible it would be well for us to find our traits first, and then seek devaluated terms with which to characterize our discoveries.

7. Acts, and even habits, that are inconsistent with a trait are not proof of the non-existence of the trait. The objection most often considered fatal to the doctrine of traits has been illustrated as follows: "An individual may be habitually neat with respect to his person, and characteristically slovenly in his handwriting, or the care of his desk."[4]

In the first place this observation fails to state that there are cases frequently met where a constant level of neatness is maintaining in all of a person's acts, giving unmistakable empirical evidence that the trait of neatness is, in some people at least, thoroughly and permanently integrated. All people must not be expected to show the same degree of integration in respect to a given trait. *What is a major trait in one personality may be a minor trait, or even nonexistent in another personality.*[5]

In the second place, we must concede that there may be opposed integrations, i.e., contradictory traits, in a single personality. The same individual may have a trait both of neatness and of carelessness, of ascendance and submission, although frequently of unequal strength.

In the third place, there are in every personality instances of acts that are unrelated to existent traits, the produce of the stimulus and of the attitude of the moment. Even the characteristically neat person may become careless in his haste to catch a train.

But to say that not all of a person's acts reflect some higher integration is not to say that no such higher integrations exist.

8. A trait may be viewed in the light of the personality which contains it, or in the light of a distribution in the population at large. Each trait has both its unique and its universal aspect. In its unique aspect, the trait takes its significance entirely from the role it plays in the personality as a whole. In its universal aspect, the trait is arbitrarily isolated for study, and a comparison is made between individuals in respect to it. From this second point of view, traits merely extend the familiar field of the psychology of individual differences.

There may be relatively few traits, a few hundred perhaps, that are universal enough to be scaled in the population at large; whereas there may be in a single personality a thousand traits distinguishable to a discerning observer. For this reason, after a scientific schedule of universal traits is compiled, there will still be the field of artistic endeavor for psychologists in apprehending correctly the subtle and unique traits peculiar to one personality alone, and in discovering the pattern which obtains between these traits in the same personality.

---

[1] With these German words, Allport is describing the range from the specific tasks an individual must perform (Aufgabe) to his or her entire view of the world (Weltanschauung).

[2] This is an all-star list of important psychologists and scientists at the time this article was written. Of these, Kurt Lewin and Allport himself had the most lasting influence on personality psychology.

[3] "Conative functions" here refer to motivation; at the time this was written statistical methods of psychological measurement (psychometrics) had been used exclusively for the measurement of intellectual skills, not motivation or personality. Over the following decades, the situation changed and psychometrics became a foundation of modern personality psychology.

[4] This comment anticipates the "person-situation" debate that flared up in 1968, almost 40 years later, with the publication of a book by Walter Mischel. Interestingly, the inconsistency of neatness, almost exactly as Allport here describes it, was used as an argument against the doctrine of traits in an even later article by Mischel and Peake (1982).

[5] This comment---that not all traits apply to all people---was developed into an important article many years later by the psychologists Daryl Bem and Andrea Allen (1974).

Chapter Four
Humanistic Perspectives

"We have, all of us, an impulse to improve ourselves, an impulse toward actualizing more of our potentialities, toward self-actualization, or full humanness, or human fulfillment, or whatever term you like. Granted this, then what holds us up? What blocks us? One such defense against growth...I call the 'Jonah Complex' or the 'fear of one's own greatness,' 'the evasion of one's destiny' or the 'running away from one's own best talents'."

Abraham Maslow

Existential Psychology---What's In It For Us?*

Abraham H. Maslow

One of the major leaders of American humanistic psychology and brilliant
proponent of the process of self-actualization was Abraham Maslow. He is best
recognized for his illustrious leadership in creating a "healthy psychology" of
personality. In this article, "Existential Psychology---What's In It for Us," Maslow
addresses the way in which European existentialist philosophy, especially the one
proposed by Sartre, is relevant to the field of psychology. Here, he discloses how
American psychologists have extracted a more optimistic message from existentialism
than did the existential philosophers themselves. Setting aside the obsession with
anguish, forlornness, and despair of the European existentialists," Maslow argues that
the loss of illusion is both exhilarating and strengthening in the final analysis.
Clearly, this article sets the underlying tone of the third force movement, humanism.

I am not an existentialist, nor am I even a careful and thorough student of
this movement. There is much in the existentialist writings that I find extremely
difficult, or even impossible, to understand and that I have not made much effort to
struggle with.

I must confess also that I have studied existentialism not so much for its own
sake as in the spirit of, "What's in it for me as a psychologist?" trying all the time to
translate it into terms I could use. Perhaps this is why I have found it to be not so
much a totally new revelation as a stressing, confirming, sharpening, and
rediscovering of trends already existing in American psychology (the various self
psychologies, growth psychologies, self-actualization psychologies, organismic

*   Maslow, Abraham.   (1969). Existential Psychology---What's In It For Us?
Existential Philosophy, 49-57. New York: McGraw Hill. Reprinted by permission.

psychologies, certain neo-Freudian psychologies, the Jungian psychology, not to mention some of the psychoanalytic ego psychologists, the Gestalt therapists, and I don't know how many more).

For this and other reasons, reading the existentialists has been for me a very interesting, gratifying, and instructive experience. And I think this will also be true for many other psychologists, especially those who are interested in personality theory and in clinical psychology. It has enriched, enlarged, corrected, and strengthened my thinking about the human personality, even though it has not necessitated any fundamental reconstruction.

First of all, permit me to define existentialism in a personal way, in terms of "what's in it for me." To me, it means essentially a radical stress on the concept of identity and the experience of identity as a *sine qua non* of human nature and of any philosophy or science of human nature. I choose this concept as the basic one partly because I understand it better in terms like essence, existence, and ontology and partly because I also feel it can be worked with empirically, it not now, then soon.

But than a paradox results, for the Americans have also been impressed with the quest for identity (Allport, Rogers, Goldstein, Fromm, Wheelis, Erikson, Horney, May, et. al.). And I must say that these writers are a lot clearer and a lot closer to the raw fact, that is, more empirical than are, e.g., the Germans Heidegger and Jaspers.[1]

1. Conclusion number one is, then, that the Europeans and Americans have been "talking prose all the time and didn't know it." Partly, of course, this simultaneous development in different countries is itself an indication that the people who have independently been coming to the same conclusions are all responding to something real outside themselves.

2. This something real is, I believe the total collapse of all sources of value outside the individual. Many European existentialists are largely reacting to Nietzsche's conclusion that God is dead and perhaps to the fact that Marx also is dead. The Americans have learned that political democracy and economic prosperity do not in themselves solve any of the basic value problems. There is no place else to turn but inward, to the self, as the locus of values.[2] Paradoxically, even some of the religious existentialists will go along with this conclusion part of the way.

3. It is extremely important for psychologists that the existentialists may supply psychology with the underlying philosophy that it now lacks. Logical positivism has been a failure, especially for clinical and personality psychologists.[3] At any rate, the basic philosophical problems will surely be opened up for discussion again, and perhaps psychologists will stop relying on pseudo-solutions or on unconscious, unexamined philosophies that they picked up as children.

4. An alternative phrasing of the core (for an American) of European existentialism is that it deals radically with that human predicament presented by the gap between human aspirations and human limitations (between what the human being *is*, what he would *like to be,* and what he *could be).* This is not so far off from the identity problem as it might at first sound. A person is both actuality and potentiality.

That serious concern with this discrepancy could revolutionize psychology, there is no doubt in my mind. Various literatures already support such a conclusion, e.g., projective testing, self-actualization, the various peak experiences (in which this gap is bridged), the Jungian psychologies, various theological thinkers.

Not only this, but they raise also the problems and techniques of integration of this twofold nature of man, his lower and his higher, his creatureliness and his Godlikeness. On the whole, most philosophies and religions, Eastern as well as Western, have dichotomized them, teaching that the way to become "higher" is to renounce and master "the lower." The existentialists, however, teach that both are simultaneously defining characteristics of human nature. Neither can be repudiated; they can only be integrated. But we already now something of these integration techniques---of insight, of intellect in the broader sense, of love, of creativeness, of human and tragedy, of play, or art. I suspect we will focus our studies on these integrative techniques more than we have in the past. Another consequence for my thinking of this stress on the twofold nature of man is the realization that some problems must remain eternally insoluble.

5. From this flows naturally a concern with the ideal, authentic, or perfect, or Godlike human being, a study of human potentialities as now existing in a certain sense, as current knowable reality. This, too, may sound merely literary, but it is not. I remind you that this is just a fancy way of asking the old, unanswered questions, "What are the goals of therapy, or education, of bringing up children?"

It also implies another truth and another problem that calls urgently for attention. Practically every serious description of the "authentic person" extant implies that such a person, by virtue of what he has become, assumes a new relation to his society and, indeed, to society in general. He not only transcends himself in various ways; he also transcends his culture. He resists enculturation. He becomes more detached from his culture and from his society. He becomes a little more a member of his species and a little less a member of his local group. My feeling is that most sociologists and anthropologists will take this hard.[4] I therefore confidently expect controversy in this area.

6. From the European writers, we can and should pick up their greater emphasis on what they call "philosophical anthropology," that is, the attempt to define man, and the differences between man and any other species, between man and objects, and between man and robots. What are his unique and defining characteristics? What is as essential to man that without it he would no longer be defined as a man?

On the whole, this is a task from which American psychology has abdicated. The various behaviorisms do not generate any such definition, at least none that can be taken seriously. (What would an S-R man be like?)[5] Freud's picture of man was clearly unsuitable, leaving out as it did his aspirations, his realizable hopes, his Godlike qualities...

7. The Europeans are stressing the self-making of the self, in a way that the Americans do not. Both the Freudians and the self-actualization and growth theorists in this country talk more about discovering the *self* (as if it were there waiting to be found) and of *uncovering* therapy (shovel away the top layers and you will see what has been always lying there, hidden). To say, however, that the self is a

project and altogether created by the "continual choices of the person himself" is almost surely an overstatement in view of what we know of, e.g., the constitutional and genetic determinants of personality. This clash of opinion is a problem that can be settled empirically.

8. A problem we psychologists have been ducking is the problem of responsibility and, necessarily tied in with it, the concepts of courage and of will in the personality. Perhaps this is close to what the psychoanalysts are now calling "ego strength."

9. American psychologists have listened to Allport's call for an idiographic psychology[6] but have not done much about it. Not even the clinical psychologists have. We now have an added push from the phenomenologists and existentialists in this direction, one that will be very hard to resist, indeed, I think, theoretically impossible to resist. If the study of the uniqueness of the individual does not fit into what we know of science, then so much the worse for the conception of science. It, too, will have to endure re-creation.

10. Phenomenology[7] has a history in American psychological thinking, but on the whole I think it has languished. The European phenomenologists, with their excruciatingly careful and laborious demonstrations, can reteach us that the best way of understanding another human being, or at least a way necessary for some purposes, is to get into his *Weltanschauung*[8] and to be able to see his world through his eyes. Of course such a conclusion is rough on any positivistic philosophy of science.

11. The existentialist stress on the ultimate aloneness of the individual is a useful reminder for us not only to work out further the concepts of decision, of responsibility, of choice, of self-creation, of autonomy, of identity itself. It also makes more problematic and more fascinating the mystery of communication between alonenesses via, e.g., intuition and empathy, love and altruism, identification with others, and homonomy in general. We take these for granted. It would be better if we regarded them as miracles to be explained.

12. Another preoccupation of existentialist writers can be phrased very simply, I think. It is the dimension of seriousness and profundity of living (or perhaps the "tragic sense of life") contrasted with the shallow and superficial life, which is a kind of diminished living, a defense against the ultimate problems of life. This is not just a literary concept. It has real operational meaning, for instance, in psychotherapy, I (and others) have been confronted with the fact that tragedy can sometimes be therapeutic and that therapy often seems to work best when people are *driven* by pain. It is when the shallow life does not work that it is questioned and that there occurs a call to fundamentals. Shallowness in psychology does not work either, as the existentialists are demonstrating very clearly.

13. The existentialists, along with many other groups, are helping to teach us about the limits of verbal, analytic, conceptual rationality. They are part of the current call back to raw experience as prior to any concepts or abstractions. This amounts to what I believe to be a justified critique of the whole way of thinking of the Western world in the twentieth century, including orthodox positivistic science and philosophy, both of which badly need reexamination.

14. Possibly the most important of all the changes to be wrought by phenomenologists and existentialists is an overdue revolution in the theory of science. I should not say "wrought by" but rather "helped along by," because there are many other forces helping to destroy the official philosophy of science or "scientism." It is not only the Cartesian split between the subject and object that needs to be overcome. There are other radical changes made necessary by the inclusion of the psyche and of raw experience in reality, and such a change will affect not only the science of psychology but all other sciences as well. For example, parsimony, simplicity, precision, orderliness, logic, elegance, definition are all of the realm of abstraction.

15. I close with the stimulus that has most powerfully affected me in the existentialist literature, namely, the problem of future time in psychology. Not that this, like all the other problems or pushes I have mentioned up to this point, was totally unfamiliar to me, nor, I imagine, to *any* serious student of the theory of personality....Growth and becoming and possibility necessarily point toward the future, as do the concepts of potentiality and hoping and of wishing and imagining; reduction to the concrete is a loss of future; threat and apprehension point to the future (no future=no neurosis); self-actualization is meaningless without reference to a currently active future life; life can be a gestalt in time, etc.

And yet the *basic and central importance* of this problem for the existentialists has something to teach us....I think it fair to say that no theory of psychology will ever be complete that does not centrally incorporate the concept that man has his future within him, dynamically active at this present moment...Also we must realize that *only* the future is in principle unknown and unknowable, which means that all habits, defenses, and coping mechanisms are doubtful and ambiguous because they are based on past experience. Only the flexibly creative person can really manage (the) future, only the one who can face novelty with confidence and without fear. I am convinced that much of what we now call psychology is the study of the tricks we use to avoid the anxiety of absolute novelty by making believe the future will be like the past.

*   *   *

It is possible that existentialism will not only enrich psychology. It may also be an additional push toward the establishment of another *branch* of psychology, the psychology of the fully evolved and authentic self and its ways of being.***

Certainly it seems more and more clear that what we call "normal" in psychology is really a psychopathology of the average, so undramatic and so widely spread that we do not even notice it ordinarily. The existentialist's study of the authentic person and of authentic living helps to throw this general phoniness, this living by illusions, and by fear, into a harsh, clear light which reveals it clearly as sickness, even though widely shared.

I do not think we need take too seriously the European existentialists' harping on dread, on anguish, on despair, and the like, for which their only remedy seems to be to keep a stiff upper life.[9] This high-IQ whimpering on a cosmic scale occurs whenever an external source of values fails to work. They should have learned from the psychotherapists that the loss of illusions and the discovery of identity, though painful at first, can be ultimately exhilarating and strengthening.

---

[1] The psychologists listed were identified with humanistic or humanistic-psychoanalytic positions; the Germans were speculative philosophers.

[2] This was a key point by Sarte.

[3] In this context, Maslow is using the term "logical positivism" to refer to the position that truth can be known with certainty if correct methods are used In psychology this leads to a superscientific outlook that emphasizes operational definitions and precise measurements over deeper meanings.

[4] Many anthropologists work from the assumption that members of different cultures are basically and even irreducibly different. But Sartre spoke of the "universal human condition," a viewpoint Maslow here seems to endorse.

[5] By "S-R man," Maslow is referring to the image of humanity implied by the behavioral approaches to psychology that were dominant when this piece was written (S-R stands for "stimulus-response").

[6] At times Gordon Allport called for an "idiographic" approach that treated each person as a unique case rather than as a point on a continuum. But neither Allport nor his successors ever seemed entirely clear about how to do this, as Maslow mentions.

[7] "Phenomenology" is the study of experience; in psychology it treats an individual's perception of reality as the essential fact about him or her.

[8] World view.

[9] This is Maslow's sarcastic construal of Sartre's call for existential courage.

Some Issues Concerning the Control Of Human Behavior: A Symposium [*]

Carl R. Rogers & B.F. Skinner

For over thirty years (1950s through 1980s), there was an ongoing debate about the control of human behavior between two intellectual leaders in psychology. These two intellectual giants were associated with two entirely different schools of psychology. One represented the behavioristic approach and its focus upon overt behavior, its consequences and the environment; the other represented the humanistic approach and its emphasis upon subjective experiences (covert behavior), free will and choice. B.F. Skinner, the leading representative of behaviorism, dedicated himself to the experimental analysis of behavior and its application to a wide variety of practical problems. Carl R. Rogers, the leading representative of humanism, accentuated the worth and dignity of the person and examined the more human side or inner essence of existence. . Central to this debate was the issue of control.

Rogers (1902-1987), originally a candidate for the ministry, became interested in helping disturbed children, so he pursued the study of clinical psychology and earned his Ph.D. from Columbia University in 1931. Skinner (1904-1990), one of the most famous and influential figures in behaviorism, earned his Ph.D. in psychology in 1931 from Harvard University. Each of these two men became intellectual giants in their respective schools of thought.

In 1956, "Some Issues Concerning the Control of Human Behavior: A Symposium," was published in Science. It highlights the debate on the control of human behavior between Rogers and Skinner at the 1956 annual meeting of the American Psychological Association in Chicago. As you will see, Skinner's view calls for an application of a behavioral technology that predicts and controls behavior to our everyday lives. Rogers, on the other hand, poses questions about the purpose of such control and maintains that there must be an agreement on values prior to the acceptance of behavioral technologies and their applications to life.

[*] Rogers, Carl and B. F. Skinner. (1956). Some Issues Concerning the Control of Human Behavior: A Symposium. *Science*, 124, 1057-1064. American Association for the Advancement of Science. Reprinted by permission.

81

I (Skinner)

Science is steadily increasing our power to influence, change, mold---in a word, control---human behavior. It has extended our "understanding" (whatever that may be) so that we deal more successfully with people in nonscientific ways, but it has also identified conditions or variables which can be used to predict and control behavior in a new, and increasingly rigorous, technology....It is the 'experimental study' of behavior which carries us beyond awkward or inaccessible "principles," "factors," and so on, to variables which can be directly manipulated.

It is also, and for more or less the same reasons, the conception of human behavior emerging from an experimental analysis which most directly challenges traditional views. Psychologists themselves often do not seem to be aware of how far they have moved in this direction. But the change is not passing unnoticed by others. Until only recently it was customary to deny the possibility of a rigorous science of human behavior by arguing, either that a lawful science was impossible because man was a free agent, or that merely statistical predictions would always leave room for personal freedom. But those who used to take this line have become most vociferous in expressing their alarm at the way these obstacles are being surmounted.

Now, the control of human behavior has always been unpopular. Any undisguised effort to control usually arouses emotional reactions. We hesitate to admit, even to ourselves, that we are engaged in control, and we may refuse to control, even when this would be helpful, for fear of criticism....

Man's natural inclination to revolt against selfish control has been exploited to good purpose in what we call the philosophy and literature of democracy. The doctrine of the rights of man has been effective in arousing individuals to concerted action against governmental and religious tyranny. The literature which has had this effect has greatly extended the number of terms in our language which express reactions to the control of men. But the ubiquity and ease of expression of this attitude spells trouble for any science which may give birth to a powerful technology of behavior....I am not so much concerned here with the political or economic consequences for psychology, although research following certain channels may well suffer harmful effects. We ourselves, as intelligent men and women, and as exponents of Western thought, share these attitudes. They have already interfered with the free exercise of a scientific analysis, and their influence threatens to assume more serious proportions.

Three broad areas of human behavior supply good examples. The first of these---*personal control*---may be taken to include person-to-person relationships in the family, among friends, in social and work groups, and in counseling and psychotherapy. Other fields are *education* and *government.* A few examples from each will show how nonscientific preconceptions are affecting our current thinking about human behavior.

Personal Control

People living together in groups come to control one another with a technique which is not inappropriately called "ethical." When an individual behaves in a fashion acceptable to the group, he receives admiration, approval, affection, and many other reinforcements which increase the likelihood that he will continue to behave in that fashion. When his behavior is not acceptable, he is criticized, censured, blamed, or otherwise punished. In the first case the group calls him "good," and in the second, "bad." This practice is so thoroughly ingrained in our culture that we often fail to see that it is a technique of control. Yet we are almost always engaged in such control, even though the reinforcements and punishments are subtle.

The practice of admiration is an important part of a culture, because behavior which is otherwise inclined to be weak can be set up and maintained with its help. The individual is especially likely to be praised, admired, or loved when he acts for the group in the face of great danger, for example, or sacrifices himself or his possessions, or submits to prolonged hardship, or suffers martyrdom. These actions are not admirable in any absolute sense, but they require admiration if they are to be strong. Similarly, we admire people who behave in original and exceptional ways, not because such behavior is itself admirable, but because we do not know how to encourage original or exceptional behavior in any other way. The group acclaims independent, unaided behavior in part because it is easier to reinforce than to help.

As long as this technique of control is misunderstood, we cannot judge correctly an environment in which there is less need for heroism, hardship, or independent action. We are likely to argue that such an environment is itself less admirable or produces less admirable people. In the old days, for example, young scholars often lived in undesirable quarters, ate unappetizing or inadequate food, performed unprofitable tasks for a living or to pay for necessary books and materials or publications. Older scholars and other members of the group offered compensating reinforcement in the form of approval and admiration for these sacrifices. When the modern graduate student receives a generous scholarship, enjoys good living conditions, and has his research and publication subsidized, the grounds for evaluation seem to be pulled from under us. Such a student no longer needs admiration to carry him over a series of obstacles (no matter how much he may need it for other reasons), and, in missing certain familiar objects of admiration, we are likely to conclude that such conditions are less admirable. Obstacles to scholarly work may serve as a useful measure of motivation---and we may go wrong unless some substitute is found---but we can scarcely defend a deliberate harassment of the student for this purpose. The productivity of any set of conditions can be evaluated only when we have freed ourselves of the attitudes which have been generated in us as members of an ethical group....

Education

The techniques of education were once frankly aversive. The teacher was usually older and stronger than his pupils and was able to "make them learn." This meant that they were not actually taught but were surrounded by a threatening world from which they could escape only by learning. Usually they were left to their own resources in discovering how to do so....

Progressive education was a humanitarian effort to substitute positive reinforcement for such aversive measures, but in the search for useful human values in the classroom it has never fully replaced the variables it abandoned. Viewed as a branch of behavioral technology, education remains relatively inefficient. We supplement it, and rationalize it, by admiring the pupil who learns *for himself*; and we often attribute the learning process, or knowledge itself, to something *inside* the individual. We admire behavior which seems to have inner sources. Thus we admire one who *recites* a poem more than one who simply *reads* it. We admire one who *knows* the answer more than one who *knows where to look it up*. We admire the *writer* rather than the *reader*. We admire the arithmetician who can do a problem in his head rather than with a slide rule or calculating machine, or in "original" ways rather than by a strict application of rules. In general, we feel that any aid or "crutch"---except those aids to which we are now thoroughly accustomed---reduces the credit due....

By admiring the student for knowledge and blaming him for ignorance, we escape some of the responsibility of teaching him. We resist any analysis of the educational process which threatens the notion of inner wisdom or questions the contention that the fault of ignorance lies with the student. More powerful techniques which bring about the same changes in behavior by manipulating *external* variables are decried as brainwashing or thought control. We are quite unprepared to judge *effective* educational measures. As long as only a few pupils learn much of what is taught, we do not worry about uniformity or regimentation....

Government

Government has always been the special field of aversive control. The state is frequently defined in terms of the power to punish, and jurisprudence leans heavily upon the associated notion of personal responsibility. Yet it is becoming increasingly difficult to reconcile current practice and theory with these earlier views. In criminology, for example, there is a strong tendency to drop the notion of responsibility in favor of some such alternative as capacity or controllability. But no matter how strongly the facts, or even practical expedience, support such a change, it is difficult to make the change in a legal system designed on a different plan. When governments resort to other techniques (for example, positive reinforcement), the concept of responsibility is no longer relevant and the theory of government is no longer applicable....

The dangers inherent in the control of human behavior are very real. The possibility of the misuse of scientific knowledge must always be faced. We cannot escape by denying the power of a science of behavior or arresting its development. It is no help to cling to familiar philosophies of human behavior simply because they are more reassuring. As I have pointed out elsewhere; the new techniques emerging from a science of behavior must be subject to the explicit countercontrol which has already been applied to earlier and cruder forms. Brute force and deception, for example, are now fairly generally suppressed by ethical practices and by explicit governmental and religious agencies. A similar countercontrol of scientific knowledge in the interests of the group is a feasible and promising possibility. Although we cannot say how devious the course of its evolution may be, a cultural pattern of control and countercontrol will presumably emerge which will be most widely supported because it is most widely reinforcing....

If the advent of a powerful science of behavior causes trouble, it will not be because science itself is inimical to human welfare but because older conceptions have not yielded easily or gracefully. We expect resistance to new techniques of control from those who have heavy investments in the old, but we have no reason to help them preserve a series of principles that are not ends in themselves but rather outmoded means to an end. What is needed is a new conception of human behavior which is compatible with the implications of a scientific analysis. All men control and are controlled. The question of government in the broadest possible sense is not how freedom is to be preserved but what kinds of control are to be used and to what ends. Control must be analyzed and considered in its proper proportions. No one, I am sure, wishes to develop new master-slave relationships or bend the will of the people to despotic rulers in new ways. These are patterns of control appropriate to a world without science. They may well be the first to go when the experimental analysis of behavior comes into its own in the design of cultural practices.

II (Rogers)

There are, I believe, a number of matters in connection with this important topic on which the authors of this article, and probably a large majority of psychologists, are in agreement. These matters then are not issues as far as we are concerned, and I should like to mention them briefly in order to put them to one side.

Points of Agreement

I am sure we agree that men---as individuals and as societies---have always endeavored to understand, predict, influence, and control human behavior---their own behavior and that of others.

I believe we agree that the behavioral sciences are making and will continue to make increasingly rapid progress in the understanding of behavior, and that as a consequence the capacity to predict and to control behavior is developing with equal rapidity....

I believe we are in agreement that the tremendous potential power of a science which permits the prediction and control of behavior may be misused, and that the possibility of such misuse constitutes a serious threat....

Points at Issue

With these several points of basic and important agreement, are there then any issues that remain on which there are differences? I believe there are. They can be stated very briefly: Who will be controlled? Who will exercise control? What type of control will be exercise? Most important of all, toward what end or what purpose, or in the pursuit of what value, will control be exercised?

It is on questions of this sort that there exist ambiguities, misunderstandings, and probably deep differences. These differences exist among psychologists, among members of the general public in this country, and among various world cultures. Without any hope of achieving a final resolution of these questions, we can, I believe, put these issues in clearer form....

Ends and Values In Relation To Science

In sharp contradiction to some views that have been advanced, I would like to propose a two-pronged thesis: (i) In any scientific endeavor---whether "pure" or applied science---there is a prior subjective choice of the purpose or value which that scientific work is perceived as serving. (ii) This subjective value choice which brings the scientific endeavor into being must always lie outside of that endeavor and can never become a part of the science involved in that endeavor.

Let me illustrate the first point from Skinner himself. It is clear that in his earlier writing it is recognized that a prior value choice is necessary, and it is specified as the goal that men are to become happy, well-behaved, productive, and so on. I am pleased that Skinner has retreated from the goals he then chose, because to me they seem to be stultifying values. I can only feel that he was choosing these goals for others, not for himself. I would have to see Skinner become "well-behaved," as that term would be defined for him by behavioral scientists. His recent article in the *American Psychologists* shows that he certainly does not want to be "productive" as that value is defined by most psychologists. And the most awful fate I can imagine for him would be to have him constantly "happy." It is the fact that he is very unhappy about many things which makes me prize him.

In the first draft of his part of this article, he also included such prior value choices, saying for example, "We must decide how we are to use the knowledge which a science of human behavior is now making available." Now he has dropped all mention of such choices, and if I understand him correctly, he believes that science can proceed without them. He has suggested this view in another recent paper, stating that "We must continue to experiment in cultural design….testing the consequences as we go. Eventually the practices which make for the greatest biological and psychological strength of the group will presumably survive."

I would point out; however, that to choose to experiment is a value choice. Even to move in the direction of perfectly random experimentation is a value choice. To test the consequences of an experiment is possible only if we have first made a subjective choice of a criterion value. And implicit in his statement is a valuing of biological and psychological strength. So even when trying to avoid such choice, it seems inescapable that a prior subjective value choice is necessary for any scientific endeavor, or for any application of scientific knowledge.

I wish to make it clear that I am not saying that values cannot be included as a subject of science. It is not true that science deals only with certain classes of "facts" and that these classes do not include values. It is a bit more complex than that, as a simple illustration or two may make clear.

If I value knowledge of the "three R's" as a goal of education, the methods of science can give me increasingly accurate information on how this goal may be achieved. . If I value problem-solving ability as a goal of education, the scientific method can give me the same kind of help….

Thus I return to the proposition with which I began this section of my remarks---and which I now repeat in different words. Science has its meaning as the objective pursuit of a purpose which has been subjectively chosen by a person or persons. This purpose or value can never be investigated by the particular scientific experiment or investigation to which it has given birth and meaning. Consequently, any discussion of the control of human beings by the behavioral sciences must first and most deeply concern itself with the subjectively chosen purposes which such an application of science is intended to implement….

Possible Concept of the Control
Of Human Behavior

It is quite clear that the point of view I am expressing is in sharp contrast to the usual conception of the relationship of the behavioral sciences to the control of human behavior....I will state this possibility (thusly:)

1) It is possible for us to choose to value man as a self-actualizing process of becoming; to value creativity, and the process by which knowledge becomes self-transcending.

2) We can proceed, by the methods of science, to discover the conditions which necessarily precede these processes and, through continuing experimentation, to discover better means of achieving these purposes.

3) It is possible for individuals or groups to set these conditions, with a minimum of power or control. According to present knowledge, the only authority necessary is the authority to establish certain qualities of interpersonal relationship.

4) Exposed to these conditions, present knowledge suggests that individuals become more self-responsible, make progress in self-actualization, become more flexible, and become more creatively adaptive.

5) Thus such an initial choice would inaugurate the beginnings of a social system or subsystem in which values, knowledge, adaptive skills, and even the concept of science would be continually changing and self-transcending. The emphasis would be upon man as a process of becoming.

I believe it is clear that such a view as I have been describing does not lead to any definable utopia. It would be impossible to predict its final outcome. It involves a step-by-step development, based on a continuing subjective choice of purposes, which are implemented by the behavioral sciences....

I trust it is also evident that the whole emphasis is on process, not on end-states of being. I am suggesting that it is by choosing to value certain qualitative elements of the process of becoming that we can find a pathway toward the open society.

Chapter Five
Behavioral Perspectives

"The mind is what the body does. It is what the person does. In other words, it is behavior, and that is what behaviorists have been saying for more than a half a century....Operant conditioning is not pulling strings to make a person dance; it is arranging a world in which a person does things that affect that world, which, in turn, affects him."

B.F. Skinner

Psychology as the Behaviorist Views It [*]

John Broadus Watson

*F*or over forty years (1920s through the 1960s), the field of psychology was largely dominated by behaviorists, who focused on the objective and empirical measurement of behavior. The founder of the American school of behaviorism was John B. Watson, whose perspective of psychology was a "purely objective experimental branch of natural science." He proposed that it would be in the best interests of the field if psychology became the science of overt behavior and modeled after the natural sciences.

In 1903, Watson (1878-1958) earned his Ph.D. in experimental psychology from the University of Chicago. Following in the footsteps of Ivan Pavlov, he began a career in teaching and research at the Johns Hopkins University in 1908 where he remained until his resignation in 1920. His most famous work is the "Case of Little Albert," which demonstrated his ability to apply the principles of classical conditioning to the acquisition of conditioned fears. Although Watson left academia after 12 years of teaching and entered the world of advertisement, his influence is still profound in the field today.

"Psychology as the Behaviorist Views It," initiates the introduction of behaviorism as a major school of thought in American psychology. In it, Watson castoffs the phenomenon of consciousness and the method of introspection from psychology and makes a case for an objective study of animal and human behavior. As you will see, his primary objective is to help psychology become more applicable to other fields such as education, law, and business as it progresses into an experimental natural science.

[*] Watson, John B. (1913). Psychology As The Behaviorist Views It. *Psychological Review*, 20, 158-177, Public Domain.

Psychology as the behaviorist views it is a purely objective experimental branch of natural science. Its theoretical goal is the prediction and control of behavior. Introspection forms no essential part of its methods, nor is the scientific value of its data dependent upon the readiness with which they lend themselves to interpretation in terms of consciousness. The behaviorists, in efforts to get a unitary scheme of animal response, recognize no dividing line between man and brute. The behavior of man, with all of its refinement and complexity, forms only a part of the behaviorist's total scheme of investigation...

The time seems to have come when psychology must discard all reference to consciousness; when it need no longer delude itself into thinking that it is making mental states the object of observation. We have become so enmeshed in speculative questions concerning the elements of mind, the nature of conscious content (for example, imageless thought, attitudes,...etc.) that I, as an experimental student, feel that something is wrong with our premises and the types of problems which develop from them. There is no longer any guarantee that we all mean the same thing when we use the terms now current in psychology. Take the case of sensation. A sensation is defined in terms of its attributes. One psychologist will state with readiness that the attributes of a visual sensation are *quality, extension, duration, and intensity.* Another will add *clearness.* Still another that of *order.* I doubt if any one psychologist can draw up a set of statements describing what he means by sensation which will be agreed to by three other psychologists of different training. Turn for a moment to the question of the number of isolable sensations. Is there an extremely large number of color sensations----or only four, red, green, yellow and blue? Again, yellow, while psychologically simple, can be obtained by superimposing red and green, spectral rays upon the same diffusing surface! If, on the other hand, we say that every just noticeable difference in the spectrum is a simple sensation, and that every just noticeable increase in the white value of a given color given simple sensations, we are forced to admit that the number is so large and the conditions for obtaining them so complex that the concept of sensation is unusable, either for the purpose of analysis or that of synthesis. Titchener, who has fought the most valiant fight in this country for a psychology based upon introspections, feels that these differences of opinion as to the number of sensations and their attributes; as to whether there are relations (in the sense of elements) and on the many others which seem to be fundamental in every attempt at analysis, are perfectly natural in the present undeveloped state of psychology. While it is admitted that every growing science is full of unanswered questions, surely only those who are wedded to the system as we now have it, who have fought and suffered for it, can confidently believe that there will ever be any greater uniformity than there is now in the answers we have to such questions. I firmly believe that two hundred years from now, unless the introspective method is discarded, psychology will still be divided on the question as to whether auditory sensations have the quality of 'extension,' whether intensity is an attribute which can be applied to color, whether there is a difference in 'texture' between image and sensation and upon many hundreds of others of like character....

I was greatly surprised some time ago when I opened Pillsbury's book and saw psychology defined as the 'science of behavior.' A still more recent text states that psychology is the 'science of mental behavior.' When I saw these promising statements I thought, now surely we will have texts based upon different lines. After a few pages the sciences of behavior is dropped and one finds the conventional treatment of sensation, perception, images, etc., along with certain shifts in emphasis and additional facts which serve to give the author's personal imprint....

This leads me to the point where I should like to make the argument constructive. I believe we can write a psychology, define it as Pillsbury, and never go back upon our definition; never use the terms consciousness, mental states, mind, content, introspectively verifiable, imagery; and the like....It can be done in terms of stimulus and response, in terms of habit integrations and the like. Furthermore, I believe that it is really worth while to make this attempt now.

The psychology which I should attempt to build up would take as a starting point, first, the observable fact that organisms, man and animal alike, do adjust themselves to their environment by means of hereditary and habit equipments. These adjustments may be very adequate or they may be so inadequate that the organism barely maintains its existence; secondly, that certain stimuli lead the organisms to make the responses. In a system of psychology completely worked out, given the response the stimuli can be predicted; given the stimuli that the response can be predicted. Such a set of statements is crass and raw in the extreme, as all such generalizations must be. Yet they are hardly more raw and less realizable than the ones which appear in the psychology texts of the day. I possible might illustrate my point better by choosing an everyday problem which anyone is likely to meet in the course of his work. Some time ago I was called upon to make a study of certain species of birds. Until I went to Tortugas I had never seen these birds alive. When I reached there I found the animals doing certain things; some of the acts seemed to work peculiarly well in such an environment, while others seemed to be unsuited to their type of life. I first studied the responses of the group as a whole and later those of individuals. In order to understand more thoroughly the relation between what was habit and what was heredity in these responses, I took the young birds and reared them. In this way I was able to study the order of appearance of heredity adjustments and their complexity, and later the beginnings of habit formation. My efforts in determining the stimuli which called forth such adjustments were crude indeed. Consequently my attempts to control behavior and to produce responses at will did not meet with much success. Their food and water, sex, and other social relations, light and temperature conditions were all beyond control in a field study. I did find it possible to control their reactions in a measure by using the nest and egg (or young) as stimuli. It is not necessary in this paper to develop further how such a study should be carried out and how work of this kind must be supplemented by carefully controlled laboratory experiments.....In the main, my desire in all such work is to gain an accurate knowledge of adjustments and the stimuli calling them forth. My final reason for this is to learn general and particular methods by which I may control behavior…..If psychology would follow the plan I suggest, the educator, the physician, the jurist and the business man could utilize our data in a practical way, as soon as we are able, experimentally, to obtain them. Those who have occasion to apply psychological principles practically would find no need to complain as they do at the present time. Ask any physician or jurist today whether scientific psychology plays a practical part in his daily routine and you will hear him deny that the psychology of the laboratories finds a place in his scheme of work. I think the criticism is extremely just. One of the earliest conditions which made me dissatisfied with psychology was the feeling that there was no realm of application for the principles which were being worked out in content terms.

What gives me hope that the behaviorist's position is a defensible one is the fact that those branches of psychology which have already partially withdrawn from the parent, experimental psychology, and which are consequently less dependent upon introspection are today in a most flourishing condition. Experimental pedagogy, the psychology of drugs, the psychology of advertising, legal psychology, the psychology of tests, and psychopathology are all vigorous growths. These are sometimes wrongly called "practical" or "applied" psychology. Surely there was never a worse misnomer. In the future there may grow up vocational bureaus which really apply psychology. At present, these fields are truly scientific and are in search of broad generalizations which will lead to the control of human behavior. For example, we find out by experimentation whether a series of stanzas may be acquired more readily if the whole is learned at once, or whether it is more advantageous to learn each stanza separately and then pass to the succeeding. We do not attempt to apply our findings. The application of this principle is purely voluntary on the part of the teachers. In the psychology of drugs we may show the effect upon behavior of certain doses of caffeine. We may reach the conclusion that caffeine has a good effect upon the speed and accuracy of work. But these are general principles. We leave it to the individual as to whether the results of our tests shall be applied or not. Again, in legal testimony, we test the effects of recency upon the reliability of a witness's report. We test the accuracy of the report with respect to moving objects, stationary objects, color, etc. It depends upon the judicial machinery of the country to decide whether these facts are ever to be applied. For a 'pure' psychologist to say that he is not interested in the questions raised in these divisions of the science because they relate indirectly to the application of psychology shows, in the first place, that he fails to understand the scientific aim in such problems, and secondly, that he is not interested in a psychology which concerns itself with human life. The only fault I have to find with these disciplines is that much of their material is stated in terms of introspection, whereas a statement of terms of objective results would be far more valuable. There is no reason why appeal should ever be made to consciousness in any of them. Or why introspective data should ever be sought during the experimentation, or published in the results. In experimental pedagogy especially one can see the desirability of keeping all of the results on a purely objective plane….

In concluding, I suppose must confess to a deep bias on these questions. I have devoted nearly twelve years to experimentation on animals. It is natural that such a one should drift into a theoretical position which is in harmony with his experimental work. Possibly I have put up a straw man and have been fighting that....Certainly the position I advocate is weak enough at present and can be attacked from many standpoints. Yet when all this is admitted I still feel that the considerations which I have urged should have a wide influence upon the type of psychology which is to be developed in the future. What we need to do is to start work upon psychology, making *behavior, not consciousness,* the objective point of our attack. Certainly there are enough problems in the control of behavior to keep us all working many lifetimes without ever allowing us time to think of consciousness....Once launched in the undertaking, we will find ourselves in a short time as far divorced from an introspective psychology as the psychology of the present time is divorced from faculty psychology.

Whatever Happened To Psychology As The Science of Behavior?

B. F. Skinner

By 1987, behaviorism had already established itself as one of the major models of psychology. Much of its fame and recognition was attributed to the lifetime work and efforts of B. F. Skinner. In this article, "Whatever Happened to Psychology as a Science of Behavior?" you will see Skinner express his disappointment and resentment about the status of this second force movement in psychology. The time had marked and witnessed the "cognitive revolution" and the re-emergence of the mind as a dominant focus in the field. Even though behaviorism had been a dominant force in the field, Skinner questions why it did not become a scientific psychology.

As you will see, Skinner identifies three villains, who played a significant role in thwarting these efforts. One is humanistic psychology and its assertion that individual have the capacity for free choice and will. The second villain is "psychotherapy" and its various forms. The third villain is cognitive psychology, which Skinner believed to be no more scientific than humanism. According to Skinner, cognitive psychologists placed too much emphasis upon the mind and unobservable mental processes, thereby distracting them from the prediction and control of behavior. Each of these villains played an important role, then, in preventing psychology from becoming a science of behavior.

There can scarcely be anything more familiar than human behavior. We are always in the presence of at least one behaving person. Nor can there be anything more important, whether it is our own behavior or that of those whom we see every day or who are responsible for what is happening in the world at large.

* Skinner, B. F. (1987). Whatever Happened To Psychology As The Science Of Behavior? *American Psychologist*, 42, 78-786, American Psychological Association (APA). Reprinted by permission.

Nevertheless, it is certainly not the thing we understand best. Granted that it is possibly the most difficult subject ever submitted to scientific analysis, it is still puzzling that so little has been done with the instruments and methods that have been so productive in other sciences***

*　　*　　*

For more than half a century the experimental analysis of behavior as a function of environmental variables and the use of that analysis in the interpretation and modification of behavior in the world at large have reached into every field of traditional psychology. Yet they have not *become* psychology, and the question is, Why not? Perhaps answers can be found in looking at three formidable obstacles that have stood in the path of an experimental analysis of behavior.

Obstacle I: Humanistic Psychology

Many people find the implications of a behavioral analysis disturbing. The traditional direction of action of organism and environment seems to be reversed. Instead of saying that the organism sees, attends to, perceives, "processes," or otherwise acts upon stimuli, an operant analysis holds that stimuli acquire control of behavior through the part they play in contingencies of reinforcement. Instead of saying that an organism stores copies of the contingencies to which it is exposed and later retrieves and response to them again, it says that the organism is changed by the contingencies and later responds as a changed organism, the contingencies having passed into history. The environment takes over the control formerly assigned to an internal, originating agent.

Some long-admitted features of human behavior are then threatened. Following the lead of evolutionary theory, an operant analysis replaces creation with variation and selection.[1] There is no longer any need for a creative mind or plan, or for purpose or goal direction. Just as we say that species-specific behavior did not evolve *in order that* a species could adapt to the environment but rather evolved *when* it adapted, so we say that operant behavior is not strengthened by reinforcement *in order that* the individual can adjust to the environment but is strengthened *when* the individual adjusts (where "adapt" and "adjust" mean "behave effectively with respect to").

The disenthronement of a creator seems to threaten personal freedom (Can we be free if the environment is in control?) and personal worth (Can we take credit for our achievements if they are nothing more than the effects of circumstances?) It also seems to threaten ethical, religious, and governmental systems that hold people responsible for their conduct. Who or what is responsible if unethical, immoral, or illegal behavior is due to heredity or personal history? Humanistic psychologists have attacked behavioral science along these lines. Like creationists in their attack on secular humanists (with the humanists on the other side), they often challenge the content or selection of textbooks, the appointments of teachers and administrators, the design of curricula, and the allocation of funds.

Obstacle 2 Psychotherapy

Certain exigencies of the helping professions are another obstacle in the path of a scientific analysis of behavior. Psychotherapists must talk with their clients and, with *rare* exceptions, do so in everyday English, which is heavy laden with references to internal causes---"I ate because I was *hungry,*" I could do it because I *knew* how to do it," and so on. All fields of science tend to have two languages, of course. Scientists speak one with casual acquaintances and the other with colleagues. In a relatively young science, such as psychology, the use of the vernacular may be challenged. How often have behaviorists heard, "You just said 'It crossed my mind!' I thought there wasn't supposed to be any mind." It has been a long time since anyone challenged a physicist who said, "That desk is made of solid oak," by protesting, "But I thought you said that matter was mostly empty space."

The two languages of psychology raise a special problem. What we feel when we are hungry or when we know how to do something are states of our bodies. We do not have very good ways of observing them, and those who teach us to observe them usually have no way at all. We were taught to say, "I'm hungry, for example, by persons who knew perhaps only that we had not eaten for some time ("You missed your lunch; you must be *hungry*") or had observed something about our behavior ("You are eating ravenously. You must be *hungry.*"). Similarly, we were taught to say "I know" by persons who had perhaps only seen us doing something ("Oh, you *know* how to do that!") or had told us how to do something and then said, "Now you *know.*" The trouble is that private states are almost always poorly correlated with the public evidence.

Reference to private events are, nevertheless, often accurate enough to be useful. If we are preparing a meal for a friend, we are not likely to ask, "How long has it been since you last ate?" or "Will you probably eat a great deal?" We simply ask, "How *hungry* are you?" If a friend is driving us to an appointment, we are not likely to ask, "Have you driven there before?" or "Has anyone told you where it is?" Instead, we ask, "Do you *know* where it is?" Being hungry and knowing where something is are states of the body resulting from personal histories, and what is said about them may be the only available evidence of those histories. Nevertheless, how much a person eats does depend upon a history of deprivation, not upon how a deprived body feels, and whether a person reaches a given destination, does depend upon whether he or she has drive there before or has been told how to get there, not upon introspective evidence of the effects.

Psychotherapists must ask people what has happened to them and how they feel because the confidential relationship of therapist and client prevents direct inquiry. (It is sometimes argues that what a person remembers may be more important than what actually happened, but that is true only if something else has happened, of which it would also be better to have independent evidence.[2]) But although the use of reports of feelings and states of mind can be justified on practical grounds, there is no justification for their use in theory making. The temptation, however, is great. Psychoanalysts, for example, specialize in feelings. Instead of investigating the early lives of their patients or watching them with their families, friends, or business associates, they ask them what has happened and how they feel about it. It is not surprising that they should then constructs theories in terms of memories, feelings, and states of mind or that they should say that an analysis of behavior in terms of environmental events lacks "depth."

Obstacle 3 Cognitive Psychology

A curve showing the appearance of the word *cognitive* in the psychological literature would be interesting. A first rise could probably be seen around 1960; the subsequent acceleration would be exponential. Is there any field of psychology today in which something does not seem to be gained by adding that charming adjective to the occasional noun? The popularity may not be hard to explain. When we became psychologists, we learned new ways of talking about human behavior. If they were "behavioristic," they were not very much like the old ways. The old terms were taboo, and eyebrows were raised when we used them. But when certain developments seemed to show that the old ways might be right after all, everyone could relax. Mind was back.

Information theory was one of those developments, computer technology another. Troublesome problems seemed to vanish like magic. A detailed study of sensation and perception was no longer needed; one could simply speak of processing information. It was no longer necessary to construct settings in which to observe behaviors; one could simply describe them. Rather than observe what people actually did, one could simply ask them what they would probably do.

The mentalistic psychologists are uneasy about these uses of introspection is clear from the desperation with which they are turning to brain science, asking it to tell them what perceptions, feelings, ideas, and intentions "really are." And brain scientists are happy to accept the assignment. To complete the account of an episode of behavior (for example, to explain what happens when reinforcement brings an organism under the control of a given stimulus) is not only beyond the present range of brain science, it would lack the glamour of a relevation about the nature of mind. But psychology may find it dangerous to turn to neurology for help. Once you tell the world that another science will explain what your key terms really mean, you must forgive the world if it decides that the other science is doing the important work.

Cognitive psychologists like to say that "the mind is what the brain does," but surely the rest of the body plays a part. The mind is what the *body does*. It is what the *person does*. In other words, it is behavior, and that is what behaviorists have been saying for more than a half century.***

*   *   *

100

Damage and Repair

By their very nature, the antiscience stance of humanistic psychology, the practical exigencies of the helping professions, and the cognitive restoration of the royal House of Mind have worked against the definition of psychology as the science of behavior. Perhaps that could be justified if something more valuable had been achieved, but, has that happened? Is there a better conception of psychology? To judge from the psychological literature, there are either many conceptions, largely incompatible, or no clear conception at all. Introductory textbooks do not help because, with an eye on their books' being adopted, the authors call their subject the "science of behavior and mental life" and make sure that every field of interest is covered. What the public learns from the media is equally confusing.

Is there a rapidly expanding body of facts and principles? Of our three obstacles, only cognitive psychology offers itself as an experimental science. It usually does so with a certain éclat, but have its promises been kept? When the journal *Psychology Today* celebrated its 15th anniversary, it asked psychologists to name the most important discoveries made during that period of time. As Nicolas Wade (1982) has pointed out, no 2 of the 10 agreed on a single achievement that could properly be called psychology. For more than two years *Science* has not published a single article on psychology, except one on memory citing work on brain-operated and brain-damaged people and one on the neurological basis of memory retrieval. Apparently the editors of *Science* no longer regard psychology itself as a member of the scientific community.

Nor has psychology developed a strong technology. Internal determiners get in the way of effective action. An article on "Energy Conservation Behavior" in the *American Psychologist* (Costanzo, Archer, Aronson, & Pettigrew, 1986) carries the significant subtitle, "The Difficult Path From Information to Action." If you take the "rational economic" path and tell people about the consequences of what they are doing or of what they might do instead, they are not likely to change. (And for good reason: Information is not enough; people seldom take advice unless taking other advice has been reinforced). If, on the other hand, you adopt the "attitude-change" approach, people are also not likely to change. Attitudes are inferences from the behavior that is said to show their presence and are not directly accessible If I turn off unnecessary lights and appliances in my home, it is not because I have a "positive attitude" toward conservation, but because doing so has had some kind of reinforcing consequence. To induce people to conserve energy, one must change contingencies of reinforcement, not attitudes. No one should try to beat a "path from information to action," because action is the problem and contingencies the solution.***

*   *   *

Beyond the current reach of all of the sciences lies an issue that cannot be safely neglected by any of them---the future of the world. For a variety of reasons all three of our "obstacles" have had special reasons for neglecting it. Humanistic psychologists are unwilling to sacrifice feelings of freedom and worth for the sake of a future, and when cognitive psychologists turn to feelings and states of mind for theoretical purposes and psychotherapists for practical ones, they emphasize the here and now. Behavior modification, in contrast, is more often preventive than remedial. In both instruction and therapy, current reinforcers (often contrived) are arranged to strengthen behavior that student and client will find useful *in the future.*

When Gandhi was asked, "What are we to do?" he is said to have replied," Think of the poorest man you have ever met and then ask is what you are doing is of any benefit to him." But he must have meant "of any benefit to the many people who, without your help, will be like him." To feed the hungry and clothe the naked are remedial acts. We can easily see what is wrong and what needs to be done. It is much harder to see and do something about the fact that world agriculture must feed and clothe billions of people, most of them yet unborn. It is not enough to *advise* people how to behave in ways that will make a future possible; they must be given effective reasons for behaving in those ways, and that means effective contingencies of reinforcement now.

Unfortunately, references to feelings and states of mind have an emotional appeal that behavioral alternatives usually lack. Here is an example: "If the world is to be saved, people must learn to be noble without being cruel, to be filled with faith, yet open to truth, to be inspired by great purposes without hating those who thwart them." That is an "inspiring" sentence. We like nobility, faith, truth, and great purposes and dislike cruelty and hatred. But what does it inspire us to *do?* What must be changed if people are to behave in noble rather than cruel ways, to accept the word of others but never without questioning it, to do things that have consequences too remote to serve as reinforcers, and to refrain from attacking those who oppose them? The fault, dear Brutus, is not in our stars *nor in ourselves* that we are underlings. The fault is in the world. It is a world that we have made and one that we must change if the species is to survive.

For at least 2,500 years philosophers and psychologists have proceeded on the assumption that because they were themselves behaving organisms, they had privileged access to the causes of their behavior. But has any introspectively observed feeling or state of mind yet been unambiguously identified in either mental or physical terms? Has any ability or trait of character been statistically established to the satisfaction of everyone? Do we know how anxiety changes intention, how memories alter decisions, how intelligence changes emotion, and so on? And, of course, has anyone ever explained how the mind works on the body or the body on the mind?

Questions of that sort should never have been asked. Psychology should confine itself to its accessible subject matter and leave the rest of the story of human behavior to physiology.

References

Costanzo, M., Archer, D., Aronson, L. & Pettigrew, T. (1986). Energy conservation behavior: The difficult path from information to action. *American Psychologist, 41,* 521-528.
Wade, N. (1982, April 30). Smart apes or dumb? *New York Times,* p. 28.

---

[1] Evolutionary theory assumes that random variation creates a variety of organisms in each generation, of which some survive and reproduce more successfully than others. Similarly, Skinner's operant behavior theory assumes that organisms begin by behaving more or less randomly, but processes of reinforcement cause some behaviors to "survive" and others to drop out of the repertoire.

[2] This is a succinct rebuttal to the phenomenological position.

The Self System
In Reciprocal Determinism [*]

Albert Bandura

Of all of the social learning theorists, Albert Bandura, is most recognized for his leadership in creating the cognitive approach of personality. Even he calls his approach social cognitive theory.

Bandura's "The Self System in Reciprocal Determinism" is considered by many to be one of the first important entries in this new approach. In it, he presents a number of relevant philosophical issues pertaining to "basic conceptions of human nature." More importantly, he shows how both behaviorists and humanists share one basic idea, that is, the unidirectional causation of behavior. Specifically, behaviorists recognize behavior as a function of environmental or situational reinforcements. Humanists, on the other hand, view behavior as a function of the person, his characteristics and capacity for free choice. Bandura attempts to present a theory that mediates between these seemingly different viewpoints.

He does this by proposing the existence of a "self-system." This cognitive system, comprised of self thoughts, feelings and perceptions, arises as a result of experience but, once established, has important effects on behavior. Essentially, it is based on the principle of reciprocal determinism which demonstrates the interactive power between the forces of person, behavior and environment. Bandura claims that "in the social learning view of interaction, which is analyzed as a process of reciprocal determinism, behavior, internal personal factors, and environmental influences all operate as interlocking determinants of each other." Clearly, Bandura has made it possible to analyze and predict behavior in a more extensive way and reinstated the relevance covert behaviors.

[*] Bandura, Albert. (1978). The Self System in Reciprocal Determinism. *American Psychologist*, 33, 344-458, American Psychological Association (APA). Reprinted by permission.

*R*ecent years have witnessed a heightened interest in the basic conceptions of human nature underlying different psychological theories. This interest stems in part from growing recognition of how such conceptions delimit research to selected processes and are in turn shaped by findings of paradigms embodying the particular view. As psychological knowledge is converted to behavioral technologies, the models of human behavior on which research is premised have important social as well as theoretical implications (Bandura, 1974).

Explanations of human behavior have generally been couched in terms of a limited set of determinants, usually portrayed as operating in a unidirectional manner. Exponents of environmental determinism study and theorize about how behavior is controlled by situational influences. Those favoring personal determinism seek the causes of human behavior in dispositional sources in the form of instincts, drives, traits, and other motivational forces within the individual.***

The present article analyzes the various causal models and the role of self influences in behavior from the perspective of reciprocal determinism.

Unidirectional environmental determinism is carried to its extreme in the more radical forms of behaviorism. For example, "A person does not act upon the world, the world acts upon him," (Skinner, 1971, p. 211). The environment thus becomes an autonomous force that automatically shapes, orchestrates, and controls behavior. ***

*   *   *

There exists no shortage of advocates of alternative theories emphasizing the personal determination of environments. Humanists and existentialists, who stress the human capacity for conscious judgment and intentional action, contend that individuals determine what they become by their own free choices. Most psychologists find conceptions of human behavior in terms of unidirectional personal determinism as unsatisfying, as those espousing unidirectional environmental determinism. To contend that mind creates reality fails to acknowledge that environmental influences partly determine what people attend to, perceive, and think. To contend further that the methods of natural science are incapable of dealing with personal determinants of behavior does not enlist many supporters from the ranks of those who are moved more by empirical evidence than by philosophical discourse.

Social learning theory (Bandura, 1974, 1997) analyzes behavior in terms of reciprocal determinism. The term *determinism* is used here to signify the production of effects by events, rather than in the doctrinal sense that actions are completely determined by a prior sequence of causes independent of the individual. Because of the complexity of interacting factors, events produce effects probabilistically rather than inevitably. In their transactions with the environment, people are not simply reactors to external stimulation. Most external influences affect behavior through intermediary cognitive processes. Cognitive factors partly determine which external events will be observed, how they will be perceived, whether they have any lasting effects, what valence and efficacy they have, and how the information they convey will be organized for future use. The extraordinary capacity of humans to use symbols enables them to engage in reflective thought, to create, and to plan foresightful courses of action in thought rather than having to perform possible options and suffer the consequences of thoughtless action. By altering their immediate environment, by creating cognitive self-inducements, and by arranging conditional incentives for themselves, people can exercise some influence over their own behavior. An act there includes among its determinants self-produced influences.

It is true that behavior is influenced by the environment, but the environment is partly of a person's own making. By their actions, people play a role in creating the social milieu and other circumstances that arise in their daily transactions. Thus, from the social learning perspective, psychological functioning involves a continuous reciprocal interaction between behavioral, cognitive and environmental influences.

Reciprocal Determinism and Interactionism

Interaction processes have been conceptualized in three fundamentally different ways. These alternative formulations are summarized schematically in Figure 48.1. In the unidirectional notion of interaction, persons and situations are treated as independent entities that combine to produce behavior. This commonly held view can be called into question on both conceptual and empirical grounds. Personal and environmental factors do not function as independent determinants; rather, they determine each other. Nor can "persons" be considered causes independent of their behavior. It is largely through their actions that people produce the environmental conditions that affect their behavior in a reciprocal fashion. The experiences generated by behavior also partly determine what individuals think, expect, and can do, which in turn, affect their subsequent behavior.

A second conception of interaction acknowledges that personal and environmental influences are bidirectional, but it retains a unidirectional view of behavior. In this analysis, persons and situations are considered to be interdependent causes of behavior, but behavior is treated as though it were only a by-product that does not figure at all in the causal process.***

*   *   *

In the social learning view of interaction, which is analyzed as a process of reciprocal determinism (Bandura, 1977), behavior, internal personal factors, and environmental influences all operate as interlocking determinants of each other. As shown in Figure 48.1, the process involves a triadic reciprocal interaction rather than a dyadic conjoint or a dyadic bidirectional one. We have already noted that behavior and environmental conditions function as reciprocally interacting determinants. Internal personal factors (e.g., conceptions, beliefs, self-perceptions) and behavior also operate as reciprocal determinants of each other. For example, people's efficacy and outcome expectations influence how they behavior, and the environmental effects created by their actions in turn alter their expectations. People activate different environmental reactions, apart from their behavior, by their physical characteristics (e.g., size, physiognomy, race, sex, attractiveness) and socially conferred attributes, roles, and status. The differential social treatment affects recipients' self-conceptions and actions in ways that either maintain or alter the environmental biases.

Unidirectional

$$B = f(P, E)$$

Partially Bidirectional

$$B = f(P \xleftarrow{\rightarrow} E)$$

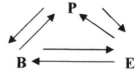

Figure 48.1 Schematic representation of three alternative conceptions of interactions: B signifies behavior, P the cognitive and other internal events that can affect perceptions and actions, and E the external environment.

The relative influence exerted by these three sets of interlocking factors will vary in different individuals and under different circumstances. In some cases, environmental conditions exercise such powerful constraints on behavior that they emerge as the overriding determinants. If, for example, people are dropped in deep water they will all promptly engage in swimming activities, however uniquely varied they might be in their cognitive and behavioral repertoires. There are times when behavior is the central factor in the interlocking system. One example of this is persons who play familiar piano selections for themselves that create a pleasing sensory environment. The behavior is self-regulated over a long period by the sensory effects it produces, whereas cognitive activities and contextual environmental events are not much involved in the process.

In other instances, cognitive factors serve as the predominant influence in the regulatory system. The activation and maintenance of defensive behavior is a good case in point. False beliefs activate avoidance responses that keep individuals out of touch with prevailing environmental conditions, thus creating a strong reciprocal interaction between beliefs and action that is protected from corrective environmental influence. In extreme cases, behavior is so powerfully controlled by bizarre internal contingencies that neither the beliefs nor the accompanying actions are much affected even by extremely punishing environmental consequences (Bateson, 1961).

In still other instances, the development and activation of the three interlocking factors are all highly interdependent. Television-viewing behavior provides an everyday example. Personal preferences influence when and which programs, from among the available alternatives individuals choose to watch on television. Although the potential televised environment is identical for all viewers, the actual televised environment that impinges on given individuals depends on what they select to watch. Through their viewing behavior, they partly shape the nature of the future televised environment. Because production costs and commercial requirements also determine what people are shown, the options provided in the televised environment partly shape the viewers' preferences. Here, all three factions---viewer preferences, viewer behavior, and televised offerings---reciprocally affect each other.

The methodology for elucidating psychological processes requires analysis of sequential interactions between the triadic, interdependent factors within the interlocking system. Investigations of reciprocal processes have thus far rarely, if ever, examined more than two of the interacting factors simultaneously. Some studies analyze how cognitions and behavior affect each other in a reciprocal fashion (Bandura, 1977a, Bandura & Adams, 1977). More often, however, the sequential analysis centers on how social behavior creates certain conditions and is, in turn, altered by the very conditions it creates (Bandura, Lipsher, & Miller, 1960, Patterson, 1975; Raush, Barry, Hertel, & Swain, 1974; Thomas & Martin, 1976).

From the perspective of reciprocal determinism, the common practice of searching for the ultimate environmental cause of behaviors is an idle exercise because, in an interactional process, one and the same event can be a stimulus, a response, or an environmental reinforcer, depending on where in the sequence of the analysis arbitrarily begins.

Regulatory processes are not governed solely by the reciprocal influence of antecedent and consequent acts. While behaving, people are also cognitively appraising the progression of events. Their thoughts about the probably effects of prospective actions partly determine how acts are affected by their immediate environmental consequences. Consider, for example, investigations of reciprocal coercive behavior in an ongoing dyadic interaction. In discordant families, coercive behavior by one member tends to elicit coercive counteractions from recipients in a mutual escalation of aggression (Patterson, 1975). However, coercion often does not produce coercive counteractions. To increase the predictive power of a theory of behavior, it is necessary to broaden the analysis to include cognitive factors that operate in the interlocking system. Counter-responses to antecedent acts are influenced not only by their immediate effects but also by judgments of later consequences for a given course of action. Thus, aggressive children will continue, or even escalate, coercive behavior in the face of immediate punishment when they expect persistence eventually to gain them what they seek. But the same momentary punishment will serve as an inhibitor rather than as an enhancer of coercion when they expect continuance of the aversive conduct to be ineffective.

Cognitions do not arise in a vacuum, nor do they function as autonomous determinants of behavior. In the social learning analysis of cognitive development, conceptions about oneself and the nature of the environment are developed and verified through four different processes (Bandura, 1977b). People derive much of their knowledge from direct experience of the effects produced by their actions. Indeed, most theories of cognitive development, whether they favor behavioristic, information-processing, or Piagetian[1] orientations, focus almost exclusively on cognitive change through feedback from direct experimentation. However, results of one's own actions are not the sole source of knowledge. Information about the nature of things is frequently extracted from vicarious experience. In this mode of verification, observation of the effects produced by somebody else's actions serves as the source and authentication of thoughts.

There are many things we cannot come to know by direct or vicarious experience because of limited accessibility or because the matters involve metaphysical ideas that are not subjected to objective confirmation. When experiential verification is either difficult or impossible, people develop and evaluate their conceptions of things in terms of the judgments voiced by other. In addition to enactive, vicarious, and social sources of thought verification, all of which rely on external influences, logical verification also enters into the process, especially in later phases of development. After people acquire some rules of inference, they can evaluate the soundness of their reasoning and derive from what they already know new knowledge about things that extend beyond their experiences.

External influences play a role not only in the development of cognitions but in their activation as well. Different sights, smells, and sounds will elicit quite different trains of thought. Thus, while it is true that conceptions govern behavior, the conceptions themselves are partly fashioned from direct or mediated transactions with the environment. A complete analysis of reciprocal determinism therefore requires investigation of how all three sets of factors---cognitive, behavioral, and environmental---interact reciprocally among themselves. Contrary to common misconception, social learning theory does not disregard personal determinants of behavior. Within this perspective, such determinants are treated as integral, dynamic factors in causal processes rather than as static trait dimensions.

Self-Regulatory Functions
Of the Self System

The differences between unidirectional and reciprocal analyses of behavior have been drawn most sharply in the area of self-regulatory phenomena. Exponents of radical behaviorism have always disavowed any construct of self for fear that it would usher in psychic agents and divert attention from physical to experiential reality. While this approach encompasses a large set of environmental factors, it assumes that self-generated influences either do not exist or, if they do, that they have no effect upon behavior. Instead events are treated simply as an intermediate link in a causal chain. Since environmental conditions presumably create the intermediate link, one can explain behavior in terms of external factors without recourse to any internal determinants. Through a conceptual bypass, cognitive determinants are thus excised from the analysis of causal processes.

In contrast to the latter view, internal determinants of behavior are gaining increasing attention in contemporary theorizing and research. Indeed, self-referent processes occupy a central position in social learning theory (Bandura, 1997b). As will be shown later, self-generated events cannot be relegated to a redundant explanatory link. In the triadic reciprocal system, they not only operate as reciprocal determinants of behavior but they play a role in the perception and formation of the environmental influences themselves.

*   *   *

In social learning theory, a self-system is not a psychic agent that controls behavior. Rather, it refers to cognitive structures that provide reference mechanisms and to a set of subfunctions for the perception, evaluation, and regulation of behavior. Before proceeding to a reciprocal analysis of self influences, the processes by which people exercise some control over their own behavior will be reviewed briefly.

Component Processes In Self-Regulation

Figure 48.2 summarizes the different component processes in the self-regulation of behavior through self-prescribed contingencies. Behavior typically varies on a number of dimensions, some of which are listed in the self-observation component. Depending on value orientations and the functional significance of given activities, people attend selectively to certain aspects of their behavior and ignore variations on nonrelevant dimensions.

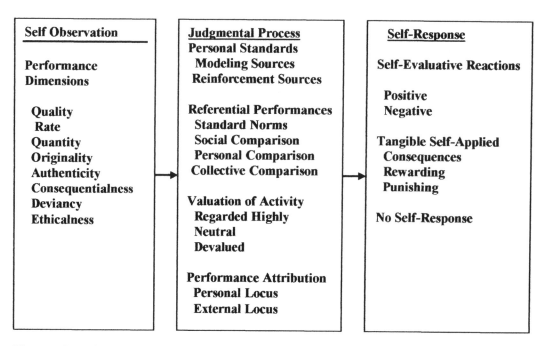

Self Observation	Judgmental Process	Self-Response
Performance Dimensions	**Personal Standards** Modeling Sources Reinforcement Sources	**Self-Evaluative Reactions**
Quality Rate Quantity Originality Authenticity Consequentialness Deviancy Ethicalness	**Referential Performances** Standard Norms Social Comparison Personal Comparison Collective Comparison **Valuation of Activity** Regarded Highly Neutral Devalued **Performance Attribution** Personal Locus External Locus	Positive Negative **Tangible Self-Applied Consequences** Rewarding Punishing No Self-Response

Figure 48.2 Component processes in the self-regulation of behavior by self-prescribed contingencies

Simply observing variations in one's performance yields some relevant information, but such data, in themselves do not provide any basis for personal reactions Behavior produces self-reactions through a judgmental function that includes several subsidiary processes. Whether a given performance will be regarded as commendable or dissatisfying depends upon the personal standards against which it is evaluated. Actions that measure up to internal standards are appraised favorably; those that fall short are judged unsatisfactory.

For most activities, there are no absolute measures of adequacy. The time in which a given distance is run, the number of points obtained on an achievement test, or the size of charitable contributions, often do not convey sufficient information for self-appraisal even when compared with an internal standard. When adequacy is defined relationally, performances are evaluated by comparing them with those of others. The referential comparisons may involve standard norms, the performances of particular individuals, or the accomplishments of reference groups.

One's previous behavior is continuously used as the reference against which ongoing performance is judged. In this referential process, it is self-comparison that supplies the measure of adequacy. Past attainments influence performance appraisals mainly through their effects on standard setting. After a given level of performance is attained, it is no longer challenging, and new self-satisfactions are often sought through progressive improvement.

Another important factor in the judgmental component of self-regulation concerns the evaluation of the activities. People do not much care how they perform on tasks that have little or no significance for them. And little effort is expended on devalued activities. It is mainly in areas affecting one's welfare and self-esteem that favorable performance appraisals activate personal consequences (Simon, 1978).

Self-reactions also vary depending on how people perceive the determinants of their behavior. They take pride in their accomplishments when they ascribe their successes to their own abilities and efforts. They do not derive much self-satisfaction, however, when they view their performances as heavily dependent on external factors. The same is true for judgments of failure and blameworthy conduct. People respond self-critically to inadequate performances for which they hold themselves responsible but not to those which they perceive are due to unusual circumstances or to insufficient capabilities. Performance appraisals set the occasion for self-produced consequences. Favorable judgments give rise to rewarding self-reactions, whereas unfavorable appraisals activate negative self-reactions. Performances that are judged to have no personal significance do not generate any reactions one way or another.

In the social learning view, self-regulated incentives alter performance mainly through their motivational function (Bandura, 1976). Contingent self-reward improves performance not because it strengthens preceding responses. When people make self-satisfaction or tangible gratifications conditional upon certain accomplishments, they motivate themselves to expend the effort needed to attain the desired performances. Both the anticipated satisfactions of desired accomplishments and the dissatisfactions with insufficient ones provide incentives for actions that increase the likelihood of performance attainments.

Much human behavior is regulated through self-evaluative consequences n the form of self-satisfaction, self-pride, self-dissatisfactions, and self-criticism. The act of writing is a familiar example of a behavior that is continuously self-regulated through evaluative self-reactions. Writers adopt a standard of what constitutes an acceptable piece of work. Ideas are generated and rephrased in thought before they are committed to paper. Provisional constructions are successively revised until authors are satisfied with what they have written. The more exacting the personal standards, the more extensive are the corrective improvements.

People also get themselves to do things they would otherwise put off by making tangible outcomes conditional upon completing a specified level of performance. In programs of self-directed change, individuals improve and maintain behavior on their own over long periods by arranging incentives for themselves (Bandura, 1976; Goldfried & Merbaum, 1973; Mahoney 7' Thoresen, 1974). In many instances, activities are regulated through self-prescribed contingencies involving both evaluative and tangible self-rewards. Authors influence how much they write by making breaks, recreational activities, and other tangible rewards contingent on completing a certain amount of work (Wallace, 1977) but they revise and improve what they write by their self-evaluative reactions.

*   *   *

Reciprocal Influence of External Factors
On Self-Regulatory Functions

Social learning theory regards self-generated influences not as autonomous regulators of behavior but as contributory influences in a reciprocally interacting system. A variety of external factors serve as reciprocal influences on the operation of a self system. They can affect self-regulatory processes in at least three major ways: They are involved in the development of the component functions in self-regulatory systems; they provide partial support for adherence to self-prescribed contingencies; and they facilitate selective activation and disengagement of internal contingencies governing conduct.

Development of Self-Regulatory Functions.

The development of capabilities for self-reaction requires adoption of standards against which performances can be evaluated. These internal criteria do not emerge in a vacuum. Behavioral standards are established by precept, evaluative consequences accompanying different performances, and exposure to the self-evaluative standards modeled by others (Bandura, 1976, 1977b; Masters & Mokros, 1974). People do not passively absorb behavioral standards from the environmental stimuli that happen to impinge upon them. They extract generic standards from the multiplicity of evaluative reactions that are exemplified and taught by different individuals or by the same individuals on different activities and in different settings (Bandura, 1976; Lepper, Sagotsky, & Mailer, 1975). People must therefore process the divergent information and eventually arrive at personal standards against which to measure their own behavior.

Associational preferences add another reciprocal element to the acquisition process. The people with whom one regularly associates partly influence the standards of behavior that are adopted. Value orientations, in turn, exercise selective influence on choices of activities and associates (Bandura & Walters, 1959; Krauss, 1964).

External Supports for Self-Regulatory Systems

In analyzing regulation of behavior through self-produced consequences, one must distinguish between two different sources of incentives that operate in the system. First, there is the arrangement of self-reward contingent upon designated performances to create proximal incentives for oneself to engage in the activities. Second, there are the more distal incentives for adhering to the self-prescribed contingencies.

Adherence to performance requirements for self-reward is partly sustained by periodic environmental influences that take a variety of forms (Bandura, 1977b). First, there are the negative sanctions for unmerited self-reward. When standards

114

are being acquired or when they are later applied inconsistently, rewarding oneself for undeserving performances is more likely than not to evoke critical reactions from others. Occasional sanctions for unmerited self-reward influence the likelihood that people will withhold rewards from themselves until their behavior matches their standards (Bandura, Mahoney, & Dirks, 1976). Personal sanctions operate as well in fostering such adherence. After people adopt codes of conduct, when they perform inadequately or violate their standards they tend to engage in self-critical and other distressing trains of thought. Anticipated, thought-produced distress over faulty behavior provides an internal incentive to abide by personal standards of performance (Bandura, 1977b).

Negative inducements, whether personal or social, are not the most reliable basis upon which to test a system of self-regulation. Fortunately, there are more advantageous reasons for exercising some influence over one's own behavior through self-arranged incentives. Some of these personal benefits are extrinsic to the behavior; others derive from the behavior itself.

People are motivated to institute performance contingencies for themselves when the behavior they seek to change is aversive. To overweight persons, the discomforts, maladies, and social costs of obesity create inducements to control their overeating. Similarly, students are prompted to improve their study behavior when failures in course work make academic life sufficiently distressing. By making self-reward conditional upon performance attainments, individuals can reduce aversive behavior, thereby creating natural benefits for their efforts.

The benefits of self-regulated change may provide natural incentives for adherence to personal prescriptions for valued activities as well as for unpleasant ones. People often motivate themselves by conditional incentives to enhance their skills in activities they aspire to master. Here the personal benefits derived from improved proficiency support self-prescription of contingencies. Self-generated inducements are especially important in ensuring continual progress in creative endeavors, because people have to develop their own work schedules for themselves. There are no clocks to punch or supervisors to issue directives. In analyzing the writing habits and self-discipline of novelists, Wallace (1977) documents how famous novelists regulate their writing output by making self-reward contingent upon completion of a certain amount of writing each day whether the spirit moves them or not.

If societies relied solely on inherent benefits to sustain personal contingencies, many activities that are tiresome and uninteresting until proficiency in them is acquired would never be mastered. Upholding standards is therefore socially promoted by a vast system of rewards including praise, social recognition, and honors. Few accolades are bestowed on people for self-rewarding their mediocre performances. Direct praise or seeing others publicly recognized for upholding excellence fosters adherence to high performance standards (Bandura, Grusec, & Menlove, 1967).

*   *   *

115

Because personal and environmental determinants affect each other in a reciprocal fashion, attempts to assign causal priority to these two sources of influence reduce to the "chicken-or-egg" debate. The quest for the ultimate environmental determinant of activities regulated by self-influence becomes a regressive exercise that can yield no victors in explanatory contests, because for every ultimate environmental cause that is invoked, one can find prior actions that helped to produce it.

Selective Activation and Disengagement of Self-Reactive Influences

The third area of research on the role of external factors in self-regulation centers on the selective activation and disengagement of self-reactive influences (Bandura, 1977b). Theories of internalization that portray incorporated entities (e.g., the conscience or superego, moral codes) as continuous internal overseers of conduct are usually at a loss to explain the variable operation of internal control and the perpetration of inhumanities by otherwise humane people.

In the social learning analysis, considerate people perform culpable acts because of reciprocal dynamics between personal and situational determinants of behavior rather than because of defects in their moral structures. Development of self-regulatory capabilities doe not create an invariant control mechanism within a person. Self-evaluative influences do not operate unless activated, and many situational dynamics influence their selective activation.

After ethical and moral standards of conduct are adopted, anticipatory self-censuring reactions for violating personal standards ordinarily serve as self-deterrents against reprehensible acts (Bandura & Walters, 1959) (i.e., you will feel guilt if you do it). Self-deterring consequences are likely to be activated most strongly when the causal connection between conduct and the detrimental effects it produces is unambiguous. There are various means, however, by which self-evaluative consequences can be dissociated from reprehensible behavior.

One set of disengagement practices operates at the level of the behavior. What is culpable can be made honorable through moral justifications and palliative characterizations (Gambino, 1973; Kelman, 1973). In this process, reprehensible conduct is made personally and socially acceptable by portraying it in the service of beneficial or moral ends. Such cognitive restructuring of behavior is an especially effective disinhibitor because it not only eliminates self-generated deterrents but engages self-reward in the service of the behavior.

Another set of dissociative practices operates by obscuring or distorting the relationship between actions and the effects they cause. By displacing and diffusing responsibility, people do not see themselves as personally accountable for their actions and are thus spared self-prohibiting reactions (Bandura, Underwood, & Fromson, 1975; Milgram, 1974). Additional ways of weakening self-deterring reactions operate by disregarding or obscuring the consequences of actions. When people embark on a self-disapproval course of action for personal gain, or because of other inducements, they avoid facing the harm they cause. Self-censuring

116

reactions are unlikely to be activated as long as the detrimental effects of conduct are disregarded.

The final set of disengagement practices operates at the level of the recipients of injurious effects. The strength of self-evaluative reactions partly depends on how the people toward whom actions are directed are viewed. Maltreatment of individuals who are regarded as subhuman or debased is less apt to arouse self-reproof than if they are seen as human beings with dignifying qualities (Zimbardo, 1969). Detrimental interactions usually involve a series of reciprocally escalative actions in which the victims are rarely faultless. One can always select from the chain of events an instance of defensive behavior by the adversary as the original instigation. By blaming victims, one's own actions are excusable. The disengagement of internal control, whatever the means, is not achieved solely through personal deliberation. People are socially aided in this process by indoctrination, scapegoating, and pejorative stereotyping of people held in disfavor.

As is evident from preceding discussion, the development of self-regulatory functions does not create an automatic control system, nor do situational influences exercise mechanical control. Personal judgments operating at each subfunction preclude the automaticity of the process. There is leeway in judging whether a given behavioral standard is applicable. Because of the complexity and inherent ambiguity of most events, there is even greater leeway in the judgment of behavior and its effects. To add further to the variability of the control process, most activities are performed under collective arrangements that obscure responsibility, thus permitting leeway in judging the degree of personal agency in the effects that are socially produced. In short, there exists considerable latitude for personal judgmental factors to affect whether or not self-regulatory influences will be activated in any given activity.

Reciprocal Influence of Personal Factors on Reinforcement Effects

Reinforcement has commonly been viewed as a mechanistic process in which responses are shaped automatically and unconsciously by their immediate consequences. The assumption of automaticity of reinforcement is crucial to the argument of unidirectional environmental control of behavior. One can dispense with the so-called internal link in causal chains only if persons are conceived of as mechanical respondents to external stimuli. The empirical evidence does not support such a view (Bandura, 1977b; Bower, 1975; Mischel, 1973, Neisser, 1976). External influences operate largely through cognitive processes.

During ongoing reinforcement, respondents are doing more than simply emitting responses. They develop expectations from observed regularities about the outcomes likely to result from their actions under given situational circumstances. Contrary to claims that behavior is controlled by its immediate consequences, behavior is related to its outcomes at the level of aggregate consequences rather than momentary effects (Baum, 1973). People process and synthesize contextual and outcome information from sequences of events over long intervals about the action patterns that are necessary to produce given outcomes.

117

The notion that behavior is governed by its consequences fares better for anticipated than for actual consequences (Bandura, 1977b). We have already reviewed research demonstrating how the same environmental consequences have markedly different effects on behavior depending on respondents' beliefs about the nature of the relationships between actions and outcomes and the meaning of the outcomes. When belief differs from actuality, which is not uncommon, behavior is weakly influenced by its actual consequences until more realistic expectations are developed through repeated experience. But it is not always expectations that change in the direction of social reality. Acting on erroneous expectations can alter how others behave, thus shaping the social reality in the direction of the expectations.

While undergoing reinforcing experiences, people are doing more than learning the probabilistic contingencies between actions and outcomes. They observe the progress they are making and tend to set themselves goals of progressive improvement. Investigators who have measured personal goal setting as well as changes in performance find that external incentives influence behavior partly through their effect on goal setting (Locke, Bryan, & Kendall, 1968). When variations in personal goals are partialed out, the effects of incentives on performance are reduced. Performance attainments also provide an important source of efficacy information for judging one's personal capabilities. Changes in perceived self-efficacy, in turn, affect people's choices of activities, how much effort they expend, and how long they will persist in the fact of obstacles and aversive experiences (Bandura, 1997a; Brown & Inouye, 1978).

Because of the personal determinants of reinforcement effects, to trace behavior back to environmental "reinforcers" by no means completes the explanatory regress. To predict how outcomes will affect behavior, one must know how they are cognitively processed. To understand fully the mechanisms through which consequences change behavior, one must analyze the reciprocally contributory influences of cognitive factors.

Reciprocal Determinism as a Generic Analytic Principle

The discussion thus far has primarily addressed issues regarding the reciprocal interactions between behavior, thought, and environmental events as they occur at the individual level. Social learning theory treats reciprocal determinism as a basic principle for analyzing psychosocial phenomena at varying levels of complexity, ranging from intrapersonal development, to interpersonal behavior, to the interactive functioning of organizational and societal systems. At the intrapersonal level, people's conceptions influence what they perceive and do, and their conceptions are in turn altered by the effects of their actions and the observed consequences accruing to others (Bandura, 1977a; Bower, 1975). Information-processing models are concerned mainly with internal operations. A comprehensive theory must also analyze how conceptions are converted to actions, which furnish some of the data for conceptions. In social learning theory, people play an active role in creating information generating experiences as well as in processing and transforming informative stimuli that happen to impinge upon them. This involves reciprocal transactions between thought, behavior, and environmental events which are not fully encompassed by a computer metaphor. People are not only perceivers, knowers, and actors. They are also self-reactors, with capacities for reflective self-awareness that are generally neglected in information-processing theories based on computer models of human functioning.

At the level of interpersonal behavior, we have previously examined how people reciprocally determine each others' actions (Bandura et. al.1960; Patterson, 1975; Rausch et. al, 1974). Although the mutuality of behavior may be the focus of study, the reciprocal processes involve cognition as well as action. At the broader societal level, reciprocal processes are reflected in the interdependence of organizational elements, social subsystems, and transnational relations (Bandura, 1973; Keohane & Nye, 1977). Here the matters of interest are the patterns of interdependence between systems, the criteria and means used for gauging systemic performances, the mechanisms that exist for exercising reciprocal influence, and the conditions that alter the degree and type of reciprocal control that one system can exert on another.

It is within the framework of reciprocal determinism that the concept of freedom assumes meaning (Bandura, 1977b). Because people's conceptions, their behavior, and their environments are reciprocal determinants of each other, individuals are neither powerless objects controlled by environmental forces nor entirely free agents who can do whatever they choose. People can be considered partially free insofar as they shape future conditions by influencing their courses of action. By creating structural mechanisms for reciprocal influence, such as organizational systems of checks and balances, legal systems, and due process and elective procedures, people can bring their influence to bear on each other. Institutional reciprocal mechanisms thus provide not only safeguards against unilateral social control but the means for changing institutions and the conditions of life. Within the process of reciprocal determinism lies the opportunity for people to shape their destinies as well as the limits of self-direction.

---

[1] Jean Piaget was a Swiss psychologist whose ideas have had an important influence on developmental psychology. The idea referred to here concerns Piaget's description of how the mind develops through an interaction between knowledge and experience.

Part One
Theoretical Foundations of Personality

Key Questions

1. What are the major differences between the developmental stage theories of Sigmund Freud and Erik Erikson? Are both of these models applicable to contemporary life? If so, in what way?

2. To what extent do the revisionist ideas of the Neo-Freudian theorists, Alfred Adler, Carl Jung, Karen Horney, and Harry Stack Sullivan truly depart from those of Sigmund Freud? Do you agree with their revisions? If so, why?

3. What do you think about Alfred Adler's ideas on birth order and earliest recollections? Do you agree that they relate to your own position in the family and your earliest remembrances? How do they enhance our understanding of personality?

4. Examine Carl Jung's proposition of Introversion-Extroversion and the dimensions of thinking-feeling, sensing-intuiting. How would you describe yourself with respect to his theory?

5. To what extent do individuals "move towards," "move away from," or "move against" sources of anxiety as Horney suggests? Do you agree with her identification of ten neurotic trends?

6. Why is it important for some personality psychologists to concentrate exclusively on the identification and measurement of such phenomena as the trait, type, need or motive? Do they lose the whole picture of an individual's personality by focusing on a single concept in the process?

7. How do you think Carl Rogers and Abraham Maslow would respond to contemporary man's or woman's striving for self-actualization if they were alive today? Would you agree that most persons are fully functioning individuals?

8. In what ways might humanistic concepts be applied to the resolution of global problems in this century?

9. What do you think of the research of John B. Watson and B. F. Skinner? Do you agree that we acquire our personalities through respondent and instrumental learning? Why?

10. In what way has Albert Bandura's theory of reciprocal determinism contributed to our understanding and assessment of personality in its entirety?

Part One
Theoretical Foundations of Personality

Suggested Readings

Adler, A. (1964). *Social Interest: A Challenge to Mankind.* New York: Putnam (Capricorn Books).

Adler, A. (1973). In H. L. Ansbacher & R. R. Ansbacher (Eds.) *Superiority and Social Interest: A Collection of Later Writings.* New York: Viking Press.

Allport, G. W. (1937). *Personality: A Psychological Interpretation.* New York: Holt, Rinehart & Winston.

Allport, G. W. (1943). *Becoming: Basic Considerations for a Psychology of Personality.* New Haven, CT: Yale University Press.

Allport, G. W. (1961). *Pattern and Growth in Personality.* New York: Holt, Rinehart & Winston.

Allport. G. W. (1968). *The Person in Psychology: Selected Essays.* Boston, MA: Beacon Press.

Bandura, A. (1965). Influences of Models' Reinforcement Contingencies on the Acquisition of Imitative Responses. *Journal of Personality and Social Psychology,* 1, 589-595.

Bandura, A. (1973). *Aggression: A Social Learning Analysis.* Englewood Cliffs, NJ: Prentice-Hall Publishers.

Bandura, A. (1977). *Social Learning Theory.* Englewood Cliffs, NJ: Prentice-Hall Publishers.

Bandura, A. (1986). *Social Foundations of Thought and Action: A Social Cognitive Theory.* Englewood Cliffs, NJ: Prentice-Hall Publishers.

Erikson, E. H. (1950). *Childhood and Society.* New York: W. W. Norton.

Erikson, E. H. (1954). The Dream Specimen in Psychoanalysis. *Journal of American Psychoanalytic Association*, 2, 5-56.

Erikson, E. H. ((1968). *Identity, Youth, and Crisis.* New York: W. W. Norton.

Erikson, E. H. (1975). *Life History and the Historical Moment.* New York: W. W. Norton.

Eysenck, H. J. (1967). *The Biological Basis of Personality.* Springfield, IL: Charles C. Thomas.

Eysenck, H. J. (1982). Development of a Theory. In C. D. Spielberger (Ed.), *Personality, Genetics and Behavior: Selected Papers* (pp. 1-38). New York: Praeger Press.

Eysenck, H. J. (1990). Biological Dimensions of Personality. In L. Pervin (Ed.), *Handbook of Personality Theory and Research* (pp. 244-276). New York: Guilford Press.

Freud, A. (1958). Adolescence. *Psychoanalytic Study of the Child,* 13, 255-278.

Freud, A. (1966). *The Ego and Mechanisms of Defense* (Rev. Ed.). New York: International Press.

Freud, A. (1966). *The Writings of Anna Freud* (Vol. 2). New York: International Press.

Freud, S. (1901). *The Psychopathology of Everyday Life.* New York: W. W. Norton.

Freud, S. (1964). *The Complete Psychological Works of Sigmund Freud.* (Vols. 1-24). London: Hogarth Press. (Original work published 1886-1936).

Freud, S., & Jung, C. G. (1974). In W. McGuire (Ed.) *The Freud/Jung Letters.* Princeton, New Jersey: Princeton University Press.

Gay, P. (1988). *Freud: A Life for Our Time.* New York: W. W. Norton.

Gay, P. (1989). *The Freud Reader.* New York: W. W. Norton.

Horney, K. (1937). *The Neurotic Personality of our Time.* New York: W. W. Norton.

Horney, K. (1939). *New Ways in Psychoanalysis.* New York: W. W. Norton.

Horney, K. (1966). *Our Inner Conflicts: A Constructive Theory of Neurosis.* New York: W. W. Norton.

Horney, K. (1967). Feminine *Psychology.* New York: W. W. Norton.

Jung, C G. (1933). *Modern Man in Search of a Soul.* New York: Hartcourt Brace Jovanovich.

Jung, C. G. (1961). *Memories, Dreams, Reflections.* New York: Pantheon Books.

Jung, C. G. (1961). *The Collected Works of Carl Jung.* (Vols. 1-17). Princeton, NJ: Princeton University Press. (Original work published 1902-1961).

Maslow, A. (1962). Lessons from Peak Experiences. *Journal of Humanistic Psychology,* 2, 9-18.

Maslow, A. (1966). *The Psychology of Science.* Chicago, IL: Regency Press.

Maslow, A. (1968). *Toward a Psychology of Being.* New York: Van Nostrand.

Maslow, A. (1970). *Motivation and Personality* (Rev. Ed.). New York: Harper & Row.

Maslow, A. (1971). *The Farther Reaches of Human Nature.* New York: Viking Press.

Rogers, C. R. (1963). The Concept of the Fully Functioning Person. *Psychotherapy: Theory, Research, and Practice,* l, 17-26.

Rogers, C. R. (1964). Toward a Science of the Person. In T. W. Wann (Ed.), *Behaviorism and Phenomenology.* Chicago, IL: University of Chicago Press.

Rogers, C. R. (1969). *Freedom to Learn: A View of What Education Might Become.* Columbus, OH: Merrill Publishers.

Rogers, C. R. (1973). Some New Challenges. *American Psychologist,* 28, 379-387.

Rogers, C. R. (1974). In Retrospect: Forty-Six Years. *American Psychologist,* 29, 115-123.

Rogers, C. R. (1977). *Carl Rogers on Personal Power.* New York: Delacorte Press.

Rogers, C. R. (1983). *Freedom to Learn for the 80s.* Columbus, OH: Charles F. Merrill.

Skinner, B. F. (1938). *The Behavior of Organisms.* New York: Appleton-Century Crofts.

Skinner, B. F. (1953). *Science and Human Behavior.* New York: MacMillan Press.

Skinner, B. F. (1974). *About Behaviorism.* New York: Knopf.

Skinner, B F. (1983). *A Matter of Consequences.* New York: Knopf.

Skinner, B. F. (1989). The Origins of Cognitive Thought. *American Psychologist,* 44, 13-18.

Sullivan, H. S. (1953). *The Interpersonal Theory of Psychiatry.* New York: W. W. Norton.

Watson, J. B. (1970). *Behaviorism.* New York: W. W. Norton. (Original work Published in 1924).

Part Two

Case Histories

Research Studies

Psychotherapies

Part Two
Case Histories, Research Studies & Psychotherapies

You may wonder how personality psychologists assess their theories, conduct their research, and establish their methods of psychological treatment. In Part Two, you will discover that these theorists relied upon an assortment of assessment tools and techniques, research methodologies, and therapeutic procedures for brining about personality change. As you will see, the range of options is extensive and closely matches the theoretical foundations of the personality psychologists previously discussed in Part One of this text.

Psychoanalysis is most famous for its use of case histories in the assessment of personality. It was Sigmund Freud's goal to transform human misery into common unhappiness and, in this quest, he sought to collect qualitative information from his patients that would enable him to gain access to the deepest regions of their minds, the unconscious. However, it is important to note that Freud himself claims that it was a merit to have created psychoanalysis, but not his merit. The honor belonged to Dr. Josef Breuer, Freud's colleague, friend, and mentor, who first dedicated himself to uncovering the origins of hysteria in a young, female patient.

Lucy Freeman's, *The Case of Anna O.*, exposes the nature of Anna O.'s illness, the historical evolution of psychoanalysis, and the fact that mental aberrations lay within the mind, itself. Even though the Case of Anna O. is not part of the collection of Freud's most famous case histories, Reuben Fine presents a number of those that are in his work, *Famous Freudian Case Histories.* Here, you will be exposed to a variety of mental disorders as evidenced in the Case of Dora (hysteria), the Case of Little Hans (phobia), the Case of the Rat Man (obsessional neurosis), the Schreber Case (paranoia), and the Case of the Wolf Man (neurosis). In *My Recollections of Sigmund Freud,* the Wolf Man offers a unique perspective of his relationship and observation of the great master, Sigmund Freud. Unprecedented, it is the only documented case history in the annals of psychoanalytic literature where we get a glimpse of psychoanalysis as a form of therapy through the eyes of the patient, himself.

Selections in Chapter Seven reflect the continued reliance upon the case history as a method for understanding personality dynamics by key revisionist theorists. In *The Anxious Young Woman and the Retired Business Man,* Carl Jung presents a comparative analysis of psychoanalysis and his analytic psychology through the case material of these two individuals. Alfred Adler's case of a fifty-year-old man, in *The Drive for Superiority,* features his basic theoretical conceptualizations of feelings of inferiority, striving for superiority, and style of life. Harry Stack Sullivan's case of *The Inefficient Wife* highlights the psychological advice he offered to one of his students concerning the schizoid personality of a young married woman. As you might guess, the suggestions given reflect his theoretical emphasis upon interpersonal relationships.

The articles presented in Chapter Eight provide insight into personality tools and techniques rather than research methodologies. Gordon Allport's *Letters from Jenny,* show us how psychologists use personal documents to obtain personality information about individuals. In this instance, correspondence between Jenny Masterson and her only son's two best friends is cleverly used to assess her trait structure. Henry Murray's *Explorations of Personality* shed some light into the construction and validation of his famous projective technique, the Thematic Apperception Test (TAT).

Case histories and archival records are not only used to diagnose the mental problems of individuals, but also to generate new theories and ideas in the field as evidenced in Chapter Nine. The case history of *The Angry Adolescent* by Carl Rogers highlights the inner workings of his nondirective, client-centered therapy. Through the eyes of a seventeen-year-old female, we learn about her discovery of the source of her problems through insight gleaned from the therapeutic relationship. In *Self-Actualizing People,* Abraham Maslow describes the sources of his motivation to develop a theory of psychological health. His personal observations of Ruth Benedict, Max Wertheimer, and others and examination of archival records led him to believe that self-actualized persons have certain personality characteristics in common. Here, he describes these characteristics in great detail.

Our final section, Chapter Ten, contains key articles illustrating some landmark studies and experiments in behaviorism. In *Conditioned Emotional*

Reactions, John B. Watson and Rosalie Rayner present their classic case of Little Albert and the merits of classical conditioning. B.F. Skinner's article, *Shaping and Maintaining Operant Behavior,* identifies the significant role played by reinforcement in the shaping of both animal and human behavior. Finally, Albert Bandura's manuscript, *Imitation of Film-Mediated Aggressive Models,* exposes the major findings of his classic Bobo Doll Study and the acquisition of aggression through observational learning.

Chapter Six
Case Histories in Psychoanalysis

"Much is won if we succeed in transforming human misery into common unhappiness."

Sigmund Freud

The Case of Anna O. *

Lucy Freeman

*F*or five months after he had concluded the treatment of his young hysterical patient, Dr. Josef Breuer told no one of her amazing "talking cure."

Then, on November 18, 1882, he spoke of what had happened to a close friend, a young physician in whom he had great faith as a research scientist. The younger man's name was Sigmund Freud.

Breuer described how his patient's paralysis, poor vision, cough, muteness, and headaches had all disappeared under hypnosis as she talked about experiences related to each symptom. She was able to recall the first time the symptom had appeared and the emotions it provoked in her even though she had lost all conscious memory of the event and the emotions.

Though Freud knew nothing about the treatment of hysteria by hypnosis, he was fascinated. He asked questions, and together they discussed the implication of such a cure. He believed that Breuer had made a revolutionary discovery in treating hysteria and should inform the medical world. Breuer disagreed, said he had enough of hysterical women, they were an ordeal and he was giving them up.

Freud was twenty-six, only three years older than Breuer's young patient. In 1880, when Breuer first visited his patient, Freud was a teaching assistant in the research laboratory of the Vienna Institute of Physiology, headed by Dr. Ernest Brucke. He was pursuing research in histology, that branch of biology concerned with the microscopic study of the structure of tissue.

Freud received his medical degree on March 31, 1881, almost on the very day---actually the day after---Breuer's patient first stepped out of the bed in which she had lain paralyzed since December 11th. In the summer of 1881, when Breuer was visiting his young patient at her country home, Freud was studying the nerve cells of the crayfish under a microscope.

As Breuer's patient ended her treatment in the spring of 1882, Freud met and fell in love with nineteen-year-old Martha Bernays, who lived in Vienna and was a friend of Breuer's young patient.

Freud first met Breuer, then a distinguished teacher, at the Institute in the late 1870s. From the first they found they shared common scientific interests. Freud

* Freeman, Lucy. (1972). The Case of Anna O. *The Story of Anna O.*, 187-202. New York: Walker and Company. Reprinted by permission.

often accompanied Breuer on visits to patients. At times Breuer loaned small sums of money to Freud, who was then penniless.

Freud became secretly engaged to Martha Bernays, on June 17, 1882, and on the advice of Brucke gave up the financially unrewarding research---which he had hoped to make his life's work---in order to prepare for general practice. He then became an intern at the Viennese General Hospital, one of the most famous teaching centers of the world. As a junior resident physician in May, 1883, he transferred from the department of medicine to the psychiatric clinic run by Dr Theodor Meynart, who had impressed Freud in medical school as the most brilliant man he had ever met. According to general medical opinion, Meynart was the most astute brain anatomist of that era, though not an outstanding psychiatrist. But Freud's study of the mental disorder called "Meynart's Amentia"---acute hallucinatory psychosis---made him aware that hallucinations might be related to wishes that the patient did not consciously realize he had.

Freud now became very interested in studying neurology. There were few neurological specialists in Vienna, but in the distance "glimmered the great name of Charcot," as Freud put it, and he went to Paris on October 11, 1885, to study under the famous Professor of Pathological Anatomy as the Salpetriere, a mammoth institution, just outside Paris, housing thousands of the chronically ill, aged, and insane. It was a "great asylum of human misery," to use Charcot's words.

Freud studied for four months with Charcot, watched him induce hysterical symptoms in a hypnotized patient, then removes the symptoms during a second hypnosis. A man in a hypnotic trance was told his right arm would feel paralyzed when he came out of the trance. Awakened, the man found he could not move his right arm. When asked why, he said he did not know of made a false reason. Then he was again hypnotized, and the suggestion made that his arm would be normal when he wok, which it proved to be.

Seeing this occur time after time, Freud concluded there was a part of the human mind outside awareness that was more powerful than the conscious, that could in fact control the conscious. The "unconscious," referred to by philosophers and poets of the past, had now, by way of hypnotism, come alive before Freud's eyes.

He recalled Breuer's young patient and told Charcot of the "talking cure." But Charcot seemed unimpressed. "So," Freud said, "I never returned to it and allowed it to pass from my mind." But only for the four months he remained in Paris. When he returned to Vienna on April 4, 1886, after spending the month of March in Berlin studying pediatrics, the memory of the "talking cure" once again haunted him. In his words, he "made" Breuer tell him "more about it." And he persuaded Breuer, who for four years had practiced only internal medicine, to resume treatment of hysterical women.

Ten years after Breuer had last seen his young patient, Freud finally persuaded him to co-author an article about the "talking cure," referring to the case from notes he had kept when he saw her. By then Freud had cured several of his own patients of hysterical symptoms. He had moved from the *Suehnhaus*, a palatial apartment house facing the *Ringstrasse*, to *Bergasse* 19, near the University of Vienna. Breuer still lived at *Brandstatte* 8.

The two authors gave their article the formidable title, "On the Psychical Mechanism of Hysterical Phenomena, Preliminary Communication." In preparation for the article Freud wrote three "memoranda," the first in the form of a letter to Breuer dated June 29, 1892. In it he says, "I am tormented by the problem of how it will be possible to give a two-dimensional picture of anything that is so much of a solid as our theory of neurosis." It is interesting that Freud uses the word, "tormented," the very word Breuer's young patient used to describe how she felt, the word which first led Breuer to question her further.

In the memoranda, Freud refers to a "second state of consciousness." This is believed to be the first time in his published scientific work that he mentions the unconscious.

The "Preliminary Communication" appeared in 1893, in two issues, January 1st and January 15th, of the periodical *Neurologisches Centralblatt* (the principal German neurological journal), which came out forthnightly in Berlin. The article was immediately reprinted in Vienna in the *Wiener Medizinischne Blatter* (The Vienna Medical Journal).

The authors referred to the hysterical young woman as "one of our patients," and described her as "a girl who, while watching a sickbed in a torment state of anxiety, fell into a twilight state and had a terrifying hallucination, while her right arm, which was hanging over the back of her chair, went to sleep. From this there developed a paresis (paralysis) of the same arm accompanied by contracture and anesthesia (loss of sensation)."

They report that in this "highly complicated case of hysteria" all the symptoms, "which sprang from separate causes, were separately removed." They also found in other cases "to our great surprise," that every hysterical symptom immediately and permanently disappeared "when we had succeeded in bringing clearly to light the memory of the event by which it was provoked and in arousing its accompanying affect (emotion), and when the patient had described that event in the greatest possible detail and had put the affect into words."

They warned, "Recollection without affect almost invariably produces no result." In other words, there had to be expression of emotion. Words alone---intellectualization---were of no help.

Freud's classic line, "Hysterics suffer mainly from reminiscences," appears in this article. He explained that the reminiscences in question relate to situations where an impulse to act was repressed. The symptoms appear "in place of" the action and represent a "strangulated" emotion. Both the traumatic incident and the emotion are lost to the patient's memory as though they had never happened. But the symptoms persist.

Hysterical symptoms arise when the emotion involved in a mental process is prevented from being worked over consciously in the normal way and is diverted into "a wrong path," such as conversion into physical illness, as in the case of Breuer's young patient. Because her emotional reaction to an event that was traumatic in her life had been repressed, the emotion remained attached to the memory, hidden in the unconscious.

The authors explained that an injury that has been repaid, even if only in words, is recollected quite differently from one that has had to be accepted without an emotional outlet. The injured person's reaction to the trauma only has a completely "cathartic" effect if it is an adequate reaction," as, for instance, revenge," if there has been hurt.

Language may serve as a substitute for action, they maintained. With the help of language, an emotion can be discharged almost as effectively as if it had been expressed at the time it was felt. Speaking itself is an adequate reaction when, for instance, "it is a lamentation or giving utterance to a tormenting secret, e.g., confession." If there is no such reaction, in deeds or words, "or in the mildest cases in tears," any recollection of the event retains its emotional tone.

But if the original experience, along with the emotions it produced, can be brought into consciousness, the "imprisoned" emotion is discharged, the force that maintains the symptom ceases to operate, and the symptom disappears. This treatment the authors call "the cathartic method."

Freud then persuaded Breuer to join him in the writing of a book, *Studies on Hysteria,* published in 1895 in Leipzig and Vienna. It is the world's first book on psychoanalysis. It contains a fuller account of the treatment of Breuer's young patient, the study of whose "remarkable case" led to the "Preliminary Communication," according to the authors.

The basic concepts of psychoanalysis appear in the book, including repression, psychic determinism, unconscious mental activity, overdetermination, defenses, resistance, and the sexual cause of neurosis, psychic trauma, conflict, conversion, transference, and ambivalence. Another of Freud's classic lines is found here: "Much is won if we succeed in transforming hysterical misery into common unhappiness."

And here, for the first time, Breuer's young patient is given a name---a pseudonym, for it was medical custom to bestow a false name on a patient to protect the identity both of the patient and his family. Breuer's patients was called Anna O.

He admitted he had, "suppressed a large number of quite interesting details" in the study. But in comparison with the medical cases of that era, it was an "extensive" case history.

He ended his description of her treatment by saying: "After this she left Vienna and traveled for a while, but it was a considerable time before she regained her mental balance entirely. Since then she has enjoyed complete health."

Though in his chapter on her treatment Breuer notes "a complete lack of sexuality" in Anna O., saying she never spoke of love, in his chapter on theory he maintains, "The sexual instinct is undoubtedly the most powerful source of persisting increases of excitation (and consequently of neurosis)." Traumatic experiences produce quantities of excitation, or energy charge, to the nerves, too large to be dealt with in the normal way and thus create neuroses.

While hysteria is usually caused by a sexual problem, the case of Anna O. "proves that a fairly severe case of hysteria can develop, flourish, and be resolved without having a sexual basis," Breuer wrote in a letter to the psychiatrist Auguste Forel on November 21st, 1907, twelve years after *Studies on Hysteria* appeared. Breuer added, "I confess that plunging into sexuality in theory and practice is not to my taste. But what have my taste and my feeling about what is seemly and what is unseemly to do with the question of what is true?"

Freud made his only trip to the United States in September, 1909, on the invitation of Clark University in Worcester, Massachusetts, to give five lectures at their Twentieth Anniversary celebration. In his first lecture, he said, "We must grant that it is a merit to have created psychoanalysis, but it is not my merit. I was a student, busy with the passing of my last examinations, when another physician of Vienna, Dr. Josef Breuer, made the first application of this method to the case of a hysterical girl (1880-1882)."

Devoting this lecture to the case of Anna O., Freud described how for years physicians had not understood hysteria and were reluctant to treat it, being unsympathetic toward it and often "punishing" the patient by withdrawing interest. He added:

"Now Dr. Breuer did not deserve this reproach in this case; he gave his patient sympathy and interest, although at first he did not understand how to help her. Probably this was easier for him on account of these superior qualities of the patient's mind and character to which he bears witness in his account of the case....His sympathetic observation soon found the means which made the first help possible."

It was especially to be noted, Freud pointed out, that Anna O., in almost all traumatic situations, "had to suppress a strong excitement, instead of giving vent to it by appropriate words and deeds....While she was seated by her father's sickbed, she was careful to betray nothing of her anxiety and her painful depression to the patient. When, later, she reproduced the same scene before the physician, the emotion which she had suppressed on the occurrence of the scene burst out with especial strength, as though it had been pent up all along."

Ending this lecture, Freud told the audience, "You have probably also felt, and rightly, that Breuer's investigations gave you only a very incomplete theory and insufficient explanation of the phenomena which we have observed. But complete theories do not fall from Heaven...."

Freud was the one who worked over the years to develop the "complete theory," the theory that started with the case of Anna O. He explored the secrets of the mind, extending the range of psychological observations made by Breuer and himself to include not only his patients but himself. He could accept the advice, "Physician, heal thyself." His own analysis opened the gates to regions of understanding, as he applied to himself the words of Terence: "Nothing that is human is alien to me."

Freud would let nothing deter him in his search for the truth and Breuer sensed this. Freud wrote to his fiancée on February 2nd, 1886, seven months before they were married;

"Do you know what Breuer said to me one evening? That he had discovered what an infinitely bold and fearless person I concealed behind my mask of shyness. I have always believed that of myself, but never dared to say it to anyone. I have often felt as if I had inherited all the passion of our ancestors when they defended their Temple, as if I could joyfully cast away my life in a great cause. And with all that I was always so powerless and could not express the flowing passions even by a word or a poem. So, I have always suppressed myself, and I believe people must notice that in me."

Anna O. had suppressed herself too, but encouraged by Breuer she had finally expressed some of her hidden emotions. This young woman, who had been helped by a devoted young physician without whose dedication she might have killed herself or spent the rest of her days in the jungle of madness, was the one whose treatment Freud described as the starting point of psychoanalysis.

Up to then, mental illness was believed to have an organic cause. It was treated mainly by physical therapy such as mild electrical shocks, drugs, change of diet, and rest cures. Anna O. proved this theory false. Her case showed that the causes of mental aberrations lay within the mind itself.

Case Histories *
Harold Greenwald

The case histories which Freud published were in themselves a unique achievement in psychiatric history. Never before had the neurotic individual been described in such intimate and human terms. It was not his fault, Freud urged rather apologetically, if the histories read like novels; it was the heart of his doctrine that the human and social circumstances of the patient were in the forefront of the causes of his neurosis, and accordingly they had to be described in the greatest of detail.

It is not easy to write up a psychoanalytic case history. In his entire life Freud published only five of major consequence. These cases all date from the period, 1905-14, although the last, written in 1914, was not published until 1918. They are so interesting in their own right, and have become such an integral part of the analytic literature that they will be reviewed here in some detail.

The Case of Dora

This, the first case Freud published after the *Studies on Hysteria* in 1895, had as its full title, "Fragment of an Analysis of a Case of Hysteria." Originally, it was to be entitled Dreams and Hysteria, and its purpose was to show the role which dreams play in the analysis of hysteria. As Freud presents this case history, it centers around two dreams produced by the patient and their detailed analysis.

Freud displayed considerable ambivalence about the publication of this particular case history. In 1901 he offered the paper to the *Monatsschrift fuer Psychiatrie und Neurologie,* in which it was ultimately published. It has been immediately accepted, but Freud asked to have the manuscript returned and kept it for another four years before he could bring himself to allow it to see the light of day. Furthermore, although the analysis itself came to an end actually at the end of 1900, Freud several times erroneously gave the date as 1899.

---

* Fine, Reuben. (1973). Famous Freudian Case Histories. *The Development of Freud's Thought,* 117-141. New York: J. Aronson. Reprinted by permission.

Dora was the younger of two children; her brother was a year and a half older. Their father was in his late forties, and had suffered from a number of illnesses throughout his life. He had been a patient of Freud's, who had treated him for the consequences of a syphilitic infection; his symptoms had cleared up entirely. Four years later he brought his daughter to Freud, and psychotherapy had been recommended. At that time, it was rejected by the girl. Two years later, however, she returned and stayed in treatment with Freud for three months.

When treatment began, Dora was eighteen years old. She had been suffering from a variety of hysterical symptoms since the age of eight. Freud says that she suffered from the commonest of all somatic and mental symptoms---breathing difficulties, nervous cough, loss of voice (sometimes for five weeks at a time), possible migraine, depression, hysterical unsociability, suicidal ideas, and a general dissatisfaction with life.

Dora's mother was described by Freud as a woman suffering from what he called "housewife psychosis"---that is, a woman who was so wrapped up in the details of housekeeping chores that she was unable to relate to any of her family.

Dora's parents had become friendly with another family, the K's. As compensation for the coldness of his wife, Dora's father had begun an affair with Mrs. K, as soon appeared in the course of Dora's analysis. Mr. K had made sexual advances to Dora and had wanted to marry her. Dora's illness was connected with her love for her father, the proposals of Mr. K, and her homosexual love for Mrs. K, as well. All this, in turn, was tied up with her own family situation, that is, her Oedipal conflict. It is to be noted, however, that at this time (1901) Freud did not trace the conflict back to the childhood Oedipal period, between three and five, but contented himself with working out the difficulties that had arisen in the period of Dora's adolescence.

As already noted, Dora remained in treatment for three months, at the end of which time she abruptly broke off without explanation. Fifteen months later, however, she returned for a consultation. It appeared that she had made some symptomatic improvement, although hysterical symptoms of one kind or another continued to crop up.

Many years later, in 1922, Dora was referred for treatment to Dr. Felix Deutsch, a Viennese practicing psychoanalyst. After Dora' death some years ago, Dr. Deutsch wrote up his experiences. Deutsch's paper is of particular interest because he had an opportunity to compare what actually happened to the patient with what Freud had predicted would happen. A number of Freud's interpretations could be confirmed in the patient's later life. For example, her attitude toward marital life, her frigidity, and her disgust with heterosexuality, bore out Freud's concept of displacement. The improvement which Freud had noted in Dora did not last very long. The same kind of rapid improvement occurred when she was under treatment by Dr Deutsch, and again failed to last. Freud, in the latter part of his paper on Dora, had discussed his omission of an analysis of various important transference phenomena. Dora, like so many hysterical women, was obviously capable of transference improvement, but had not been completely analyzed.

The Case of Little Hans

Little Hans was a five-year-old boy who developed such a fear that a horse would bite him that he refused to go out of doors. The child's father was an adherent of Freud's and came to him with the problem. Freud treated the child through the father, and saw the boy only once. The case was written up in 1909 in a paper entitled "Analysis of a Phobia in a Five-Year-Old Boy."

The dynamics of the phobia were traced by Freud and tied up with the Oedipal situation. The father brought the various productions of the child to Freud, who interpreted them, and these interpretations were then given back to the child by the father. It turned out that the phobia had started after the birth of a sister when Little Hands was three and one-half years old. This started the child on a train of thought about where babies come from, the difference between the sexes, and related questions. Hans was much preoccupied with his penis, which he called his "widdler," and with castration fears. These eventually led to the horse phobia. The phobia was directly derived from the Oedipus complex; the horse was equated with the father who, Hans thought, would castrate him for wanting mother. For protection Hans stayed home with mother.

The therapeutic result was excellent. The child got over the phobia completely. His interest turned to music, which was his father's profession, and he later pursued a musical career. According to all reports, he has led a comparatively normal life since.

Fourteen years after the therapy, little Hans, then nineteen years old, appeared in Freud's office and announced himself. "I am little Hans." He had forgotten the whole incident completely and no longer recalled anything, either of his phobia or of his treatments.

The case is important because it is the first time that infantile sexuality was demonstrated to exist in a child. As Freud says, strictly speaking, the case taught him nothing new, but he was able to show directly in a child the suppositions which he had derived from the analyses of adults. It is surprising that Freud saw it only as an exception, and did not utilize the opportunity to make this the beginning of child analysis. Evidently here Freud still retained traces of hesitation about getting too far into the sex life of the child. Since then, of course, especially since the 1920s, child analysis has become a full-fledged specialty, and cases such as those of little Hans are now everyday occurrences.

The Case of the Rat Man

This is the only complete successful analysis which Freud ever published. The case of Dora cannot be considered a complete analysis, since she broke off treatment prematurely; furthermore, it was not really successful. Other cases which Freud published were only fragmentary.

The official title of the paper is "Notes upon a Case of Obsessional Neurosis." Freud's main purpose in publishing the case was to show the structure of an obsessional neurosis. This he did admirably in the theoretical portion.

The analysis began on October 1, 1907, and lasted eleven months. The treatment ended very successfully. The symptoms cleared up, the man re-established himself in his vocation and in his love life. Unfortunately, he died in World War I.

The nickname, "The Rat Man," derives from the great obsessive fear which brought the patient to analysis. The patient was a lawyer of almost thirty, who had been drafted into the army. During maneuvers, he had had various obsessional ideas, all of which, however, had passed off rather quickly. On one occasion, however, during a march, he lost his pince-nez and wired to his optician in Vienna to send him another pair by the next mail. During the same stop, he sat between two officers, one of whom, a captain with a Czech name, was obviously fond of cruelty. This captain defended the introduction of corporal punishment and in this connection told of an especially horrible punishment used in the East. This punishment consisted of tying the criminal up, turning a pot full of rats upside down on his buttocks, and allowing the rats to bore their way into his anus.

As soon as the patient heard the captain tell of this punishment, the idea flashed through his mind that this was happening to a person who was very dear to him. This person was the woman he loved. At the same time, he was afraid that the punishment would be visited upon his father, despite the fact that his father had died many years previously. Whenever he though that a punishment would be carried out, there always appeared a "sanction," that is, a defensive measure which he was obliged to adopt in order to prevent the fantasy from being fulfilled. In this way, many obsessional maneuvers had been built up.

The case history reveals many features which are seen over and over again in similar patients today. For example, in the earliest sessions the patient began to relate details of his sex life. He remembered, from his fourth or fifth year, a scene where he had some sex play with a pretty young governess, which left him with a burning and tormenting curiosity to see the female body. At six he had erections and once went to his mother to complain about them. He used to have a morbid idea that his parents knew his thought; he explained this to himself by supposing that he had spoken them out loud without having heard himself do it.

The theoretical explanation which Freud gives to the obsessional neurosis on the basis of this case is still essentially true today, although it would be expanded in a number of directions in terms of present-day concepts. Although at that time ego psychology had not yet been explicitly formulated. Freud's description of the illness is really much more in terms of the ego structure of the patient than in terms of the id.

By chance, Freud's daily life notes of the first four months of treatment have been found posthumously among his papers. The first third roughly, of these notes were published by Freud in the case history. The remainder appeared for the first time in the Standard Edition. They give a vivid picture of how Freud worked.

The notes on a few of the sessions are reproduced here.

Nov. 8---When he was a child he suffered much from worms. He probably used to put his fingers up his behind and was an awful pig, he said, like his brother. Now carries cleanliness to excess.

Phantasy, before sleep:---He was married to his cousin (the lady). He kissed her feet; but they weren't clean. They had black marks on them, which horrified him. During the day he had not been able to wash very carefully and had noticed the same thing on his own feet. He was displacing this on to his lady. During the night he dreamt that he was licking her feet, which were clean, however. This last element is a dream-wish. The perversion here is exactly the same as the one we are familiar with in its undistorted form.

That the behind was particularly exciting to him is shown by the fact that when his sister asked him what it was that he like about his cousin, he replied jokingly "her behind." The dressmaker whom he kissed today first excited his libido when she bent down and showed the curves of her buttocks especially clearly.

Postcript to the rat-adventure. Captain Novak said that this torture ought to be applied to some members of Parliament. The idea came to him, that he must not mention Gisa, and to his horror immediately afterwards he did mention Dr. Hertz, which once more seemed to him a fateful occurrence. His cousin is actually called Hertz and he at once thought that the name Hertz would make him think of his cousin, and he sees the point of this. He tries to isolate his cousin from everything dirty.

He suffers from sacrilegious compulsion, like nuns. A dream had to do with joking terms of abused used by his friend V.---"son of a whore," "son of a one-eyed monkey" (Arabian Nights).

When he was eleven, he was initiated into the secrets of sexual life by his (male) cousin, whom he now detests, and who made out to him that all women were whores, including his mother and sisters. He countered this with the question, "Do you think the same of your mother?"

Nov. 11---During an illness of his (female) cousin's (throat trouble and disturbances of sleep), at the time when his affection and sympathy were at their greatest, she was living on a sofa and he suddenly though "may she be like this for ever." He interpreted this as a wish that she should be permanently ill, for his own relief, so that he could be freed from his dread of her being ill. An over-clever misunderstanding! What he has already told me shows that this was connected with a wish to see her defenseless, because of her having resisted him by rejecting his love; and it corresponds crudely to a necrophilic phantasy which he once had consciously but which did not venture beyond the point of looking at the whole body.

He is made up of three personalities---one humorous and normal, another ascetic and religious, and a third immoral and perverse.

Inevitable misunderstanding of the Ucs by the Cs, or rather, distortion of the shape of the Ucs wish.

The hybrid thoughts resulting from these.

The Schreber Case

The fourth of Freud's case histories was actually not a case of his at all; it was based on the published account of a paranoid illness by Dr. Daniel Paul Schreber, who in 1903 had written a book, *Memoirs of My Nervous Illness.* As justification for the choice of the publication of a case from the literature rather than one from his own practice, Freud cited the fact that the practicing analyst who is not attached to institutions rarely has the opportunity to see a case of paranoia at first hand. As a result of Freud's pioneering efforts, the situation today is of course quite different, and there are many analytically oriented psychiatrists who have done detailed studies of paranoid and other psychotic illnesses.

The full title of the paper is "Psycho-Analytic Notes on an Autobiographical Account of a Case of Paranoia (Dementia Paranoides)."

It is one of the anomalies of history that Freud, who in many respects is the founder of modern psychiatry, was not a practicing psychiatrist at all in our present-day sense. As has been noted he did not treat psychosis, and his only concern with it, apart from the theoretical one, was to make sure in the beginning of analysis that he was not dealing with an underlying or incipient psychotic. The conflict between the organic and the psychological points of view in psychiatry is still be waged in some respects, although it is by now generally agreed, at least among American psychiatrists, that psychoanalysis furnishes the basis for all dynamic understanding in psychiatry, even though in many cases its therapeutic efforts may have to be modified in many important ways before the technique can be adapted to the psychotic.

Freud himself spoke of the Schreber case as the boldest adventure into psychiatry that he had yet undertaken. He wrote that he expected either scornful laughter or immortality, or both.

Daniel Paul Schreber was a judge presiding over a division of an appeals court in Saxony. He was by profession a lawyer; the title of doctor is customarily used by European lawyers. His first attack of nervous illness was recorded in 1885, and at that time was called "hypochondria." He spent six months in Flechsig's clinic in Leipzig; the attack lasted in all about fifteen months and he recovered from it.

He was apparently well until the summer of 1893 when he was notified of his prospective appointment as a judge, an appointment that was to start in October, 1893. Between these dates he had a number of bad dreams. One morning he woke up with the thought that, after all, it really must be very nice to be a woman submitting to the act of copulation.

The second illness set in at the end of October, 1893, with a torturing bout of sleeplessness. He went back to Flechsig's clinic, where he got worse. He had hypochondriacal ideas (apparently what today would be called somatic delusions), ideas of persecution and suicidal ideas. He gradually developed a complete delusional system, although in other respects he was quite rational. The worst of the illness disappeared, but he never got over his belief in much of his delusional system.

His civil rights were restored in July, 1902, and his book, *Memoirs of My Nervous Illness,* on which Freud based his analysis, was published in 1903.

The two principal elements in Schreber's delusional system were his transformation into a woman and his favored relationship to God. One of his delusions was:

He believed that he had a mission to redeem the world and to restore it to its lost state of bliss. This, however, he could only bring about if he were first transformed from a man into a woman.

Schreber had a variety of other delusions which fitted in with the two main ones. Thus he believed that his nerves were in a condition of great excitement, and nerves such as this had precisely the property of exerting an attraction upon God. Further, inasmuch as he is the only object upon which divine miracles are worked, he believed himself the most remarkable man who ever lived on earth. During the first years of his illness certain of his bodily organs suffered such destructive injuries as would inevitably have led to death of any other man: he lived for a long time without a stomach, without intestines, almost without lungs, with a torn esophagus, without a bladder, and with shattered ribs; he used sometimes to swallow part of his own larynx with his food, and so on. But divine miracles ("rays") always restored what had been destroyed and therefore as long as he remains a man he is not in any way mortal. These alarming phenomena stopped a long time ago and instead of "femaleness" became prominent. This involved a process of development which will probably require decades, if not centuries, for its completion, and it is unlikely that anyone now living will survive to see the end of it. He had a feeling that great numbers of "female nerves" have already passed over into his body, and out of them a new race of men will proceed, through a process of direct impregnation by God. He held that God had played a part in a plot in which his soul was to be murdered and his body was to be used like a strumpet's.

The delusion of the transformation into a woman readily lends itself to the interpretation of a homosexual panic, and to the theoretical delineation of a relationship between homosexuality and paranoia.

In fact, the dynamic character of all of Schreber's delusions is so obvious that it is most remarkable that it escaped the attention of previous psychiatrists. Of course we can readily understand this difficulty of Freud's predecessors, in that they were always looking for some kind of organic explanation of the phenomena and totally ignored the psychological material which was so readily at hand.

Freud used the material to elucidate the nature of libidinal development and the relationship between the various neuroses and the psychoses, the distinction between which had at that time not yet been clarified. Freud himself did suggest a diagnostic category, paraphrenia, to take the place of Bleuler's schizophrenia, but the suggestion never caught on.

Freud based his analysis of paranoia on its close connection with homosexuality. The paranoiac begins with the statement, I love a man. He then can deny this statement in one of four different ways, by denying the subject, the predicate, the object, or by denying the sentence altogether, and each of these denials leads to a different clinical picture.

1. *Delusions of persecution*, which say: "I do not *love* him---I *hate* him." Such a delusion then becomes transformed by *projection* into another one: "He hates (persecutes) me, which will justify me in hating him."

2. The predicate is contradicted in *erotomania*. Here the man says first: "I do not love *him*---I love *her*. By projection, this is transformed into: "I observe that *she* loves *me*." Then it is enlarged into: "I do not love *him*---I love *her*, because *she* loves *me*." (It is in this way that many apparent Don Juans cover up their homosexual desires.)

3. The third way in which the proposition can be contradicted is by contradicting the subjects, which leads to *delusions of jealousy*. Here the man says: "It is not I who loves the man---*she* love him." And he suspects the woman in relation to all men who he himself is tempted to love. Projection does not play a role here.

4. A fourth kind of contradiction is possible, namely one which rejects the proposition altogether. Here the man says: "I do not love *at all*---I do not love *anyone*." In this case, something must be done with the libido, which then turns back upon itself and the man says: "I love only *myself*." This leads to *megalomania*.

A very significant factor in the mechanism of symptom formation in paranoia is the use of *projection*. Projection is the process by virtue of which internal perceptions of feelings which are unacceptable to the individual are projected to an outsider or to some outside force.

The illness in the paranoiac is precipitated by a profound inner change, which Freud sees as a detachment of libido from persons in the paranoiac's environment and from the external world generally. The end of the world, which is so frequently part of paranoid delusion formation, is the projection of this internal catastrophe; the individual's subjective world has come to an end since his withdrawal of his love from it. The delusional formation, which psychiatrists had previously taken to be the pathological product, is now seen to be in the reality an attempt at recovery, a process of reconstruction.

Freud's illuminating insights concerning paranoia and psychosis in general have stood the test of time. However, as clinical experience with the psychoses has grown, it has become particularly evident that these disorders are intimately tied up with the oral stage, and the image of the bad mother, a concept which Freud did not have.

The Schreber case in itself has become the hub of considerable literature, and there have been many subsequent re-evaluations of the material.

The Case of the Wolf Man

The last of Freud's great case histories, "The Wolf Man," is in many respects the best. It has the most exhaustive analysis to be found in any of Freud's writings of the development in childhood of a neurosis in an adult. The full title of the work is "From the History of an Infantile Neurosis." It was finished in 1914, several months after the patient terminated treatment, but was not published until 1918 because of conditions created by World War I.

The nickname of the patient derives from his childhood phobia of wolves, which he knew only from stories and picture books.

The patient was a wealthy Russian who was completely incapacitated by his neurotic illness. At the time he came to Freud he was twenty-three years old. For years he had traveled around accompanied by a private doctor and a valet, unable event to dress himself or face any aspect of life.

The bizarre character of his ideation is sufficiently indicated by his offer in the first hour of treatment with Freud to have rectal intercourse with him and then defecate on his head.

The Wolf Man was in treatment with Freud for five years, from 1909 to 1914, at the end of which time he was fully recovered. The revolution in Russia left him penniless, and in 1919, he escaped from Russia and managed to find his way once again to Vienna. There Freud analyzed him for another four months (November, 1919 to February, 1920) because of a symptom of constipation, which then finally disappeared entirely. In this period Freud not only treated him free of charge, but regularly for the next six years collected money for the patient and his invalid wife.

For twelve years after Freud's first treatment, the patient remained free of any serious neurosis, and then developed an entirely different illness, a paranoiac psychosis. This time Ruth Mack Brunswick treated him for four or five months (October, 1826 to February, 1927) and he once more recovered. Two years later he came back to her and she treated him at various times for several years. Her last report of him was in 1940 when he was in excellent health, a similar report has been published more recently by Muriel Gardiner. At the time that Jones wrote his biography of Freud, he that that he (Jones) was still in correspondence with the patient.

Because of the unusual interest that attaches to this case, it has been possible to follow it up for a period of almost fifty years. The patient is still (1961) alive, now in his seventies, and apparently in good health. This is one case where there is certainly adequate and intensive follow-up of Freud's original treatment. The patient is a highly intelligent man and has written a number of papers about his contacts with Freud which have been published in psychoanalytic journals.

One of the Wolf Man's most recent communication, "How I Came into Analysis with Freud," was published in 1958 and gives an unusually perceptive account of the problems facing a psychiatric patient in those early days of psychoanalysis. A portion of this paper is worth quoting here: The Wolf Man says:

I first met Freud in the year 1910. At that time psychoanalysis and the name of its founder were practically unknown beyond the borders of Austria. Before I report on how I came into analysis with Freud, however, I should like to recall to you the desolate situation in which a neurotic found himself at that period before psychoanalysis. A sufferer from neurosis is trying to find his way back into normal life, as he has come into conflict with his environment and then lost contact with it. His emotional life has become "inadequate," inappropriate to outer reality. His goal is not a real, known object, but rather some other object, hidden in his unconscious, unknown to himself. His affect by-passes the real object, accessible to his consciousness. As long as nothing is know of this state of affairs, only two explanations were possible; one, that of the layman, concerned itself with the increase in intensity of affect, which, was out of proportion to the real situation, it was said that the neurotic exaggerated everything. The other explanation, that of the neurologist or psychiatrist, derived the mental and emotional from the physical, and sought to persuade the patient that his trouble was due to a disease of the nervous system. The neurotic went to a physician with the wish to pour out his heart to him, and was bitterly disappointed when the physician would scarcely listen to his problems, much less try to understand them. But that which to the doctor was only a superficial manifestation of the illness was for the neurotic himself a profound inner experience. So there could be no real contact between the patient and physician. The treatment of emotional illness seemed to have got into a dead-end street.

It was a revelation to me to hear the fundamental concepts of a completely new science of the human psyche from the mouth of its founder. I perceived at once that Freud had succeeded in discovering an unexplored region of the human soul and that if I could follow him along this path, a new world would open for me. The error of "classical" psychiatry had been that, ignorant of the existence and laws of the unconscious, it derived everything from the physical. A further consequence of this error was a too sharp distinction between healthy and sick. Everything the neurotic undertook was considered sick. If, for example, he fell in love with a woman, this was described as "manic," or as a "compulsion." But for Freud the "break-through to the woman" would under certain circumstances be considered a healthy achievement, a sign of the neurotic's will to live, an attempt at restitution. This followed from the psychoanalytic point of view that there was no sharp division between sick and healthy, that in the healthy person also the unconscious may dominate. Although Freud certainly did not underestimate the neurotic in his patients, he attempted always to support and strengthen the kernel of health, separated from the chaff of neurosis.

It will be easy to imagine the sense of relief I now felt, when Freud asked me various questions about my childhood and about the relationships in my family, and listened with the greatest attention to all I had to say. Occasionally, he let fall some remark which was witness to his complete understanding of everything I had experienced. My new knowledge, the feeling that I had, so to speak, "discovered" Freud, and the hope of regaining my health made my condition rapidly improve. But now Freud warned me against overoptimism, foreseeing quite rightly that resistance and its attendant difficulties were still to come.

Freud did not publish the entire history of the case, as he had done with the Rat Man, just the reconstruction of the patient's infantile neurosis, as the title of the paper indicates. His main theoretical interest in publishing the case was to show how it is possible from an exhaustive analysis to reconstruct the infantile history of a patient. It is this reconstruction which particularly captured the imagination of the psychoanalytic world and became the model which many analysts aimed to imitate for along time to come.

Freud maintained that the adult neurosis was understandable only in the light of the infantile material, which in such a person would necessarily have to be regarded as neurotic. He declared

I am ready to assert that every neurosis in an adult is built upon a neurosis which has occurred in his childhood but has not invariably been severe enough to strike the eye and be recognized as such.

In 1923 Freud added a footnote to the case in which he set out the chronology of the main events listed in the case history. This chronology gives those events which Freud considered of particular significance in the formation of the patient's personality. It is reproduced here with some explanation of the events to which Freud makes reference.

Born on Christmas Day: The fact that the patient was born on Christmas Day was significant because it helped to date some of the other events in his life.

1-1/2 years old: Malaria, Observation of his parents copulation, or observation of them when they were together, into which I later introduced a phantasy of them copulating.

The question of whether an infant a year and a half old can recognize that his parents are having sexual intercourse has been much discussed among psychoanalysts since this publication of Freud's. It is to be noted that Freud himself specifically maintained that he is not sure whether the recollection is a phantasy or an actual event, and in any case, does not feel that it really makes any difference so far as the formation of the personality is concerned. Since Freud, there has been much more direct observation of children. While it is clear enough that infants often do see the parents having sexual intercourse, the precise meaning of this to them is still not at all clear.

Just before 2-1/2: scene with Grusha, a maid in his parents' household.

This scene with the maid Grusha was finally worked out as follows: Grusha was kneeling on the floor, and beside her was a pail and a short broom made of a bundle of twigs; he was there and she was teasing him or scolding him. When he had seen the girl scrubbing the floor, he had urinated in the room, and she had rejoined, no doubt jokingly, with a threat of castration.

When he saw the girl upon the floor engaged in scrubbing and kneeling down, with her buttocks projecting and her body horizontal, he was faced once again with the attitude which his mother had assumed in the coitus scene. She became his mother to him, he was seized with sexual excitement, owing to the activity of this picture; and like his father (whose action he can only be regarded at this time as urination) he behaved in a masculine way towards her. *His urinating on the floor was in reality* an attempt at a seduction and the girl replied to it with a threat of castration just as though she had understood what he meant.

It was to this scene that Freud traced a peculiar love-competition which the patient showed later on in life. Whenever he saw someone leaning over washing clothes he was seized by an irresistible sexual desire or an irresistible love feeling toward her. From one such woman whom he met in his eighteenth year he had contracted gonorrhea which incapacitated him for some time.

2-1/2: Screen memory of is parents' departure with his sister. This showed him along with his Nanya (nurse) and so disowned Grusha and his sister. His sister was two years older.

Before 3-1/2: His mother's laments to the doctor. This refers to the following: His mother had once taken him with her when she was walking down to the station with a doctor who had come to visit her. During this walk she had lamented over her pains and hemorrhages and had broken out into the words, "I cannot go on living like this," without imagining that the child whose hand she was holding would keep these words in his memory. The patient repeated this lament on innumerable occasions during his later illness, this lament thus has the significance of an identification with his mother.

3-1/4: Beginning of his seduction by his sister. Soon afterward, the threat of castration from his Nanya.

The patient suddenly called to mind the fact that when he was still very small his sister had seduced him into sexual practices. First came a recollection that in the lavatory which the children frequently used to visit together she had made this proposal, "Let's show our bottoms," and had proceeded from words to deeds. Subsequently the more essential part of this seduction came to light and there were full particulars as to time and place. It was in the spring, at a time when his father was away, the children were in one room playing on the floor while the mother was working in the next room. His sister had taken hold of his penis and played with it, at the same time telling him incomprehensible stories about his Nanya, as though by way of explanation. His Nanya, she said, used to do the same thing with all kinds of people---for instance, with the gardener. She used to stand him on his head and then take hold of his genitals.

In reaction to the seduction by his sister, the boy refused her, and her solicitations soon ceased, but he tried to win instead of her another person whom he was fond of, the information which his sister herself had given him---and in which his Nanya was a model---turned his choice in that direction. He therefore began to play with his penis in his Nanya's presence, and this must be regarded as an attempt at seduction. His Nanya disillusioned him, she made a serious face and explained that that wasn't good. Children who did that, she said, got a wound in that place.

With this new frustration he secretly began to look about for another sexual object. His sexual researches began, and he soon came upon the problem of castration. He succeeded in observing two girls, his sister and a friend of hers, while they were urinating. This gave rise to all kinds of thoughts about the body.

Soon after the refusal of his Nanya and the threat of castration he gave up masturbation. His sexual life, therefore, which was beginning to come under the sway of the genital zone gave way before an external obstacle, and was thrown back by its influence into an earlier phase of pregenital organization. The boy regressed to the sadistic anal stage.

Eventually, he again became attached to his father in a passive way.

3-1/2: The English governess. Beginning of the change in his character. When the child was 3 ½ the family engaged in an English governess for him. At roughly the same time a decided change in his character took place. Where before he was sweet and gentle, now he entered a phase of naughtiness and perversity. Freud traced this to the regression to the sadistic anal stage. The boy became irritable and a tormenter, and gratified himself in this way at the expense of animals and humans. His principal object was his beloved Nanya and he knew how to torment her so she would burst into tears. He began to be cruel to small animals, to catch flies and pull off their wings, and to crush beetles underfoot. In his imagination he liked beating large animals (horses) as well. There were also masochistic phantasies which came to light. The content of these was of boys being chastised and beaten, and especially being beaten on the penis. This kind of constant ambivalence was peculiarly characteristic of the obsessional individual. Freud generalized from here to say that a child behaves in such an unmanageable way is making a concession and trying to provoke punishment. He hopes for a beating as a simultaneous means of setting at rest his sense of guilt and of satisfying his masochistic sexual urge.

4: The wolf dream. Origin of the phobia.

Freud traced this dream to a precise age in the patient's childhood because of the accidental fact that he was born on Christmas Day. The dream, which came when the child was four, was:

I dreamt that it was night and that I was lying in my bed. (My bed stood with its foot toward the window; in front of the window there was a row of old walnut trees. I know it was winter when I had the dream, and night-time). Suddenly the window opened of its own accord and I was terrified to see that some white wolves were sitting on a big walnut tree in front of the window. There were six or seven of them. The wolves were quite white, and more like foxes or sheep dogs, for they had big tails like foxes and that had their ears pricked like dogs when they pay attention to something. In great terror, evidently of being eaten up by the wolves, I screamed and woke up.

Freud, through the analysis, traced this as the first anxiety dream which the boy had in the course of his life, stemming from the fear of his father which from that time forward was to dominate his life.

The form taken by the fear of his father, the fear of being eaten by the wolf, was only the regressive transposition of the wise to be copulated with by his father, that is, to be given sexual satisfaction in the same way as his mother. This explained why the dream ended in a state of anxiety from which he did not recover until he had his nurse with him. He therefore fled from his father to her.

To understand this anxiety, Freud hypothesized that what sprang into activity the night of the dream out of the chaos of the dream is unconscious memory traces, was the picture of copulation between his parents, copulation in circumstances which were not entirely usual and were especially favorable for observation. This *primal scene* (the term is here used for the first time in this paper, although it had been mentioned earlier by Freud in one of his letters to Fleiss) occurred when the infant was a year and a half old.

Freud himself considered the tracing of the infantile neurosis back to a primal scene at the age of one and a half years to be a reconstruction which required extraordinary documentation. He expressed the fear that at that point the reader's belief would abandon him. He said:

I have now reached the point at which I must abandon the support which I have hitherto had from the course of analysis, I am afraid it will also be the point at which the reader's belief will abandon me.

He considered the doubts as to the probability of such an occurrence in considerable detail. He fell back upon his theory of deferred action, which he had already put forward in the *Studies on Hysteria.* This was the idea that a sexual scene in childhood in itself has no pathogenic effect, but at some later date when the child becomes more mature sexually, he suddenly remembers the earlier sexual experience and it then has a traumatic effect on him. In the *Studies on Hysteria,* however, the primal scenes were considered to be of a much later date, and the effects of them were deferred at least until the age of puberty. Here Freud proposed that the primal scene trauma occurred at the age of one and a half and that its activation which led to the neurotic transformation occurred at the age of four.

4-1/2: *Influence of the Bible story. Appearance of the obsessional symptoms.*

At the age of about four and a half occurred his initiation into religion and from them onward the period of obsessional neurosis up to a time later than his tenth year. His mother told him the sacred story herself and also made his nurse read aloud to him about it from a book adorned with illustrations. The chief stress in the story was laid upon the story of the Passion. His Nanya, who was very pious and superstitious, added her own comments on it, but was obliged to listen to all the little critic's objections and doubts.

Freud had already, in a paper published in 1907, called attention to the close connection between obsessional actions and religious practices. Here he produced more evidence along the same lines. For example, the little boy had no sooner heard the Bible story than he began to add illuminations and doubts of all kinds. One of the first questions which he addressed to his nurse was whether Christ had a behind too. Nanya informed him that He had been a God and also a man, and as a man had had all the same things as other men. This did not satisfy him, but he succeeded in reconciling himself to the situation by telling himself that the behind is really only a continuation of the legs. But then came another question, whether Christ used to shit. He did not venture to put this question to his pious nurse, but he himself found a way out. Since Christ had made wine out of nothing, he could also make food out of nothing and in this way have avoided defecating. (It is to be noted that serious difficulties connected with defecation were part of the patient's neurotic symptomatology when he came to Freud and that severe constipation was the reason for the re-analysis by Freud from 1919 to 1920).

Marked ambivalence toward God took the place of the marked ambivalence toward his father, and was part of the obsessional neurosis. One of the last flickerings of his neurosis was the obsession of having to think of the Holy Trinity whenever he saw three heaps of dung lying together on the road.

Just before 5: Hallucination of the loss of his finger.

The patient described the following experience at the age of five:

When I was five years old, I was playing in the garden near my nurse, and was carving with my pocket-knife in the bark of one of the walnut trees that come into my dream as well. Suddenly, to my unspeakable terror, I noticed that I had cut through the little finger of my (right or left?) hand, so that it was only hanging on by its skin. I felt no pain, but great fear, I did not venture to say anything to my nurse, who was only a few paces distant, but I sank down on a near seat and sat there, incapable of casting another glance at my finger. At last I calmed down, took a look at the finger, and saw that it was entirely uninjured.

It turned out that this hallucination was instigated by a story that a female relative of his had been born with six toes, and that the extra toe had immediately afterwards been chopped off with an axe. Women, then, had no penis because it was taken away from them at birth. The hallucination of the severed finger was an obvious substitute for a castration fear.

5: Departure from the first estate.

The family's move from one estate to another helped to date a number of events in the patient's life. It was shortly after this move that the father became mentally ill and had to be confined to a sanitarium.

After 6: Visits to his sick father.

The patient had developed a pious ritual by means of which he eventually atoned for his blasphemies. Part of this was to breathe in a ceremonious manner under certain conditions. Each time he made the sign of the Cross he was obliged to breathe in deeply or exhale forcibly. In his native tongue "breath" is the same as "spirit" so that here the Holy Ghost came in. He was obliged to breathe in the Holy Spirit, to breathe out the evil spirits which he had heard and read about. He ascribed to these evil spirits the blasphemous thoughts for which he had to inflict such heavy penance upon himself. He was also obliged to exhale when he saw beggars or cripples; ugly, old, or wretched-looking people, but he could think of no way of connecting this obsession with the spirits. The only account he could give to himself was that he did it so as not to become like such people.

Eventually, the analysis showed that this breathing out at the sight of pitiable-looking people had begun only after his sixth year and was related to his father. Shortly after he was six, when he had not seen his father for some time, his mother took the children to a sanitarium where they saw their father again; he looked sick and the boy felt very sorry for him. His father was thus the prototype of all the cripples, beggars, and poor people in whose presence he was obliged to breathe out. And thus his determination not to become like cripples (which was the motive for his breathing out in their presence) was his old identification with his father, transformed into the negative. But in this he was also imitating his father in the positive sense, for the heavy breathing was an imitation of the noise which he had heard coming from his father during intercourse.

8-10: Final outbreaks of the obsessional neurosis.

The obsessional neurosis came to an end when he was given a German tutor when he was ten years old. This German tutor very soon exerted a great influence over him. The whole of his strict piety faded away, never to be revived, after he had noticed and learned from enlightening conversations with his tutor that his father substitute attached no importance to piety and set no store by the truth of religion. His religion sank away along with his dependence upon his father who was now replaced by a new and more sociable father.

Under the influence of the German tutor there arose a new and better sublimation of the patient's sadism, which then gained the upper hand over his masochism. He developed an enthusiasm for military affairs, for uniforms, weapons and horses, and used them as food for continual daydreams. Thus, for the first time, he found himself, for the time being at any rate, on fairly normal lines.

17: Breakdown, precipitated by gonorrhea.

23: Beginning of treatment.

Summary

In reviewing these case histories, one is struck above all by Freud's incredible capacity to master an enormous number of details and to organize them in a coherent fashion. It is this very difficulty in handling the tremendous complexity of a case history that has stopped others from writing up their cases. None of Freud's contemporaries or successors has ever provided anything remotely comparable. One result is that while one has a reasonably good idea of how Freud analyzed, the same cannot be said for other analysts.

Freud's emphasis was on tracing the precise connections between the symptoms and the infantile sexuality, as reconstructed in the course of the analysis. By this meticulous attention to the actual events in the patient's life, Freud was able to draw the necessary connections and effects the disappearance of symptoms. When others began to philosophize or introduce social or moral questions he objected on the grounds that this did not help the patient. This was one of his objections to both Adler and Jung---they did not explain the specific neurotic conflict with which they were dealing, but resorted rather to broad generalities.

Once Freud described his manner of work as follows:

When I recollect isolated cases from the history of my work, I find my working hypothesis invariably came about as a direct result of a number of impressions based on experience. Later on, whenever I have the opportunity of recognizing an hypothesis of this kind to be erroneous was always replaced---and I hope improved---by another idea which occurred to me (based on the former as well as new experiences) which I then submitted the material.

It is this painstaking attention to the specific genetic development of any symptom or character pattern that makes Freud's histories so unique in the analytic literature.

Each case history that he wrote had a specific purpose, to be evaluated with that in mind. The case of Dora was written to show how dreams can be used in therapy. Little Hans was analyzed to show that the Oedipal conflict inferred from the anality in adults could be directly observed in children. The Rat Man demonstrates the intricate structure of an obsessional neurosis. The Schreber case casts light on paranoid mechanisms which were so severe that they require hospitalization; in his office practicing physicians did not encounter such cases, and few hospital psychiatrists of that day were alive to the teachings of psychoanalysis. The Wolf Man was in part a reply to Jung and his more general theory of the libido; Freud was here trying to show exactly how the reconstruction of the patient's childhood confirmed his hypothesis about psychosexual development.

At the same time careful perusal of the cases discloses weaknesses in Freud's approach, some of which have been corrected. Actually, as already pointed out, Freud published one really complete history of psychoanalysis, that of the Wolf Man. Dora interrupted treatment prematurely, and later died. It is odd that Freud never described a really successful analysis with a woman. Of the five case histories, that of Dora, the only one which was a partial failure. The other four were all men, including the spontaneous recovery in Schreber.

Perhaps the major lack in these early case histories is theory of systematic character analysis. It was still mainly the theory that concerned Freud here; understanding of the total picture came only later, in the 1920s. Even then, however, as the many autobiographical accounts of his students show, Freud frequently did not practice the strict classical technique he himself had devised. He would interrupt, engage in conversations, at times conduct analysis for only a few months, and so on.

As with his self-analysis, in some ways Freud was too modest about his achievement. The careful unraveling of the patient's childhood, as described particularly in the Wolf Man, was something Freud could do, but few others. The attempt to imitate this particular achievement of Freud's led in the 1920s to many disappointments and many attempts to revise analytic technique.

My Recollections of Sigmund Freud [*]
The Wolf Man

I first met Freud in the year 1910. At that time psychoanalysis and the name of its founder were practically unknown beyond the borders of Austria. Before I report on how I came into analysis with Freud, however, I should like to recall to you the desolate situation in which a neurotic found himself at that period before psychoanalysis. A sufferer from neurosis is trying to find his way back into normal life, as he has come into conflict with his environment and then lost contact with it. His emotional life has become "inadequate," inappropriate to outer reality. His goal is not a real, known object, but rather some other object, hidden in his unconscious, unknown to himself. His affect by-passes the real object, accessible to his consciousness. As long as nothing is know of this state of affairs, only two explanations were possible; one, that of the layman, concerned itself with the increase in intensity of affect, which, was out of proportion to the real situation, it was said that the neurotic exaggerated everything. The other explanation, that of the neurologist or psychiatrist, derived the mental and emotional from the physical, and sought to persuade the patient that his trouble was due to a disease of the nervous system. The neurotic went to a physician with the wish to pour out his heart to him, and was bitterly disappointed when the physician would scarcely listen to his problems, much less try to understand them. But that which to the doctor was only a superficial manifestation of the illness was for the neurotic himself a profound inner experience. So there could be no real contact between the patient and physician. The treatment of emotional illness seemed to have got into a dead-end street.

Clearly, I was not better off than my companions-in-suffering, who at that time were grouped together under the catch-all name of "neurasthenics." In less serious cases, the suggestive effect of physical therapy, hydrotherapy, electric treatments, etc., might cause some improvement; in my case these treatments had

[*] Gardiner, Muriel (Ed.). (1971). My Recollections of Sigmund Freud. *The Wolf Man by the Wolf Man: The Double Story of Freud's Most Famous Case*, 135-152. New York: Basic Books, Inc. Reprinted by permission.

completely failed. Whenever I went into a sanitarium, my condition became so much worse that I had to leave again as soon as possible. I had consulted a considerable number of the most famous neurologists, as, for example, Professor Ziehen in Berlin and Professor Kraepelin in Munich, without the slightest improvement in my condition. Professor Kraepelin, who was world-famous, was himself honest enough to confess failure. He explained to me finally that he had been mistaken in his diagnosis. When I asked what I should do now, he always replied: "You see, I made a mistake." Finally, he advised me again to go into a sanitarium. After all this, it was scarcely strange that I had at last given up all hope of receiving any medical help.

Then by chance I made the acquaintance of a young physician, Dr. D., who took an interest in me, and with extraordinary energy, tried to persuade me that my case was by no means hopeless and that previous attempts to help me had failed only because of mistaken methods of treatment. Dr. D., was a passionate believer in psychotherapy, and frequently mentioned the name of Dubois and Freud. He spoke also of "psychoanalysis," of which, however, as I later discovered, he had only the most nebulous ideas. His powers of persuasion were so great, and my emotional condition was one of such misery, that I finally decide, as a last resort, to attempt therapy with Dr. D.

This was the beginning of my "analysis" with Dr. D. which was simply a free, conversational exchange between patient and doctor. Although this touched only the conscious surface of my problems, the good thing was that I had now found a physician in whom I had complete confidence and to whom I could talk about whatever concerned me, to my heart's content. So, for a time, I held myself above water, until finally Dr. D. himself had the insight to confess that the task he had undertaken was beyond his powers, saying he thought I should try something else. At first he spoke of a journey around the world, but then suggested something which appealed to me much more that I should seek treatment from Dubois in Switzerland, and Dr. D. himself would accompany me there. Had Dr. D. stuck to his first suggestion to travel, my life would certainly have taken quite a different course, but apparently fate wanted it otherwise.

Our journey took us through Vienna, where we intended to remain about two weeks. There Dr. D. met some of his colleagues, who pointed out that psychoanalysis was really the creation of Freud and that we should therefore "attempt" it first with him. I agreed to this, and the very next day we visited Freud.

Freud's appearance was such as to win my confidence immediately. He was then in his middle fifties and seemed to enjoy the best of health. He was of medium height and figure. In his rather long face, framed by a closely clipped, already graying beard, the most impressive features was his intelligent dark eyes, which looked at me penetratingly but without causing me the slightest feeling of discomfort. His correct, conventional way of dressing, and his simple but self-assured manner, indicated his love of order and his inner serenity. Freud's whole attitude, and the way in which he listened to me, differentiated him strikingly from his famous colleagues whom I had hitherto known and in whom I had found such a lack of deeper psychological understanding. At my first meeting with Freud I had the feeling of encountering a great personality.

Freud told us he found my case suitable for psychoanalytic treatment but that he was at present so busy that he could not immediately take any new patients. However, we might make a compromise. He was visiting a patient every day in the Cottage Sanitarium, and following this visit he would begin my treatment there, if I agreed to spend a few weeks in the sanitarium. This proposal disconcerted us, and we reconsidered continuing our journey to Switzerland. But Freud had made such a favorable impression upon me that I persuaded Dr. D. that I should follow Freud's suggestion. So I moved into the Cottage Sanitarium where Freud visited me every afternoon. After the first few hours with Freud, I felt that I had at last found what I had so long been seeking.

It was a revelation to me to hear the fundamental concepts of a completely new science of the human psyche from the mouth of its founder. I perceived at once that Freud had succeeded in discovering an unexplored region of the human soul and that if I could follow him along this path, a new world would open for me. The error of "classical" psychiatry had been that, ignorant of the existence and laws of the unconscious, it derived everything from the physical. A further consequence of this error was a too sharp distinction between healthy and sick. Everything the neurotic undertook was considered sick. If, for example, he fell in love with a woman, this was described as "manic," or as a "compulsion." But for Freud the "break-through to the woman" would under certain circumstances be considered a healthy achievement, a sign of the neurotic's will to live, an attempt at restitution. This followed from the psychoanalytic point of view that there was no sharp division between sick and healthy, that in the healthy person also the unconscious may dominate. Although Freud certainly did not underestimate the neurotic in his patients, he attempted always to support and strengthen the kernel of health, separated from the chaff of neurosis. It is hardly necessary to underline the fact that this separation of the two elements requires a large measure of emotional penetration and is one of the psychiatrist's more difficult tasks.

It will be easy to imagine the sense of relief I now felt, when Freud asked me various questions about my childhood and about the relationships in my family, and listened with the greatest attention to all I had to say. Occasionally, he let fall some remark which was witness to his complete understanding of everything I had experienced.

"Up to now you have been looking for the cause of your illness in your chamber pot," remarked Freud aptly, referring to the methods of physical therapy to which I had submitted.

When I told Freud of my doubts and brooding as a child, his opinion was that "only a child can think so logically." And once, in this connection, he spoke of a "thinker of the first rank," which filled me with no little pride, since in my childhood I had suffered from competition with my sister, who was two and a half years older than I and far ahead of me. Later, however, we understood each other very well.

My new knowledge, the feeling that I had, so to speak, "discovered" Freud, and the hope of regaining my health made my condition rapidly improve. But now Freud warned me against overoptimism, foreseeing quite rightly that resistance and

161

its attendant difficulties were still to come. At the time agreed upon, I returned to my pension and continued my analysis in Freud's apartment.

From the beginning, I had the impression that Freud had a special gift for finding a happy balance in everything he undertook. This characteristic expressed itself also in the appearance of his home in the Bergasse. I can remember, as though I saw them today, his two adjoining studies, with the door open between them and with their windows opening onto a little courtyard. There was always a feeling of sacred peace and quiet here. The rooms themselves must have been a surprise to any patient, for they in no way reminded one of a doctor's office but rather of an archeologist's study. Here were all kinds of statuettes and other unusual objects, which even the layman recognized as archeological finds from ancient Egypt. Here and there on the walls were stone plaques representing various scenes of long vanished epochs. A few potted plants added life to the rooms, and the warm carpet and curtains gave them a homelike note. Everything here contributed to one's feeling of leaving the haste of modern life behind, of being sheltered from one's daily cares. Freud himself explained his love for archeology in that the psychoanalyst, like the archeologist in his excavations, must uncover layer after layer of the patient's psyche, before coming to the deepest, most valuable treasures.

In view of the mass of work Freud set himself to accomplish, he of course had to distribute his time most carefully. His medical practice began early in the morning and, except for meals and a short walk, lasted the whole day. One cannot help wondering how, in spite of this, it was possible for him to devote himself to science and writing to such an extent. He did, it is true, allow himself a long vacation of about two and a half months every year in the late summer.

This is not the place to speak of all the phases of my treatment, I can only say that in my analysis with Freud I felt myself less as a patient than as a co-worker, the younger comrade of an experienced explorer setting out to study a new, recently discovered land. This new land is the realm of the unconscious, over which the neurotic has lost that mastery which he now seeks, through analysis, to regain.

This feeling of "working together" was increased by Freud's recognition of my understanding of psychoanalysis, so that he even once said it would be good if all his pupils could grasp the nature of analysis as soundly as I. We were talking about how hard it is for a healthy person to accept the principles of Freud's teaching, as they wound his vanity. It is different for the neurotic, who has, in the first place, experienced in his own person the force and aims of his unconscious drives, and secondly, in submitting to analytic therapy, has acknowledged his inability to manage without help.

But there is another type of person accessible to all theoretical knowledge, and therefore also to psychoanalysis. These are the persons whose unimpeachable intelligence seems to be cut off from their instinctive drives.[1] Such persons are capable of thinking things through to the last logical conclusion, but they do not apply the results of this thinking to their own behavior. Freud mentions this curious characteristic in one of his essays, but does not treat this theme in detail. It is an obscure region of the human soul, but I believe one must seek the explanation in the fact that the "object cathexis" of these persons is too much under the influence of the unconscious. They pursue not real objects but fantasy images; even though they know what dangers threaten them thereby from the side of reality. They face an insoluble problem: either to disregard the pleasure-principle and follow the dictates of their intellect, or to act as their feelings force them to act. So, they are always talking very reasonably and acting just as unreasonably.

Primitivism in modern art and existentialism in philosophy have both stressed the emotional in contrast to the intellectual. And when Jean Jacques Rousseau declares: *"la prevoyance, la prevoyance, voila la source de toutes mes souffrances,"* he deliberately takes a stand against the reality-principle. But Freud, although he assailed repression as a harmful by-product of the cultural development of mankind, nevertheless was not an enemy of culture. He believed that culture develops under the iron pressure of the reality principle, which requires giving up the immediate gratification of instinctual drives for a later, more realistic satisfaction. This leads to the reawakening of various interests and to forming relationships once more with the outer world. Freud himself believed that the treatment of a patient's severe neurosis was at the same time an education of the patient. I need hardly emphasize the fact that Freud practiced this educational task in the most tactful way, and that his purely human influence on his patients, by virtue of the greatness of his personality, was bound to be profound and lasting. Even Freud's sharp way of expressing his opinion, which always struck at the heart of the matter in most telling words, afforded one great enjoyment. Freud's memory was absolutely astonishing; he retained everything in his mind, noticed the smallest details, and never mixed up family relationships or anything of the sort.

But a too close relationship between patient and doctor has, like everything else in life, its shadow side. Freud himself believed that if the friendly relations between the two overstep a certain boundary, this will work against the therapy. It is easy to understand why: on the one hand, there is the danger that the physician may become too forbearing and too compliant toward the patient; on the other hand, resistances in the transference increase when the patient looks upon the analyst as a father substitute. Although Freud, in keeping with his character, put everything personal into the background and always made every effort to be completely objective, the attractive power of his personality was so great that there were certain dangers involved.

As an analysis requires a great deal of time, it raises difficulties for those not well-to-do. "We have made it a rule," Freud once said to me, "always to treat one patient without remuneration." He added that such an analysis often meets with greater resistance than one that is paid for, as feelings of gratitude appear with special strength and hamper the treatment. I myself know of a case in which Freud treated a patient, who had lost his fortune, for many months and also aided him financially.[2]

During a psychoanalytic treatment of long duration the patient often has the opportunity of discussing all manner of things with the physician. Freud told me once, for example, how the "psychoanalytic situation" came about. This "situation" as is well known, is that of the patient lying on the couch with the analyst sitting near the couch in a position where he cannot be seen by the analysand. Freud told me that he had originally sat at the opposite end of the couch, so that the analyst and analysand could look at each other. One female patient, exploiting this situation, made all possible---or rather all impossible---attempts to seduce him. To rule out anything similar, once and for all, Freud moved from his earlier position to the opposite end of the couch.

One story of Freud's was not lacking in a certain irony. He told me once a little, insignificant-looking man had come into his office complaining of severe depressions. When Freud inquired as to his work, it turned out that he was the greatest contemporary Viennese comedian, the late Eisenbach.

Once when I wanted to explain some emotional process---I no longer remember what---by the force of habit, Freud would not accept my explanation. He said: "If a mother, worried about her son on the high seas, prays every evening for his speedy return, do you think that after he comes safely home she would still say the same prayer from force of habit?" I understood this reaction of Freud's very well, because at that time, when so little was known of man's real instinctual life, much was erroneously put down to "habit." Later Freud modified the pleasure principle, in that he subscribed also to a repetition compulsion, independent of the pleasure principle. This is, so to speak, a psychic law of inertia, a tendency innate in all living things to seek rest, with the final goal of death. So Freud came to accept a death instinct, opposed to Eros. He deals with this question in *Beyond the Pleasure Principle,* but without mentioning habit. But it is an obvious step to trace habit also back to the repetition compulsion. So this remark of Freud's could be understood to mean that one should not overestimate the importance of habit, as it appears as a kind of repetition compulsion only when outer and inner conditions favor this psychic automatism and when no stronger impulse works against it.

As at that time the "storm and stress" period of psychoanalysis was not yet over, Freud often touched on this theme. His view, as well as his whole theory, were so new that they were bound to meet with the most violent opposition everywhere. In the beginning no one had found it necessary to refute psychoanalysis, people simply took no notice of it. But in the long run it was impossible to ignore it completely, so psychoanalysis, along with its founder Freud, was furiously attacked from all sides. The preachers of morality rejected it because it gave too much important to sexuality, and official medicine condemned it as "unscientific." Freud once told me that he far preferred these attacks to the former total silence. For it followed from them that he had serious opponents with whom he was forced to join issue. It seems Freud never took the moralists' indignation very seriously. He once told me laughing, that a meeting in which psychoanalysis was sharply attacked as "immoral" ended up with those present telling each other the most indecent jokes.

These attacks confirmed Freud in feeling bound to show the greatest objectivity and to exclude everything of an emotional or subjective nature from his arguments. And, as is well known, he was never afraid to revise his theories, insofar as this seemed to him called for by his practice, that is, through observation and experience. In justification he could cite the fact that even such an exact science as physics proceeds in the same way, adjusting its theories to the specific state of empirical research. The same was true of Freud in regard to the detailed work of therapy. If one of his hypotheses was not confirmed by the associations and dreams of the patient, he dropped it immediately. Even at that time Freud expressed greater confidence in the future of psychoanalysis, believing that its continued existence was assured and that it would achieve its due place in medicine and other fields.

Freud very seldom spoke of his family relationships, which was natural considering the conditions of psychoanalytic treatment (transference, etc.). I occasionally met his wife as well as his three sons and two daughters on the stairs, so I knew them only by sight. Later I became acquainted with his oldest son, Dr. Martin Freud, who had become a lawyer and was occupied in the world of business, but this was in no way connected with my analysis with Freud. I had the impression that Freud's family life was very tranquil and harmonious. Once during an analytic hour Freud told me that he had just received word that his youngest son[3] had broken a leg skiing, but that luckily it was a mild injury with no danger of lasting damage. Freud went on to say that of his three sons the youngest was the most like him in character and temperament. Freud came back to his youngest son later in another connection. This was a time when I was occupied with the idea of becoming a painter. Freud advised me against this, expressing the opinion that although I probably had the ability, I would not find this profession satisfying. He believed that the contemplative nature of the artist was not foreign to me but that the rational (he once called me a "dialectician") predominated. He suggested that I should strive for a sublimation that would absorb my intellectual interest completely. It was on this occasion that he told me that his youngest son had also intended to become a painter, but had then dropped the idea and switched over to architecture. "I would have decided on painting," he had told his father, "only if I were either very rich or very poor." The grounds for this decision were that one should either regard painting as a luxury, pursuing it as an amateur or else take it very seriously and achieve something really great since to be a mediocrity in this field would give no satisfaction. Poverty and the "iron necessity" behind it would serve as a sharp spur goading one on to notable achievements. Freud welcomed his son's decision and thought his reasoning well founded.

Freud's dedication to psychoanalysis was so great that in many ways it influenced his other interests also. As regards painting, he had the greatest esteem for the old masters. He engaged in a searching study of one of Leonardo da Vinci's paintings and published a book about it. It is clear that the painters of the Renaissance had a particular fascination for Freud, s at that time man was the center of universal interest and therefore also the subject matter of painting. On the other hand, Freud had little interest in landscape painting, including the work of the Impressionists. Modern art in general had no great appeal for him. He had no affinity to music either.

World literature, as one might expect, claimed Freud's interest in the highest degree. He was enthusiastic about Dostoevsky, who, more than any other, has the gift of piercing the depths of the human soul and searching out the most hidden stirrings of the unconscious, to give them expression in a work of art. In *The Brothers Karamazov*, Dostoevsky deals with patricide, that is, with the Oedipus complex. Dreams also appear in his works. I can remember that in one of my analytic hours Freud made a psychoanalytic interpretation of a dream of Raskolnikov's. Freud saw Dostoevsky's weakness as a political thinker in the fact that he had to take such a long-drawn-out and wearying way to arrive at his later political convictions, whereas smaller minds came to the same conclusions more rapidly and with less expenditure of energy. As is well known, Dostoevsky was in his youth a member of a secret conspiracy and was banished to Siberia. He returned from there, after serving his sentence, an advocate of a conservative philosophy of life.

Freud gave high praise to the novel, *Peter and Alexis*, by the Russian writer Merezhkovsky, in which the emotional ambivalence between father and son is treated in an extraordinary psychoanalytic manner. Freud had less appreciation of Tolstoi. The world in which Tolstoi lived and which he described was too alien to Freud. Tolstoi was an epic writer, who sketched marvelous pictures of the life of the Russian upper classes of the nineteenth century, but as a psychologist he did not penetrate as deeply as Dostoevsky. And Freud must have had little sympathy for Tolstoi's sharply critical stand against sexuality.

When I told Freud of my liking for Maupassant, he remarked "Not bad taste." As at this time the French author, Mirbeau, who embarked on very daring themes, was in fashion. I asked Freud how he like him. His answer was quite unfavorable.

Freud had a special liking for Anatole France. I remember how he once described to me a scene from one of Anatole France's books which had evidently made a strong impact on him. Two distinguished Romans are arguing which one of the many mythological deities will be the leading god of the future. At this instant a disciple of Christ, clad in beggar's garments, walks past them. The two Romans, scarcely noticing him, have not the faintest idea that he is the prophet of a new religion which will overturn the old gods and start on a triumphal procession through the world.

Freud also fully appreciated humorists, and greatly admired Wilhelm Busch. Once we happened to speak of Conan Doyle and his creation, Sherlock Holmes. I had thought that Freud would have no use for this type of light reading matter, and was surprised to find that this was not at all the case and that Freud had read this author attentively. The fact that circumstantial evidence is useful in psychoanalysis when reconstructing a childhood history may explain Freud's interest in this type of literature. By the way, the spiritual father of Conan Doyle's famous hero, the amateur detective who gets the better of all the official agencies is really not Conan Doyle himself but none other than Edgar Allan Poe with his Monsieur Dupin (for more details see Marie Bonaparte's extremely interesting psychoanalytic study of Edgar Allan Poe). It was natural for a *"raisonneur infaillible"* like Poe to endow Monsieur Dupin with the gift of arriving at the most extraordinary conclusions by means of exact observation of human behavior and weighing all the circumstances. Thanks to these unusual gifts, which Poe designates as "analytic," Monsieur Dupin, this prototype of Sherlock Holmes succeeds in reconstructing and solving a most complicated and mysterious crime in the Rue Morgue.

Freud was quite indifferent to political questions. They occupied a different sphere, too far from the realm of psychoanalysis and Freud's work. In this connection, Freud's conclusions about Dostoevsky as a political thinker seem to me noteworthy. Usually a person making such observations takes as a starting point whatever philosophy he considers the right one. Thus some people would think that lesser minds than Dostoevsky's reached the same conclusions, he did more quickly only because they adopted these conservative views uncritically, without giving them much thought. Others holding political view opposite to Dostoevsky's conservative conclusions could reproach him for not living up to his principles firmly enough to retain his earlier revolutionary convictions, in spite of his misfortune. Both views would contain value judgments, which Freud evidently wished to avoid. Therefore his purely scientific reflections on psychic processes, the comparison of the two amounts of energy necessary to attain the same result. Here lie the borders of psychoanalysis, which Freud did not wish to overstep.

Now I would like to touch on another question, which also occupies one of the border regions. I mean the problem so disputed in philosophy that of free will. As psychoanalysis recognizes a causal relationship between a neurotic's repressions, that is, his unconscious processes and the symptoms of his illness, one would assume that it uncompromisingly rejects free will and takes a strictly deterministic stand. That proves to be true, for instance, in *The Criminal, the Judge and the Public*, by Franz Alexander and Hugo Staub. According to this book, a decision results from the working together of various forces, constituting, so to speak, their meaning. One might follow this train of thought further and say that these forces often work in opposite directions. As they are invisible to us the outcome of this working together and working against, that is the decision itself, does not appear to be determined by definite causes.

A remark of Freud's occurs to me, however, which can be understood as intimating at least the possibility of free will. Freud said that even when the repressed becomes conscious, and when an analysis could be regarded as successful, this does not automatically bring about the patient's recovery. After such an analysis the patient has been placed in a position in which he can get well, before analysis this was not possible. But whether or not he really will get well depends on his wish to recover, on his will. Freud compared this situation with the purchase of a travel ticket. This ticket only makes the journey possible; it does not take its place. But what is this will to recover, really? And what determines it?

Freud's attitude to religion is well known. He was a freethinker and an adversary of all dogmatism. Notwithstanding this, he insisted that there was no fundamental opposition between religion and psychoanalysis and that therefore a religious adherent could readily become a follower of psychoanalysis.

Psychoanalysis assumes the task of bringing repressed ideas into consciousness, a task which necessitates overcoming resistances. In accordance with this, Freud considered the attacks against him in a psychoanalytic sense as the expression of inner resistance. He regarded them as a matter of course, since our ego defends itself against admitting the repressed to consciousness. Freud stated that the human race had in the course of its development suffered three hard blows to its self-love, to its narcissism: first, the realization that our earth is not the center of the universe, that the sun does not revolve around the earth but the earth around the sun, then Darwin's theory of evolution; and now, through psychoanalysis, the dethronement of our sphere of consciousness in favor of the unconscious, which determines our emotional life and so, in the long run, our relationship to everything.

This position of Freud's---following the maxim that to understand all is to forgive all---naturally led to his unresentful attitude to those who rejected his teaching. Personal hatred was foreign to Freud's nature. It is well-known, for example, that there was tension between Freud and Wagner-Jauregg, but I never perceived that Freud nourished any feelings of enmity toward him. Freud simply thought that Wagner-Jauregg was lacking in deeper psychological understanding. But as Wagner-Jauregg's merits lay in quite a different field---I mean the malaria treatment of paresis---this judgment of Freud's in no way detracted from the other's fame.

(By the way, years later, after Freud had emigrated to England, I once had the opportunity of discussing with Wagner-Jauregg a case I was very concerned about. This was about six months before Wagner-Jauregg died. He was a very old man but still looked quite robust. I found him very likable as a person. Whereas Freud's most striking characteristics were his seriousness and his concentration on a certain sphere of ideas. Wagner-Jauregg made the impression of being a genial, easygoing Viennese of a past epoch).

In spite of Freud's forbearance and tolerance of his adversaries personally, he made no concessions or compromises about questions to which he believed he had found the true answers. To search for the truth was for Freud the first principle. Human intelligence and the triumphs of the mind were for Freud the highest excellence, important is not what man does, but what he thinks. By this Freud evidently meant to express the idea that feeling and thinking should be regarded as primary, and the actions resulting therefrom as secondary. Nevertheless, Freud was no stranger to the "human, the all too human." This is shown by a remark he once let fall that the satisfaction gained from intellectual work and success cannot match in intensity the feelings of pleasure achieved through the immediate gratification of instinctual aims. In intellectual achievement, the immediacy of the experience is lacking, just that feeling characterized by Freud's rather coarse but to-the-point expression---I still remember his words very well---"damn good." Through this remark of Freud's shimmers the wistful consciousness that intellectuality can be purchased only by sacrifice: the renunciation of immediate instinctual satisfaction.

In the week before the end of my analysis, we often spoke of the danger of the patient's feeling too close a tie to the therapist. If the patient remains "stuck" in the transference, the success of the treatment is not a lasting one, as it soon becomes evident that the original neurosis has been replaced by another. In this connection, Freud was of the opinion that at the end of treatment a gift from the patient could contribute, as a symbolic act, to lessening his feeling of gratitude and his consequent dependence on the physician. So we agreed that I would give Freud something as a remembrance. As I knew of his love for archeology, the gift I chose for him was a female Egyptian figure, with a miter-shaped headdress. Freud placed it on his desk. Twenty years later looking through a magazine, I saw a picture of Freud at his desk. "My" Egyptian immediately struck my eye, the figure which for me symbolized my analysis with Freud, who himself called me "a piece of psychoanalysis."

The end of my analysis with Freud coincided with the period of world political agitation in the summer of 1914. It was a hot and sultry Sunday, this fateful 28 of June 1914, on which the Austrian Crown Prince Franz Ferdinand and his wife were assassinated. On this day I took a walk through the Prater, and as my treatment with Freud was about to end in a few days, I let these years that I had spent in Vienna flow through my thoughts. During this time my resistances in the transference had sometimes become so strong that I despaired of bringing my analysis with Freud to a successful conclusion. Now this period was over, and I was filled with the heartening feeling that, in spite of all the difficulties, I had persevered with Freud and could now leave Vienna a healthy man. I was also very happy that my future wife, whom I had presented to Freud a short time before, had made an excellent impression on him and that he approved my choice. I saw the future in a very rosy light, and in this hopeful mood I returned home from my walk. Scarcely had I entered my apartment when the maid brought me the extra edition of the newspaper, reporting the assassination of the archducal couple.

When I saw Freud the following day, of course, we spoke of this event. At this time a very excited anti-Serbian spirit dominated Vienna. I felt it was false reasoning to condemn a whole people, lock, stock, and barrel, and to ascribe certain bad qualities whatever they might be, to one and all. Freud apparently did not share this view, as he observed that there are indeed nations in which certain bad qualities are more marked than in others. In talking about the situation, Freud remarked that if Franz Ferdinand had come to power, we would certainly have had a war with Russia. Obviously, he could have had no idea that the assassination at Sarjevo would start the ball rolling.

When I saw Freud again after World War I, in the spring of 1919, and spoke of how absolutely incomprehensible it was that such mass slaughter could take place in the twentieth century, Freud did not pursue this them but remarked, somewhat resignedly, that we have a "wrong attitude" toward death. To the great political events of the world following the war, Freud took a wait-and-see position. He said something to the effect that one could not expect a psychoanalyst to judge these events correctly or to foresee their outcome. It was at this time also that I learned from Freud that Jung, whom Freud had always praised highly and whom he had formerly designated as his successor, had broken away from him and was now going his own way.

I have spoken of Freud's composure and self-control. He constructed a whole new world of thought which apart from everything else, required great energy and perseverance. His strength of mind, although it sometimes lent him the semblance of harshness, was most admirable, and never deserted him, even when he was subjected to fate's hardest blows.

In the winter of 1919-1920 Freud suffered an extremely painful loss through the death of his oldest daughter, to whom, I have heard, he was especially attached. I saw him the day following this tragic event. He was calm and composed as usual, and did not betray his pain in any way.

When some years later Freud was taken ill with a growth in the oral cavity, he conducted himself as resolutely as before. He had to have an operation, and when I visited him after this and asked how he felt he behaved as though nothing had happened. "One just grows old," he said, making a gesture with his hand of the sort people make to brush away trivial things. Freud as a physician was of course fully aware of the seriousness of his illness. And in fact the first operation was followed by a second, in which a part of his palate was removed, so that he had to wear prosthesis. It impeded his speech slightly, but one hardly noticed this. But this misfortune did not have the power to subdue Freud or rob him of his passion for work. He devoted himself to writing as he had formerly done, and still continued his analytic practice, though to a limited degree. After Hitler's annexation of Austria, Freud emigrated to England, where he died early in World War II.

"A prophet is without honor in his own country," according the proverb, and this has been, alas, true of Freud. Although Freud spent most of his entire life in Vienna, where he for many decades carried on work that proved to be so important for mankind, psychoanalysis meets with less acceptance in Vienna than elsewhere. To what can this be attributed? Perhaps it is because Austria, in her recent history, has undergone so many political and economic crises. But something else may also play a role: the fact that Austrians possess the happy aptitude of making light of many things, and, like the French, take life more from its bright and pleasant side. It may follow that they suffer less from their complexes and get over them more easily.

However that may be, the time is more than due, ten years after Freud's death, to place a fitting memorial plaque on the house in the Bergasse where he lived. It is still sadly missing when one walks past.[4]

---

[1] Cf., p. 157 in this volume to which Freud writes of the Wolf Man: "His unimpeachable intelligence was, as it were, cut off from the instinctual forces which governed his behavior in the few relations of life that remained to him." (Translator's note.)

[2] In his *Memoirs, 1919-1938* (p. 113), the Wolf Man wrote of the year 1920 when he was completing four months of reanalysis with Freud. "Our situation was such that we could hardly even have paid our rent had not Professor Freud, who had some English patients, given us a few English pounds from time to time." Replying to a question of mind, the Wolf Man wrote me in a letter of September 14, 1970: "My reanalysis in 1919 took place not at my request, but at the wish of Professor Freud himself. When I explained to him that I could not pay for this treatment, he expressed his readiness to analyze me without remuneration." (Translator's note.)

[3] Anna Freud states that it was not the youngest but the oldest son who broke his leg. This is the only factual error she has found in these *Recollections*. The rest of what is written about his youngest son, the architect, correctly applies to him. (Translator's note.)

[4] On May 6, 1954, more than two years after the Wolf Man wrote this paper, the World Organization for Mental Health placed a commemorative plaque on the door. (Translator's note.)

Chapter Seven
Case Histories in Neo-analysis

"The case history is living drama...
   the drama of a woman who feels that everyone is against her;
   of a man falsely accused of murder, helpless to defend himself;
   of a small child who cannot sleep...
Each drama is unique to the individual involved, but, like all real
experience, each has something to say to all people."

Harold Greenwald

The Anxious Young Woman and The Retired Business Man [*]

Carl Gustave Jung, M.D.
Translated by R. F. C. Hull

Carl Gustave Jung (1875-1961) met Freud in 1906, after having corresponded with him for some time. In 1909, he came to America with Freud and Ferenczi to lecture on psychoanalysis. When he returned to middle-class Switzerland, he became increasingly uneasy about Freud's emphasis on sexual matters and broke with him in 1913, to establish his own school of thought, generally referred to as "Analytical Psychology."

While formally breaking with Freud, Jung has granted that the problems of the neurotic patient under forty years old can well be helped by utilizing the techniques of Freud or Adler. However, Jung believes that older patients require a different approach because they are suffering from the senselessness and aimlessness of their lives rather than from a definite neurosis (an idea currently emphasized by the "existential" analysts). In his technique, Jung appears to stress the uniqueness of the individual and the desirability of the individual's acceptance and full development of all sides of his personality.

Jung is responsible for the popularity of the term "introvert" and "extravert" which he saw as one-sided developments of the personality.

In the following material, Jung illustrates first the Freudian, and second the Jungian theory, and in doing so, demonstrates how his theory both resembles and differs from Freudian psychoanalysis.

[*] Jung, Carl. (1973). The Anxious Young Woman and the Retired Business Man. In Greenwald, Harold (Ed.), *Great Cases in Psychoanalysis*, 155-174. New York: J. Aronson. Reprinted by permission.

173

I remember a young woman who suffered from acute hysteria following a sudden fright. She had been to an evening party and was on her way home about midnight in the company of several acquaintances, when a cab came up behind them at full trot. The others got out of the way, but she, as though spellbound with terror, kept to the middle of the road and ran along in front of the horses. The cabman cracked his whip and swore; it was no good, she ran down the whole length of the road, which led across a bridge. There her strength deserted her, and to avoid being tramples on by the horses she would in her desperation have leapt into the river had not the passers-by prevented her. Now, this same lady had happened to be in the St. Petersburg on the bloody twenty-second of January, in the very street which was cleared by the volleys of soldiers. All round her people were falling to the ground dead or wounded; she, however, quite calm and clear-headed, espied a gate leading into a yard through which she made her escape into another street. These dreadful moments caused her no further agitation. She felt perfectly well afterwards---indeed, rather better than usual.

Essentially similar reactions can frequently be observed. Hence it necessarily follows that the intensity of a trauma has very little pathogenic significance in itself, but it must have a special significance for the patient. That is to say, it is not the shock as such that has a pathogenic effect, it must impinge on a special psychic disposition, which may, in certain circumstances, consist in the patient's unconsciously attributing a specific significance to the shock. Here we have a possible key to the "predisposition." We have, therefore, to ask ourselves: what are the special circumstances of the scene with the cab? The patient's fear began with the sound of the trotting horses; for an instant it seemed to her that this portended some terrible doom---her death, or something as dreadful; the next moment she lost all sense of what she was doing.

The real effect evidently comes from the horses. The patient's predisposition to react in so unaccountable a way to this unremarkable incident might there consist in the fact that horses have some special significance for her. We might conjecture, for instance, that she once had a dangerous accident with horses. This was actually found to be the case. As a child of about seven she was out for a drive with her coachman, when suddenly the horses took fright and at a wild gallop made for the precipitous bank of a deep river-gorge. The coachman jumped down and shouted to her to do likewise, but she was in such deadly fear that she could hardly make up her mind. Nevertheless she jumped in the nick of time, while the horses crashed with the carriage into the depths below. That such an event would leave a very deep impression scarcely needs proof. Yet it does not explain why at a later date such an insensate reaction should follow the perfectly harmless hint of a similar situation. So far we only know that the later symptom had a prelude in childhood, but the pathological aspect of it still remains in the dark. In order to penetrate this mystery, further knowledge is needed. For it had become clear with increasing experiences that in all the cases analyzed so far, there existed, apart from the traumatic experiences, another, special class of disturbances which lie in the province of love. Admittedly "love" is an elastic concept that stretches from heaven to hell and combines in itself good and evil, high and low. With this discovery Freud's views underwent a considerable change. He had formerly sought the cause of the neurosis in traumatic experiences, now the center of gravity of the problem shifted to an entirely different point. This is best illustrated by our case; we can understand well enough why horses should play a special part in the life of the patient, but we do not understand the later reaction, so exaggerated and uncalled for. The pathological peculiarity of this story lies in the fact that she is frightened of quite harmless horses. Remembering the discovery that apart from the traumatic experience there is often a disturbance in the province of love, we might inquire whether perhaps there is some peculiarity in this connection.

The lady knows a young man to whom she thinks of becoming engaged; she loves him and hopes to be happy with him. At first nothing more is discoverable. But it would never do to be deterred from investigation by the negative results of the preliminary questioning. There are indirect ways of reaching the goal when the direct way fails. We therefore return to that singular moment when the lady ran headlong in front of the horses. We inquire about her companions and what sort of festive occasion it was in which she had just taken part. It had been a farewell party for her best friend, who was going abroad to a health resort on account of her nerves. This friend is married and, we are told, happily; she is also the mother of a child. We may take leave to doubt the statement that she is happy; for, were she really so, she would presumably have no reason to be "nervous" and in need of a cure. Shifting my angle of approach, I learned that after her friends had rescued her they brought the patient back to the house of her host---her best friend's husband---as this was the nearest shelter at that late hour of the night. There she was hospitably received in her exhausted state. At this point the patient broke off her narrative, became embarrassed, fidgeted, and tried to change the subject. Evidently some disagreeable reminiscence had suddenly bobbed up. After the most obstinate resistance had been overcome, it appeared that yet another very remarkable incident had occurred that night; the amiable host had made her a fiery declaration of love, thus precipitating a situation which, in the absence of the lade of the house, might well be considered both difficult and distressing. Ostensibly this declaration of love came to her like a bolt from the blue, but these things usually have their history. It was now the task of the next few weeks to dig out bit by bit a long love story, until at last a complete picture emerged which I attempt to outline somewhat as follows:

As a child the patient had been a regular tomboy, caring only for wild boys' games, scorning her own sex, and avoiding all feminine ways and occupations. After puberty, when the erotic problem might have come too close, she began to shun all society, hated and despised everything that even remotely reminded her of the biological destiny of man, and lived in a world of fantasies which had nothing in common with rude reality. Thus, until about her twenty-fourth year, she evaded all those little adventures, hopes, and expectations which ordinarily move a girl's heart at this age. Then she got to know two men who were destined to break through the thorny hedge that had grown up around her. Mr. A was her best friend's husband, and Mr. B was his bachelor friend. She liked them both. Nevertheless it soon began to look as though she liked Mr. B a vast deal better. An intimacy quickly sprang up between them and before long there was talk of a possible engagement. Through her relation with Mr. B and through her friends she often came into contact with Mr. A, whose presence sometimes disturbed her in the most unaccountable way and made her feel nervous. About this time the patient went to a larger party. Her friends were also present. She became lost in thought and was dreamily playing with her ring when it suddenly slipped off her finger and rolled under the table. Both gentlemen looked for it and Mr. B succeeded in finding it. He placed the ring on her finger with an arch smile and said, "You know what that means!" Overcome by a strange and irresistible feeling, she tore the ring from her finger and flung it through the open window. A painful moment ensued, as may be imagined, and soon she left the party in deep dejection. Not long after this, so-called chance brought it about that she should spend her summer holidays in a health resort where Mr. And Mrs. A were also staying. Mrs. A then began to grow visibly nervous, and frequently remained indoors because she felt out of sorts. The patient was thus in a position to go out for walks alone with Mr. A. On one occasion, they went boating. So boisterous was she in her merriment that she suddenly fell overboard. She could not swim, and it was only with great difficulty that Mr. A pulled her half-unconscious into the boat. And then it was that he kissed her. With this romantic episode the bonds were tied fast. But the patient would not allow the depths of this passion to come to consciousness, evidently because she had long habituated herself to pass over such things or, better, to run away from them. To excuse herself in her own eyes she pursued her engagement to Mr. B all the more energetically, telling herself every day that it was Mr. B whom she loved. Naturally this curious little game had not escaped the keen glances of wifely jealousy. Mrs. A, her friend, had guessed the secret and fretted accordingly, so that her nerves only got worse. Hence it became necessary for Mrs. A to go abroad for a cure. At the farewell party the evil spirit stepped up to our patient and whispered in her ear. "Tonight he is alone. Something must happen to you so that you can go to his house." And so indeed it happened: through her own strange behavior, she came back to his house, and thus she attained her desire.

After this explanation, everyone will probably be inclined to assume that only a devilish subtlety could devise such a chain of circumstances and set it to work. There is no doubt about the subtlety, but its moral evaluation remains a doubtful matter, because I must emphasize that the motives leading to this dramatic denouement were in no sense conscious. To the patient, the whole story seemed to happen of itself, without her being conscious of any motive. But the previous history makes it perfectly clear that everything was unconsciously directed to this end, while the conscious mind was struggling to bring about the engagement to Mr. B. The unconscious drive in the other direction was stronger.

So once more we return to our original question, namely, whence comes the pathological (i.e., peculiar or exaggerated) nature of the reaction to the trauma? On the basis of a conclusion drawn from analogous experiences, we conjectures that in this case too there must be, in addition to the trauma, a disturbance in the erotic sphere. This conjecture has been entirely confirmed, and we have learnt that the trauma, the ostensible cause of the illness, is no more than an occasion for something previously not conscious to manifest itself, i.e., an important erotic conflict. Accordingly the trauma loses its exclusive significance, and is replaced by a much deeper and more comprehensive conception which sees the pathogenic agent as an erotic conflict.

One often hears the question: why should the erotic conflict be the cause of the neurosis rather than any other conflict? To this we can only answer: no one asserts that it must be so, but in point of fact it frequently is so. In spite of all indignant protestations to the contrary, the fact remains that love, its problems and its conflicts, is of fundamental importance in human life and, as careful inquiry consistently shows, is of far greater significance than the individual aspects.

The trauma theory has therefore been abandoned, as antiquated; for with the discovery that not the trauma but a hidden erotic conflict is the root of the neurosis; the trauma loses its causal significance.

Once, in America, I was consulted by a business man of about forty-five. He was a typical American self-made man who had worked his way up from the bottom. He had been very successful and had founded an immense business. He had also succeeded in organizing it in such a way that he was able to think of retiring. Two years before I saw him he had in fact taken his farewell. Until then he had lived entirely for his business and concentrated all his energies on it with the incredible intensity and one-sidedness peculiar to successful American business men. He had purchased a splendid estate where he thought of "living," by which he meant horses, automobiles, golf, tennis, parties and what not. But he had, reckoned without his host. The energy which should have been at his disposal would not enter into these alluring prospects, but went capering off in quite another direction. A few weeks after the initiation of the longed-for-life of bliss, he began brooding over peculiar, vague sensations in his body, and a few weeks more sufficed to plunge him into a state of extreme hypochondria. He had a complete nervous collapse. From a healthy man, of uncommon physical strength and abounding energy, he became a peevish child. That was the end of all his glories. He fell from one state of anxiety to the next and worried himself almost to death with hypochondriacal mopings. He then consulted a famous specialist, who recognized at once that there was nothing wrong with the man but lack of work. The patient saw the sense of this, and returned to his former position. But, to his immediate disappointment, no interest in the business could be aroused. Neither patience nor resolution was of any use. His energy could not by any means be forced back into the business. His condition naturally became worse than before. All that had formerly been living, creative energy in him now turned against him with terrible destroying force. His creative genius rose up, as it were, in revolt against him; and just as before he had built up great organizations in the world, so now his daemon spun equally subtle systems of hypochondriacal delusion that completely annihilated him. When I saw him he was already a hopeless moral ruin. Nevertheless I tried to make clear to him that though such a gigantic energy might be withdrawn from the business, the question remained, where should it go? The finest horses, the fastest cars, and the most amusing parties may very likely fail to allure the energy, although it would be rational enough to think that a man who had devoted his whole life to serious work had a sort of natural right to enjoy himself. Yes, if fate behaved in a humanly rational way, it would certainly be so: first work, then well-earned rest. But fate behaves irrationally, and the energy of life inconveniently demands a gradient agreeable to itself; otherwise it simply gets dammed up and turns destructive. It regresses to former situations---in the case of this man, to the memory of a syphilitic infection contracted twenty-five years before. Yet even this was only a stage on the way to the resuscitation of infantile reminiscences which had all but vanished in the meantime. It was the original relations to his mother that mapped the course of his symptoms: they were an "arrangement" whose purpose it was to compel the attention and interest of his long-dead mother. Nor was this stage the last; for the ultimate goal was to drive him back, as it were, into his own body. After he had lived since his youth only in his head. He had differentiated one side of his being; the other side remained in an inert physical state. He would have needed this other side in order to "live." The hypochondriacal "depression" pushed him down into the body he had always overlooked. Had he been able to follow the direction indicated by his depression and hypochondriacal illusion, and make himself conscious of the fantasies which proceed from such a condition, that would have been the road to salvation. My arguments, naturally met with no response, as was to be expected. A case so far advanced can only be cared for until death, it can hardly be cured.

This example clearly shows that it does not lie in our power to transfer "disposable" energy at will to a rationally chosen object. The same is true in general of the apparently disposable energy which is disengaged when we have destroyed its unserviceable forms through the corrosive of reductive analysis. This energy, as we have said, can at best be applied voluntarily for only a short time. But in most cases it refuses to seize hold, for any length of time, of the possibilities rationally presented to it. Psychic energy is a very fastidious thing which insists on fulfillment of its own conditions. However much energy may be present, we cannot make it serviceable until we have succeeded in finding the right gradient.

This question of the gradient is an eminently practical problem which crops up in most analyses. For instance, when in a favorable case the disposable energy, the so-called libido, does seize hold of a rational object, we think we have brought about the transformation through conscious exertion of the will. But I that we a re deluded, because even the most strenuous exertions would not have sufficed had there not been present at the same time a gradient in that direction. How important the gradient is can be seen in cases when, despite the most desperate exertions, and despite the fact that the object chosen or the form desired impresses everybody with its reasonableness, the transformation still refuses to take place, and all that happens is a new repression.

It has become abundantly clear to me that life can flow forward only along the path of the gradient. But there is no energy unless there is a tension of opposites, hence it is necessary to discover the opposite to the attitude of the conscious mind. It is interesting to see how this compensation by opposites also plays its part in the historical theories of neurosis. Freud's theory espoused Eros, Adler's the will to power. Logically, the opposite of love is hate, and of Eros, Phobos (fear); but psychologically it is the will to power. Where love reigns, there is no will to power;

and where the will to power is paramount, love is lacking. The one is but the shadow of the other: the man who adopts the standpoint of Eros finds his compensatory opposite in the will to power, and that of the man who puts the accent on power is Eros. Seen from the one-sided point of view of the conscious attitude, the shadow is an inferior component of the personality and is consequently repressed through intensive resistance. But the repressed content must be made conscious so as to produce a tension of opposites, without which no forward movement is possible. The conscious mind is on top, the shadow underneath, and just as high always longs for low and hot for cold, so all consciousness, perhaps without being aware of it, seeks the unconscious opposite, lacking which it is doomed to stagnation, congestion, and ossification. Life is born only of the spark of opposites.

It was a concession to intellectual logic on the one hand to psychological prejudice on the other that impelled Freud to name the opposite of Eros the destructive or death instinct. For in the first place, Eros is not equivalent to life; but for anyone who thinks it is, the opposite of Eros will naturally appear to be death. And in the second place, we all feel that the opposite of our own highest principle must be purely destructive, deadly, and evil. We refuse to endow it with any positive life-force, hence we avoid and fear it.

As I have already indicated, there are many highest principles both of life and of philosophy, and accordingly there are just as many different forms of compensation by opposition. Earlier on I singled out the two---as it seems to me---main opposite types, which I have called introverted and extraverted. William James had already been struck by the existence of both these types among thinkers. He distinguished them as "tender-minded" and "tough-minded." Similarly Ostwald found an analogous division into "classical" and "romantic" types among men of learning. So I am not alone in my idea of types, to mention only these two well-known names among many others. Inquiries into history have shown me that not a few of the great spiritual controversies rest upon the opposition of the two types. The most significant case of this kind is the opposition between nominalism and realism which, beginning with the difference between Platonic and Megaric schools, became the heritage of scholastic philosophy, where it is Abelard's great merit to have hazarded at least the attempt to unite the two opposed standpoints in his "conceptualism." This controversy has continued right into our own day, as is shown in the opposition between idealism and materialism. And again, not only the human mind in general, but each individual has a share in this opposition of types. It has come to light on closer investigation that either type has a predilection to marry its opposite, each being unconsciously complementary to the other. The reflective nature of the introvert causes him always to think and consider before acting. This naturally makes him slow to act. His shyness and distrust of things induces hesitation, and so he always has difficulty in adapting to the external world. Conversely the extravert has a positive relation to things. He is, so to speak, attracted by them. New, unknown situation fascinate him. In order to make closer acquaintance with the unknown he will jump into it with both feet. As a rule he acts first and thinks afterwards. Thus his action is swift, subject to no misgivings and hesitations. The two types therefore seem created for a symbiosis. The one takes care of reflection and the other sees to the initiative and practical action. When the two types marry they may effect an ideal union. So long as they are fully occupied with their adaptation to the manifold external needs of life they fit together admirably. But when the man has made enough money, or if a fine legacy should drop from the skies and external necessity no longer presses, then they have time to occupy themselves with one another. Hitherto they stood back to back and defended themselves against necessity. But now they turn face to fact and look for understanding---only to discover that they have never understood one another. Each speaks a different language. Then the conflict between the two types begins. This struggle is envenomed, brutal, full of mutual depreciation, even when conducted quietly and in the greatest intimacy. For the value of the one is the negation of value for the other. It might reasonably be supposed that each, conscious of his own vague, could peaceably recognize the other's value, and that in this way any conflict would be superfluous. I have seen a good number of cases where this line of argument was adopted, without, however, arriving at a satisfactory goal. Where it is a question of normal people, such critical periods of transition will be overcome fairly smoothly. By "normal" I mean a person who can somehow exist under all circumstances which afford him the minimum needs of life. But many people cannot do this, therefore not so very many people are normal. What we commonly mean by a "normal persona" is actually an ideal person whose happy blend of character is a rare occurrence. By far the greater number of more or less differentiated persons demand conditions of life which afford considerably more than the certainty of food and sleep. For these ending of a symbiotic (mutually dependent) relationship comes as a severe shock.

It is not easy to understand why this should be so. Yet if we consider that no man is simply introverted or simply extraverted, but has both attitudes potentially in him---although he has developed only one of them as a function of adaptation---we shall immediately conjecture that with the introvert extraversion lies dormant and undeveloped somewhere in the background, and that introversion leads a similar shadowy existence in the extravert. And this is indeed the case. The introvert does possess an extraverted attitude, but it is unconscious, because his conscious gaze is always turned to the subject. He sees the object, of course, but has false or inhibiting ideas about it, so that he keeps his distance as much as possible, as though the object were something formidable and dangerous. I will make my meaning clear by a simple illustration.

Let us suppose two youths rambling in the country. They come to a fine castle; both want to see inside it. The introvert says, "I'd like to know what it's like inside." The extravert answers, "Right, let's go in," and makes for the gateway. The introvert draws back---"Perhaps we aren't allowed in," says he, with visions of policemen and fierce dogs in the background. Whereupon the extravert answers, "Well, we can ask. They'll let us in all right."---with visions of kindly old watchmen, hospitable seigneurs, and the possibility of romantic adventures. On the strength of extraverted optimism they at length find themselves in the castle. But now comes the denouement. The castle has been rebuilt inside, and contains nothing but a couple of rooms with a collection of old manuscripts. As it happens, old manuscripts are the chief joy of the introverted youth. Hardly has he caught sight of them when he becomes as one transformed. He loses himself, in contemplation of the treasures, uttering cries of enthusiasm. He engages the keeper in conversation so as to extract from him as much information as possible, and when the result is meager the youth asks to see the curator in order to propound his questions to him. His shyness has vanished, objects have taken a seductive glamour, and the world wears a new face. But meanwhile the spirits of the extraverted youth are ebbing lower and lower. His face grows longer and he begins to yawn. No kindly watchmen are forthcoming here, no knightly hospitality, not a trace of romantic adventure---only a castle made over into a museum. These are manuscripts enough to be seen at home. While the enthusiasm of the one rises, the spirits of the other fall, the castle bores him, the manuscripts remind him of a library, library is associated with university, university with studies and menacing examinations. Gradually a veil of gloom descends over the once so interesting and enticing castle. The object becomes negative "Isn't it marvelous," cries the introvert, "to have stumbled on this wonderful collection?" "The place bores me to extinction," replies the other with undisguised ill humor. This annoys the introvert, who secretly vows never again to go rambling with an extravert. The latter is annoyed with the other's annoyance, and he thinks to himself that he always knew the fellow was an inconsiderate egotist who would, in his own selfish interest, waste all the lovely spring day that could be enjoyed so much better out of doors.

What has happened? Both were wandering together in happy symbiosis until they discovered the fatal castle. Then the for-thinking, or Promethean, introvert said it might be seen from the inside, and the after-thinking, or Epimethean, extravert opened the door. At this point the types invert themselves: the introvert, who at first resisted the idea of going in, cannot now be induced to go out, and the extravert curses the moment when he set foot inside the castle. The former is now fascinated by the object, the latter by his negative thoughts. When the introvert spotted the manuscripts, it was all up with him. His shyness vanished, the objects took possession of him, and he yielded himself willingly. The extravert, however, felt a growing resistance to the object and was eventually made the prisoner of his own ill-humored subjectivity. The introvert became extraverted, the extravert introverted. But the extraversion of the introvert is different from the extraversion of the extravert, and vice versa. So long as both were wandering along in joyous harmony, neither fell foul of the other, because each was in his natural character. Each was positive to the other, because their attitudes were complementary. They were complementary, however, only because the attitude of the one included the other. We can see this from the short conversation at the gateway. Both wanted to enter the castle. The doubt of the introvert as to whether an entry were possible also held good for the other. The initiative of the extravert likewise held good for the other. Thus the attitude of the one included the other, and this is always in some degree true if a person happens to be in the attitude natural to him, for this attitude has some degree of collective adaptation. The same is true of the introvert's attitude, although this always comes from the subject. It simply goes from subject to object, while the extravert's attitude goes from object to subject.

But the moment when, in the case of the introvert, the object overpowers and attracts the subject, his attitude loses its social character. He forgets the presence of his friend, he no longer includes him, he becomes absorbed into the object and does not see how very bored his friend is. In the same way the extravert loses all consideration for the other as his expectations are disappointed and he withdraws into subjectivity and moodiness.

We can therefore formulate the occurrence as follows: in the introvert the influence of the object produces an inferior introversion, while in the extravert an inferior introversion takes the place of his social attitude. And so we come back to the proposition from which we started, "The value of the one is the negation of value for the other."

Positive as well as negative occurrences can constellate the inferior counter-function. When this happens, sensitiveness appears. Sensitiveness is a sure sign of the presence of inferiority. This provides the psychological basis for discord and misunderstanding, not only as between two people, but also in ourselves. The essence of the inferior function is autonomy, it is independent, it attacks, it fascinates and so spins us about that we are no longer masters of ourselves and can no longer rightly distinguish between ourselves and others.

And yet it is necessary for the development of character that we should allow the other side, the inferior function, to find expression. We cannot in the long run allow one part of our personality to be cared for symbiotically by another, for the moment when we might have need of the other function may come at any time and find us unprepared, as the above example shows. And the consequences may be bad: the extravert loses his indispensable relation to the object, and the introvert loses his to the subject. Conversely, it is equally indispensable for the introvert to arrive at some form of action not constantly bedeviled by doubts and hesitations, and for the extravert to reflect upon himself, yet without endangering his relationships.

In extraversion and introversion it is clearly a matter of the two antithetical, natural attitudes or trends, which Goethe once referred to as diastole and systole. They ought, in their harmonious alternation, to give life a rhythm, but it seems to require a high degree of art to achieve such a rhythm. Either one must do it quite unconsciously, so that the natural law is not disturbed by any conscious act, or one must be conscious in a much higher sense, to be capable of willing and carrying out the antithetical movements. Since we cannot develop backwards into animal unconsciousness, there remains only the more strenuous way forwards into higher consciousness. Certainly that consciousness, which would enable us to live the great Yea and Nay of our own free will and purpose, is an altogether superhuman ideal. Still, it is a goal. Perhaps our present mentality only allows us consciously to will the Yea and to bear with the Nay. When that is the case, much is already achieved.

The problem of opposites, as an inherent principle of human nature, forms a further stage in our process of realization. As a rule it is one of the problems of maturity. The practical treatment of a patient will hardly ever begin with this problem, especially not in the case of young people. The neuroses of the young generally come from a collision between the forms of reality and an inadequate, infantile attitude, which form the casual point of view which is characterized by an abnormal dependence on the real or imaginary parents, and from the teleological point of view by unrealizable fictions, plans, and aspirations. Here the reductive methods of Freud and Adler are entirely in place. But there are many neuroses which either appear only at maturity or else deteriorate to such a degree that the patients become incapable of work. Naturally one can point out in these cases that an unusual dependence on the parents existed even in youth, and that all kinds of infantile illusions were present; but all that did not prevent them from taking up a profession, from practicing it successfully, from keeping up a marriage of sorts until that moment in riper years when the previous attitude suddenly failed. In such cases, it is of little help to make them conscious of their childhood fantasies, dependence on the parents, etc., although this is a necessary part of the procedure and often has a not unfavorable result. But the real therapy only begins when the patient sees that it is no longer father and mother who are standing in this way, but himself---i.e., an unconscious part of his personality which carries on the role of the father and mother. Even this realization, helpful as it is, is still negative; it simply says, "I realize that it is not father and mother who are against me, but I myself." But who is it in him that is against him? What is this mysterious part of his personality that hides under the father-and mother-images, making him believe for years that the cause of his trouble must somehow have got him into him from outside? This part is the counterpart to his conscious attitude; and it will leave him no peace and will continue to plague him until it has been accepted. For young people liberation from the past may be enough; a beckoning future lies ahead, rich in possibilities. It is sufficient to break a few bonds; the life-urge will do the rest. But we are faced with another task in the case of people who have left a large part of their life behind them, for whom the future no longer beckons with marvelous possibilities, and nothing is to be expected but the endless round of familiar duties and the doubtful pleasures of old age.

If ever we succeed in liberating young people from the past, we see that they always transfer the images of their parents to more suitable substitute figures. For instance, the feeling that clung to the mother now passes to the wife, and the father's authority passes to respected teachers and superiors or to institutions. Although this is not a fundamental solution, it is yet a practical road which the normal man treads unconsciously and therefore with no notable inhibitions and resistances.

The problem for the adult is very different. He has put this part of the road behind him with or without difficulty. He has cut loose from his parents, long since dead perhaps, and has sought and found the mother in the wife, or, in the case of a woman, the father in the husband. He has duly honored his fathers and their institutions, has himself become a father, and, with all this in the past, has possibly come to realize that what originally meant advancement and satisfaction has now become a boring mistake, part of the illusion of youth, upon which he looks back with mingled regret and envy, because nothing now awaits him but old age and the end of all illusions. Here there are no more fathers and mothers; all the illusions he projected upon the world and upon things gradually come back to him, jaded and way-worn. The energy streaming back from these manifold relationships fall into the unconscious and activates all the things he had neglected to develop.

In a young man, the instinctual forces tied up in the neurosis give him, when released, buoyancy and hope and the chance to extend the scope of his life. To the man in the second half of life, the development of the function of opposites lying dormant in the unconscious means a renewal, but this development no longer

183

proceeds via the solution of infantile ties, the destruction of infantile illusions and the transference of old images to new figures; it proceeds via the problem of opposites.

The principle of opposition is, of curse, fundamental even in adolescence, and a psychological theory of the adolescent psyche is bound to recognize this fact. Hence the Freudian and Alderian viewpoints contradict each other only when they claim to be generally applicable theories. But so long as they are content to be technical, auxiliary concepts, they do not contradict or exclude one another. A psychological theory, if it is to be more than a technical makeshift, must base itself on the principle of opposition; for without this it could only reestablish a neurotically unbalanced psyche. There is no balance, no system of self-regulation, without opposition. The psyche is just such a self-regulating system.

If, at this point, we take up the thread we let fall earlier, we shall now see clearly why it is that the values which the individual lacks are to be found in the neurosis itself. At this point, too, we can return to the case of the young woman and apply this insight we have gained. Let us suppose that this patient is "analyzed," i.e., she has, through the treatment, come to understand the nature of the unconscious thoughts lurking behind her symptoms, and has thus regained possession of the unconscious energy which constituted the strength of those symptoms. The question then arises: what to do with the so-called disposable energy? In accordance with the psychological type of the patient, it would be rational to transfer this energy to an object—to philanthropic work, for example, or some useful activity. With exceptionally energetic natures that are not afraid of wearing themselves to the bone, if need be, or with people who delight in the toil of such activities, this way is possible, but mostly it is impossible. For—do not forget—the libido, as this psychic energy is technically called, already possesses its object unconsciously in the form of the young Italian or some equally real human substitute. In these circumstances sublimation is an impossible as it is desirable, because the real object generally offers the energy a much better gradient than do the most admirable ethical activities. Unfortunately far too many of us talk about a man only as it would be desirable for him to be, never about the man as he really is. But the doctor has always to do with the real man, who remains obstinately himself until all sides of his reality are recognized. True education can only start from naked reality, not from a delusive ideal.

It is unhappily the case that no man can direct the so-called disposable energy at will. It follows its own gradient. Indeed, it had already found the gradient even before we set the energy free from the unserviceable form to which it was linked. For we discover that the patient's fantasies, previously occupied with the young Italian, have now transferred themselves to the doctor. The doctor has himself become the object of the unconscious libido. If the patient altogether refuses to recognize the fact of the transference, or if the doctor fails to understand it, or interprets it falsely, vigorous resistances supervene, directed towards making the relation with the doctor completely impossible. Then the patient goes away and looks for another doctor, or for some one who understands; or, if he gives up the search, he gets stuck in his problem.

If, however, the transference to the doctor takes place, and is accepted, a natural form is found which supplants the earlier one and at the same time provides the energy with an outlet relatively free from conflict. Hence if the libido is allowed to run its natural curse, it will find its own way to the destined object. Where this does not happen, it is always a question of willful defiance of the laws of nature, or of some disturbing influence.

In the transference all kinds of infantile fantasies are projected. They must be cauterized, i.e., resolved by reductive analysis, and this used to be called "severing the transference." Thereby the energy is again released from an unserviceable form, and again we are faced by the problem of its disposability. Once more we shall put our trust in nature, hoping that, even before it is sought, an object will have been chosen which will provide a favorable gradient.

The Drive for Superiority
Alfred Adler, M.D.

Alfred Adler (1870-1937 was one of the founding members of the Vienna Psychoanalytic Society and was later its president. Even during the period from 1902 to 1911 when he worked with Freud he began to develop ideas which were different from those of Freud and others in the Vienna Society. When these differences became too wide, he presented his view to the Society and as a result of the criticism and denunciation his position was accorded by other members of the Society, he resigned to develop his own school of psychotherapy under the name of Individual Psychology.

Adler de-emphasized Freud's findings in sexual matters. A term which has passed into general usage as "inferiority complex" was coined by Adler and is the one thing most people think of in connection with his name. However, Adler actually contributed many other ideas and had great influence outside the field of psychoanalysis---in education, criminology, and medicine, for instance, as well as on the development of American psychoanalysis in particular. His emphasis on social factors probably influenced American therapists like Erich Fromm, Carl Rogers, Karen Horney and Harry Stack Sullivan.

Adler saw the inevitable result of feelings of inferiority as would be strivings for superiority. He later developed the theory that social interest rather than striving for superiority is the only true and natural compensation for feelings of inferiority.

In the case described, Adler stresses some of the neurotic ways in which striving for superiority is sometimes carried out. The case also illustrates Adler's emphasis on the life style, that is, the way in which the individual organizes his life to compensate for feelings of inferiority.

A curious case of depression which I once treated illustrates very clearly how sadness may be used to heighten the feeling of superiority. This was the case of a man of fifty, who said he felt perfectly healthy except when he was in a notably

* Adler, Alfred. (1973). The Drive for Superiority. In Greenwald, Harold (Ed.), *Great Cases in Psychoanalysis*, 175-186. New York: J. Aronson. Reprinted by permission.

comfortable situation. It was when he was at a concert or theatre with his family, for instance, that a fit of melancholy would descend upon him and in such depression he always remembered an intimate friend who had died when he was twenty-five. This friend had been his rival, not only in business but as a suitor for the hand of his wife---an unsuccessful rival, however, for by the time he contracted his fatal illness, my patient already had the advantage over him both in love and in business.

Success had been his lot, both before and after the friend's death; he was the favorite of his parents, unsurpassed by brothers and sisters, and prosperous in the world. His wife, however, was an ambitious character who strove to solve every domestic problem by a personal triumph or conquest, moral or otherwise, and between two such persons, the struggle was naturally continuous and severe. The wife sometimes gained ascendancy very cleverly, not by quarrelling or domineering in any way, but by becoming very nervous in disadvantageous situations, and conquering him by her painful condition. She never expressed her excessive jealousies, but sought to shackle him as required by her fits of anxiety. Thus, successful as he was in all but one relation of life, the man felt uncertain of having reached his goal of superiority, and his excessive ambition was demanding compensation.

I know that many psychologists would seek for a "guilt complex" to explain this depression. They would investigate the patient's childhood to find out a very early desire to kill someone---probably the father. This patient, however, had been the favorite of his father, and there was not the least reason why he should every have desired his death, as he had always been able to mange him in his own interest. Such a mistaken search for a "guilt complex" might also lead a psychologist to think that the patient had secretly wished to murder his friend and rival; and that after having triumphed over him and having had the death-wish granted by fate, he remained still unsatisfied. If that were so, the guilt complex might be developed by the striving of the patient to see himself in an intense light. He would want to express his good feeling and liking for his former rival with the highest sincerity and honesty; and at the same time he would be shaken by the memory of his rival's fatal end and the thoughts which he had been unable wholly to dismiss before it happened. This would amount to the complicated state of self-accusation and repentance at the same time, which we call a guilt complex, which is always a superiority-striving on the useless side of life. As I have already observed, it means: "I have reached the summit of error" or "My virtue is so lofty that this slight stain upon it is killing me."

However, in this case, I found no indications of the kind, and the man's valuation of honesty as a virtue was not abnormally developed. His depressions were an attempt to show himself superior to his wife. To be depressed in very favorable situations called attention to his good fortune much more than if he had allowed himself to enjoy them. Everyone was surprised at his depression, and he constantly asked himself, "You happy being, why are you depressed when you have everything you want?" The unmanageable wife was the one sorrow in his comfortable life, and he compensated for this by *remembering his victory* in the most difficult phase of his history---when he outstripped his friend and won the woman from him. Loyalty forbade him to rejoice in the money of his dead friend: but he could nevertheless feed upon this ancient triumph by being depressed in the box of the theatre. The more melancholy he was and upon the brighter the occasion, the more he was able to think of his past conquest and to elevate the consciousness of his estate. Deeper enquiries confirmed my conclusion. His friend had died from paralysis after syphilis, a disease which they had both contracted at the same time. My patient was cured, however; and now, surrounded by his healthy wife and six children, could not but recall, together with the triumph over his friend, his conquest of the disease.

Such, then, were his conclusions. In his marriage this man did not feel superior; but at least his wife was the woman his friend had desired, and she had chosen him instead. By contemplating his friend's disaster in a discreet gloom he heightened the sense of victory. Consolation of this nature is on the useless side, however, and tends, as we see, towards disease.

A man of thirty-six came to me for advice about sexual impotence after having tried various treatments. He was a self-made man, in a good position, and physically healthy, but not very well education; and he had a love relation with a well-educated girl. He was a second child between two girls, and had lost both parents at the age of five. He remembered that his family had been very poor, but that he had been a spoilt child, very pretty and quiet, to whom the neighbors liked to give presents; and that he exploited their generosity, behaving like a beggar. One of his earliest remembrances was of walking the streets on Christmas Eve and looking into the shop windows at the Christmas trees destined for *others*. In the orphanage, to which he was transferred at the age of five, he was strictly treated, but his habitual docility and the striving nature he possessed as a second child enabled him to surpass others. His servility stood him in good stead, for he was promoted to be the principal servant of the institution. In this occupation he had sometimes to wait for a long time at an old and deserted railway station in the country; and at these times, when only the humming of the telegraph wires relieved the dead stillness of the night, he felt utterly isolated and alone in a friendless world. He preserved strong memories of this experience.

Often, in later life, he complained of buzzing in the ears, for which no aurist could find the cause. It proved, however, to be quite coherent with his style of life. When he felt isolated, which happened very often, the memory of the humming wires returned with all the liveliness of a hallucination. After this had been explained to him, and he had been a little more socially reconciled and encouraged to marry his sweetheart, the humming ceased.

It is quite usual for children who are brought up in an orphanage to make the strongest efforts to hide the fact, as though it were a disgrace. This man justified his concealment by asserting that many orphans do not succeed in later life. He regarded failure in life as the inexorable fate of orphans, which gave him his tense and striving attitude in business. For the same reason he halted before the problem of love and marriage, and his neurotic impotence was the immediate result of this profound hesitation.

This man's style of life, as we have seen, was to be a beggar. In business, however, (as previously in the orphanage), begging had paved the way to domination. In business he enjoyed nothing more than a begging attitude on the part of his subordinates. He was only a beggar until he could be a conqueror, and he played the second role as heartily as the first. There is no need to drag in the idea of "ambivalent" characteristics, as some psychologists would do immediately. Rightly understood, the whole of this mental process---working from below to above, expressing inferiority but compensating with superiority---is not ambivalence but a dynamic unity. Only if it is not understood as a whole do we see it as two contradictory and warring entities. In his business we find the man with a "superiority complex;" but if he were to lose his position and have to start again he would promptly go back to the expression of inferiority and make capital out of it. In his love-problem he was, for the time being, upon the submissive line of action, begging for love, but trying to reach domination. His sweetheart like him and wanted to marry him, so she responded to his hesitancy by taking up more and more of a begging attitude towards him! He was well on the way, in fact, towards getting the upper hand with her, and frequently did so in minor matters.

He had still not overcome his hesitant attitude but after having had his style of life explained to him and having been encouraged, his state improved and his impotence disappeared. He then set up a second resistance, which was that every woman attracted him, and these polygamous desires were an escape from marriage. At this time he dreamt that he was lying upon a couch in my room, and he became sexually excited and had pollution.

There is no couch in my consulting room. My patients sit, stand, or move about as they please; but the couch in this dream was in the room of a doctor who had formerly treated him for a few months. This dream extracted a confession which he had never made before. He believed that both the other doctor and I belonged to a secret society, the object of which was to cure patients such as him by providing sexual intercourse for them. For this reason he had been trying to find out which of my woman patients would be chosen for him. The fact that he missed the couch in my room was like an accusation against me. I was not the right doctor. He had come to me *begging,* expecting me to settle his difficulties, take over his responsibilities, and to assist him to escape from marriage. My collusion in stopping his marriage was to go to the length of being his procurer, a fantasy to which his fright, his impotence and his polygamous tendencies were all contributory. Failing that, he would solve his sexual problem by pollutions, as others might resort to masturbation or perversion.

He married, but it was difficult to prevent him from developing a tyrannical attitude towards his conciliatory wife.

Another case of the begging attitude was brought to me by a man of fifty years old, the youngest of a very poor family. He had been indulged by his mother and the neighbors because of an apparent weakness, and early developed a very timid manner. He always tried to lean upon his mother and to appeal to the sympathies of weak persons, especially in difficult times when he exhibited great depression and cried until help came. We have already seen the use which is made of crying by both children and adults. This ma's earliest memory was that he had fallen down and hurt himself. The choice of this incident to treasure in the memory out of all possible recollections is explained only by his desire to impress himself with the danger of life. His technique of life was to perfect himself in the role of a beggar, to attract support, consolation and favor by calling attention to his infirmities. Every incident was made into a matter for tears.

As a child the man had been very backward in learning to talk, and his mother, as always happens in such cases, had to attend all the more carefully to him to find out what he wanted. In this way he was able to feel like a little king. As Lessing said, "The real beggar is the only real king." He became a master of the begging art, expressing his inferiority in the power of his plight over others; "How can I make the poor weak child a king?" was the problem of life as he saw it, and he answered it by elaborating his own individual and essentially mendicant style.

This is one way of living, and so early an apprentice becomes a past master of its technique. He will not change it, unless the cost becomes clearly too great, when he may be brought to see that his childish method is inadequate for present problems. Otherwise change is impossible for him, because he has all his life ascribed every success to the begging act and every failure to lack of proficiency in it. Such a goal as this is not calculable from the inheritance or the environmental stimuli, or the child's individual conception of the future is the dominant causal factor, and this patient's conception was such that whenever he wanted to attain superiority he had to make a mistake or get himself into a mess of some kind. All his feelings were appropriately ordered towards the goal of thus getting something for nothing.

After a few days' treatment this man was very much impressed by what I told him, and he sent me a pamphlet he had written some years before. It was entitled "An Association of Beggars."

Habitual criticism, anger, and envy are indications of a useless striving for superiority. The are motions towards the suppression of others, either in reality or fancy, so as to be supreme. Useful criticism of a constructive tendency is always in some comprehensible relation with social feeling, but where the motive is merely relative self-elevation by lowering or degrading others the tendency is neurotic. Neurotics often make use of the truth in order to undervalue others, and it is important, when checking a neurotic criticism, not to overlook the element of truth in the observation.

Anger is usually a sign that the person who is angry feels at a disadvantage--- at least temporarily. Neurotics use it freely as a weapon to intimidate those who are responsible for them. Although occasional anger is an understandable attitude in certain critical relations, when it is habitual it is a sign of anxiety, of impatience, or of feelings of helplessness or suppression. Patients of this habit are often very clever in the selection of vulnerable points to attack in others, and are also great strategists in preparing such situations that they put others slightly in the wrong before they begin a fight.

Envy is universally an expression of inferiority, though it may sometimes be a stimulus to useful action. In neurosis, however, envy of another's good does not go so far as practical emulation. It stops like a tram before the journey's end, leaving the patient irritable and depressed.

In a certain popular music-hall turn the "strong man" comes on and lifts an enormous weight with care and immense difficulty, and then, during the hearty applause of the audience, a child comes in and give away the fraud by carrying the dummy weight off with one hand. There are plenty of neurotics who swindle us with such weights, and who are adept in the art of appearing overburdened. They could really dance with the load under which they stagger like Atlas bearing the world on his shoulders. Yet it cannot be denied that neurotics feel their burden very keenly. They may be continually tired. They may sometimes perspire very freely, and their symptoms may suggest the possibility of tuberculosis. Every movement is very tiring, and they often suffer from palpitation of the heart. Usually depressed, they continually demand more zealous care from others, and yet find it continually insufficient.

I had a case of agoraphobia (fear of open places) in a man of fifty-three, who found that he could not breathe properly when he was in company with others. He was living with his sister, and had a son whose characteristics were very much like his own. When I investigated the cause of this man's unusual concentration of interest upon himself, I found that he had been orphaned at ten years of age, and there were two elder brothers in the home. It was when they quarreled that he had had his first attack. This indicates the tendency to meet a difficult situation by breakdown. The man was the youngest of a family of eight, and education by his grandfather. A grandparent is almost invariable a spoiling foster-parent. The patient's father and mother had been happily married; the father was superior and the mother rather cold, so the boy was attracted to the father.

A child's first good-fellowship in life is always with the mother if she is present, so that if it inclines more towards the father we may assume that the mother does not give the child sufficient attention; she is probably unkind, otherwise occupied, or more attentive to a younger child. In such circumstances the child turns to the father if possible, and in this case the resistance to the mother was very marked.

People are often unable correctly to remember their earliest situations, but experience enables us to reconstruct their circumstances from comparatively slight indications. One man said he could only remember three incidents from early childhood which had deeply impressed his memory. The first of these occurred at the age of three, when his brother died. He was with his grandfather on the day of the funeral, when his mother returned from the cemetery, sorrowful and sobbing, and when the grandfather kissed her, whispering some words of kindness and consolation, the boy saw that his mother smiled a little. He was very much upset by this, and for long afterwards resented his mother's smile on the day that her child was buried. A second memory that he had preserved was of a friendly reproof from his uncle, who had asked him, "Why are you always so rough towards your mother? A third remembrance from the same period of his life related to a quarrel between his parents, after which he turned to his father, saying, "You were brave, daddy, like a soldier!" He depended much upon his father, and was pampered by him: and he always admired his father more than his mother, although he realized that his mother's character was of a better type.

All these memories, which appeared to date from his third or fourth year, showed the fighting attitude towards the mother. The first and the third remembrances were clearly ruled by his goal, which was to criticize the mother and to justify him in turning towards the father. His reason for turning away from the mother is easy to guess: he had been too much spoilt by her to be able to put up with the younger brother's appearance upon the scene,---the same younger brother who figures in an apparently innocent manner in the first recollection.

This patient had married at the age of twenty-four, and marriage had disappointed him, because of his wife's demands upon him. Marriage between two spoilt children is always unhappy, because both remain in the expectant attitude and neither begins to give. This man went through varied experiences and tried different occupations without success. His wife was not sympathetic, and complained that she would rather be the mistress of a rich man than the wife of a poor one, and the union ended in divorce. Although the man was not really poor, he was very stingy towards his wife, and she divorced him by way of revenge.

After his divorce he turned misogynistic, and developed homosexual tendencies; he had no actual relationships with men, but felt a desire to embrace men. This homosexual trend was as usual a kind of cowardliness. He had been twice defeated and baulked by women---first by his mother and afterwards by his wife---and he was now trying to divert his sexuality towards men so as to evade women and further possibilities of humiliation. To confirm himself in such a tendency a man can easily falsify the past by recollecting and magnifying the importance of certain common experiences which are then taken by him as proofs of inborn homosexual tendencies. Thus, this patient remembered that he had been in love with a schoolmaster, and that in h is youth a boy friend had seduced him into mutual masturbation.

The determining factor in this man's behavior was that he was a spoiled child who wanted everything for nothing. His agoraphobia resulted from the fear of meeting a woman on the one hand, and on the other hand it was also dangerous to meet men, because of possible erotic inclination towards them. In this tension of feelings about going out of doors he developed stomach and respiratory troubles. Many nervous people begin to swallow air when they get into a state of tension, which causes flatulence, stomach trouble, anxiety and palpitation, besides affecting the breathing. When I made him realize that this was his condition, he asked the usual question: "What shall I do not to swallow air?" Sometimes I reply: "I can tell you how to mount a horse, but I can't tell you how *not* to mount a horse." Or sometimes I advise: "If you want to go out, and feel in a conflict about it, swallow some air quickly." This man, like some other patients, swallowed air even in sleep, but after my advice he began to control himself, and discontinued the habit. Air-swallowing at night and vomiting upon waking occur in these patients who suffer from stomach trouble and anxiety when they are bothered by a difficulty which must be confronted upon the following day. The patient in question began to recuperate when he came to understand that, as a pampered child, he expected continually to take without giving. He now realized that he had first stopped his normal sexual life, looking for something easier, and afterwards adopted a fictitious homosexuality in which he also stopped short of danger, the whole process being an elaborate way of coming to a standstill. The last obstacle to be removed was his fear of mixing with strangers who did not care for him, such as the people in the streets. This fear is produced by the deeper motive of agoraphobia, which is to exclude all situations in which one is not the center of attention.

The Inefficient Wife

Harry Stack Sullivan, M.D.

Harry Stack Sullivan's (1892-1949) chief emphasis in psychoanalysis was on the critical importance of interpersonal relations. He did not believe that personality could be separated from interpersonal situations and that therefore the only thing that could be interpreted would be interpersonal behavior. Thus he did not consider the individual himself as the object of study but rather the individual's interaction with people around him. He felt that even a hermit carries with him his memories of relationships with others. Like Adler and Horney with whom he joined in de-emphasizing the role of instinct, Sullivan saw the field of psychoanalysis as being closely allied to social psychology. In his therapy he stressed the interview and the technique of the interview. He felt that the skill of the analyst in person to person interviews was of fundamental importance. Sullivan was the leader of the William Alanson White Psychiatric Foundation.

Like most leading practitioners, Sullivan spent a great deal of time in teaching. The case that follows then is not a case that Sullivan himself treated, but rather his advice to a student on how to deal with a specific problem which the patient had presented. The advice that Sullivan gives is focused on the interpersonal relations between the patient and her husband.

Sullivan commented on the therapeutic problems of eliciting and interpreting communication. The therapist's problem is to find a way to relate to what is communicative in the patient's productions. Such communications are, of course, fragmentary, and therefore Sullivan's comments on the problems presented by his colleagues are fragmentary. For this reason, we have included h ere, as a case illustration of his therapeutic approach, his comments on the case of a schizoid (unsocial, introverted) who---while relatively inarticulate----was able to communicate something of her problems to her therapist.

* Sullivan, Harry Stack. (1959). The Inefficient. In Greenwald, Harold (Ed.), *Great Cases in Psychoanalysis*, 201-208. New York: J. Aronson. Reprinted by permission.

The case is then that of a schizoid---a young married woman who is extremely tense, apprehensive, and inarticulate. Her main difficulty, as she describes it, is that she is an inefficient housekeeper who "lazes" most of the day away. She looks upon herself as a failure. Treatment in the case has bogged down, after several months, and the question raised in the presentation of the problem is, What techniques can be used to get things moving again?

The patient is a product of an extremely traumatic childhood, during which she was deserted by her mother and later abandoned to the care of the maternal grandparents by her father, who was himself unreliable. In the grandparents' home, she was treated more or less as a servant; but as she was very gifted intellectually, she managed to finish college and earn a Ph.D. in economics. She married a fellow-student in the same field and became a housewife. Her husband is extremely critical of her as a housekeeper, and has frequently told her about romantic entanglements with other women, always presenting these women to her as romantic ideals. During the ten years of marriage, in which two children have been born, the relationship has steadily worsened, with the husband threatening divorce and immersing himself in his work, and the wife leading an increasingly inactive and isolated life.

Sullivan: I have a number of considerations in mind, the first of which is to get the patient to notice that, even before her husband's recent promotion, they were perfectly able to afford at least a part-time maid. And as the patient finds herself showing, I suppose, unrecognized resentment of the burdens of her life every morning, I would start therapy by asking, "Well, why haven't you a maid?" And I want to know, in a fashion that makes it perfectly clear to me why they don't have a maid. If there isn't any adequate explanation, I would then ask, "How about getting one?"

I would go on by saying that her training seems to be rather exceptional for a person who has accepted a purely domestic role all these years and that, under the circumstances, her feeling of helplessness to get along in the morning rather encourages me than otherwise. Has she never heard of a woman who preferred something else to domestic preoccupations? I would ask, "Has this never occurred to you, or has it occurred to you as something morbid and strange?" (I would suppose it had actually never occurred to her at all). Then I would want to know how it happened that she went through college and took a graduate degree in economics; since women economists are not the most common thing in the world, I would point out that it looks to me as if she must have followed some natural bent. Now of course it may come out that she did it because great-aunt Catherine recommended it, something of that kind, but that immediately excited me about great-aunt Catherine, who seems to have had ideas, you know

What I am attempting to do here is to get her mind open a little bit to the fact that not only is she in a disagreeable situation, but she finds it disagreeable. And by sort of hounding her to prove that she is an exceptional woman with an exceptional education---and an exceptional inclination to go on suffering an impossibly silent domestic involvement---I am simply hoping to crack the shell that surrounds all her feelings. Until she raises her sights to something, I think that an attempt to get her clear on how much she resents her husband all that would be merely an intellectual exercise. She would catch on very quickly, and nothing would happen, except possibly that she would feel that things were getting a little worse. But I start the other way---if I get her to wondering what the hell she has been doing all this time and why she has never felt entitled to object to any of it---then I can anticipate that she will be equal to feeling some very real anger at times.

I would sort of hound her with commonplace things, not because I care too much about the facts themselves at the moment, but because I want her mind to being to reach a little outside the magic circle of insulation in which she has been living all this time. Otherwise, we are just going to get some fine thinking. There must be an outward movement of her interest, a beginning suspicion, "Well, this really wasn't all necessary and inevitable," before I can expect her to do much real observing of the play of interpersonal movement that probably has characterized her, as it does all of us, all her life. The very lack of outward signs of suffering indicates how early she accepted as fit and inevitable that she should be the slave in her maternal grandparents' home and that she should in some fashion be kept from associations with other people, presumably because she wasn't good enough or trustworthy enough or just didn't have sense enough. I would lead her to talk a little bit about how she explained this tacit ban on her developing ordinary relationship, and I would expect that she would then hint of her acceptance of her unworthiness for a free life. At this point I would ask, "Well, now, how do you explain college and the rather original choice of subject that you carried through so well?" Then, after I had listened to a good deal of that, I would come down like a ton of bricks on economics. "Well, how about economics? Why has that interest vanished from your life without a trace? You take a Ph.D., in economics, marry an economist, and as far as I can discover, from then on research in economics has been left exclusively to him. Did that suit him? Was that what he insisted on? Did you just accommodate his feeling that it was awkward to have a wife who knew something about his business, or what?"

Thus, by that remote route, I hope that I would begin to get her resentments toward her husband. They will be so far back in experience, you see, that immediate explosive danger will be diminished by the time she gets anywhere near the present. It seems to me that the big problem for the therapist in dealing with a person like this is to close in on areas that inevitably must open her mind to a reassessment of what has been taken more or less for granted as a continuing act of God.

The thing I would be determined that this woman should tell me sometime or other is that she has discussed with her husband just what he had in mind in advising her in long, ecstatic letters of his great love for another woman some years back, and I would try to get her to look at that simply as a piece of research or investigation. "Now here is a very interesting research problem," I would say, "One's husband goes off and becomes terribly enamored of some goddess and writes his wife all about it. Now what was he doing? What did he think he was doing?" She doesn't know, of course, she hasn't had any experience in being anybody's husband. Then I ask her, "But why not find out?" Here again, I hope that I would be pushing on something far enough away and essentially intriguing enough so that she will rather calmly ask him a few questions. I think they will be very profoundly

197

embarrassing questions. My notion of why a husband does things like that is not to the husband's credit at all. And maybe she will have the privilege of seeing him quite disconcerted in explaining this, and maybe that will introduce the idea to her, "Well, this bird who has always said he was horribly insecure and so on, *is* horribly insecure. Why is he picking on me then? Why should I be his whipping-boy?" And I am pretty sure that he will respond very hastily to good management on her part. I may be wholly wrong, but he sounds to me like a person who has been getting away with murder because he was fortunate enough to find one of these incredible women to whom it has never occurred that there is any fun in life or any give-and-take, and I think one starts her education in which I call the *middle distance*, before college and through early marriage, winding up with the great love that came into the husband's life and had to be embalmed in letters to his wife. I do not take an interest in current events with her husband, first, because I wouldn't know what on earth they meant, for she is a poor observer and has carefully looked the other way a great part of her life, and, second, because I wouldn't know what foolishness she might think I wanted her to engage in. You see, I particularly don't want her to get the impression that I think she ought to rough-house him and throw some of the bric-a-brac at him, because the poor man might take flight. He might become completely undone. And I am pretty certain that he is insecure enough so that she will find, to her great astonishment and permanent gratitude, that she can manage with him if she proceeds slowly enough along the line I have suggested.

I am not after anything here that is going to be very difficult to recall. It would be well within the realm of reasonable recall for all of us. What I am trying to do with the middle distance is literally to lift her eyes about this tiny little irregular area in which she lives. Pat of that will be done by getting her to review this utterly slavery existence that was so convenient for the relations with whom she lived in her girlhood. Why did she never suspect that anything else was possible? Where has she been all her life? What was the doom, the inherent handicap that made her so practically resigned at all stages of her life to what I think is best summed up as an almost complete lack of any fun? There wouldn't be anything at all odd about this woman if she had been born a century earlier in middle New England. She might in that setting have had a placid life. But a hundred little times she seems never to have noticed that a life for her in the world of today was a poor imitation of what other people in similar circumstances had been having all this time.

Now I approach the situation in this way because I don't see anything malignant anywhere in it. The husband sounds more like an insecure tyrant than anything else. Maybe he is also schizoid. He also has apparently no grasp on the principle of fun in life than to have an almost classically autistic love affair every now and then; I wouldn't be a bit surprised if some of the women he has been so enamored of have known nothing about it. Also, I do not feel completely discouraged about his perhaps ultimately finding that psychotherapy for himself, though undesirable, is inescapable. I think that he, too, can lift his sights a little bit without any serious upheaval of personality and without this marital group breaking up. I would hope that together they might even emerge from this sort of numb dullness that almost asphyxiates them at time, and get a little bit of pleasure out of life.

Chapter Eight
Research in the Dispositional Model

"This is a test of your creative imagination. I shall show you a picture and I want you to make up a plot or a story for which it might be used as an illustration. What is the relation of the individuals in the picture? What happened to them? What are their present thoughts and feelings? What will be the outcome? Do your very best. Since I am asking you to indulge your literary imagination, you may make your story as long and as detailed as you wish."

Henry Murray

Letters from Jenny *

Gordon Allport

Given Allport's emphasis on the individual, how does one go about attempting to understand a specific personality? Allport believed that one of the best methods was to use personal documents such as diaries, autobiographies, letters or interviews. Allport's most thorough use of personal documents to describe an individual's personality was a collection of 301 letters written by Jenny Grove Masterson (a pseudonym) during an 11 year period. The final version of this study was published as *Letters from Jenny* in 1965, although Allport had worked on the case for a number of years prior to that time.

Jenny was born in Ireland in 1868 and moved to Canada when she was 5. She had five younger sisters and one younger brother, all of whom were very dependent on her because her father had died when she was 18. Jenny outraged her family when she married a divorced railway inspector. She and her husband moved to Chicago, where she described life as boring. Her husband died in 1897, when she was 29 years old. Shortly after her husband's death, Jenny gave birth to her only child, whom she named Ross. She worked hard and devoted herself to Ross. When Ross reached puberty she enrolled him in an expensive boarding school. In order to afford this private school, she took a job as a librarian and lived primarily on milk and cereal in a small windowless room. Until Ross was 17, he and his mother were very close, but at that time he left home to go to Princeton. In his sophomore year Ross enlisted in the army, in the Ambulance Corps. Before he went overseas to France, Jenny visited him at Princeton and met two of his friends, Glenn and Isabel. It was with Glenn and Isabel that Jenny was later to correspond.

When Ross returned home, he had changed completely and, except for finishing his degree at Princeton, his life was characterized by a series of failures and quarrels with his mother. The most intense quarrel followed Jenny's discovery of Ross's secret marriage. On this Allport commented, "On his first visit to her

* Allport, Gordon. (2003). Letters from Jenny. In Hergenhahn, B. R. and M. H. Olson. (2003). *An Introduction to Theories of Personality (Sixth Edition).* Upper Saddle River, New Jersey: Prentice Hall/Pearson Education, 218-220. Reprinted by permission.

(Jenny) following her discovery she drove him out of her room with violent denunciations and a threat to have him arrested if he ever tried to see her again" (1965, p. 6). Following this encounter, Jenny contacted Ross's old friends, Glenn and Isabel, who were now married and teaching in an n eastern college town. They offered to "keep in touch' with Jenny, and the result was 301 letters The correspondence started in March 1926, when Jenny was 58, and continued until October 1937, when Jenny died, at the age of 70. She outlived her son Ross by 8 years.

By 1928, Ross had abandoned his wife and begun a relationship with another woman named Marie. In a letter written in 1929, Jenny mentioned Ross's poor health. He suffered from an ear infection and, when they operated, the doctors found a tumor on the inner ear and an abscess on the outer tissue covering of the brain. Ross did not recover from his illness and died shortly afterward. In a letter written toward the end of 1929, Jenny blames Marie, who she refers to as a "chip" (whore), for Ross's death.

> My affairs. Oh, they are all in turmoil. The chip lady (although)
> all dissolved in tears, and of course heartbroken, is not too liquid
> to forget that material things count in this mundane sphere, and
> lo! She claimed Ross's clothes, and Ross's car. (She claims to be
> Ross's closest relative.) If she is Ross's nearest relative it is she
> who will received the (Veteran's administrations) compensation,
> and that would be tragic enough to make one die of laughter.
> She has only known him 6 months. February was the beginning
> of their "Great Romance"---dirty and low as they are made—
> the low contemptible street dog. She killed Ross---morally and
> physically. (Allport, 1965, pp. 73-74).

Following Ross's funeral and cremation, Jenny was reported to have said, "The body is consumed, now we'll have a good steak dinner" (recollection of Isabel, in Allport, 1965, p. 153).

In 1931, Jenny entered a home for women where she lived until her death. The superintendent of the home reported that she had become unbearably difficult during the year prior to her death. For example, she swept her dinner on the floor if it displeased her, and she hit one of her fellow boarders over the head with a pail. The superintendent considered moving her to an institution for the insane shortly before she died.

Allport had 36 judges read Jenny's letters in sequence and they, along with Allport, used 198 trait names to describe Jenny. But when synonymous traits were lumped together, it was observed that Jenny could be described accurately using eight trait names. They were:
1. Quarrelsome---suspicious
2. Self-Centered
3. Independent
4. Dramatic
5. Aesthetic—Artistic
6. Aggressive

7. Cynical—Morbid

8. Sentimental

Using a computer, Jeffrey Paige (1966), one of Allport's students, performed a complex statistical factor analysis of Jenny's letters and isolated eight "factors" characterizing them.

1. Aggression
2. Possessiveness
3. Need for Affiliation
4. Need for Autonomy
5. Need for Familial Acceptance
6. Sexuality
7. Sentience (love of art, literature, etc.)
8. Martyrdom

On reviewing Paige's study, Allport concluded that the automated approach yielded about the same traits as did his longhand approach. There is probably no better example of what Allport meant by idiographic research than his analysis of Jenny's letters. It is because of this type of research that Allport has been accused of being more of an artist than a scientist.

Study of Expressive Behavior and Values

Besides his studies of religion, prejudice, humor, and his extensive idiographic study of Jenny through her letters, Allport also investigated expressive behavior and values. His studies of both expressive behavior and values reclaimed his emphasis on the importance of the individual. His research on expressive behavior, for example, investigated a person's unique "facial expressions, style of walking, speech mannerism, and handwriting" (Allport & Cantral, 1934; Allport & Vernon, 1933). His *Study of Values* first published wit Vernon in 1931 is now in its third edition. To study values, Allport and his collaborators (Allport, Vernon & Lindzey, 1960) devised a scale that attempted to determine the extent to which a person emphasized certain values in his or her life. Allport observed that the scale of values, actually combines nomothetic and idiographic methodologies. "We being with an instrument that measures six common traits (values) but end with a profile that is strictly personal and individual" (quoted in Evans, 1976, p 211). The following six values measured by the scale of values were first proposed by Eduard Spranger (1882-1963) in 1913:

1. <u>Theoretical:</u> "The person emphasizing this value is primarily concerned with the search for truth.

2. <u>Economic:</u> "The person emphasizing this value is very pragmatic and interested in the relevance of knowledge.

3. <u>Aesthetic:</u> The persona emphasizing this value is strongly inclined toward artistic experiences.

4. <u>Social:</u> The person emphasizing this value gives high priority to developing and maintaining warm human relationships.

5. <u>Political:</u> The person emphasizing this value is primarily interested in attaining power.

6. <u>Religious:</u> The person emphasizing this value gives great importance to seeking unity and harmony in the universe.

Allport, Vernon and Lindzey (1960) reported that the scale produced the expected results, for example, clergymen scored highest on the religious value, art students scored highest on the aesthetic value, and business students scored highest on the economic value.

Explorations in Personality[*]
Henry A. Murray

In the field of personality tests and measurement, you will find several projective techniques including such tools as the Rorschach Inkblot Test, Holtzman Inkblot Test, Blacky Picture Cards and Sentence Completions. Henry A. Murray, Director of the Harvard Psychological Clinic and Father of Modern Need Theory, and his assistant, Christiana D. Morgan, created a very unique form of projective tests. They named their instrument the Thematic Apperception Test, or "TAT," which focused entirely on the content of the subject's interpretations of 20 pictures of people in various social situations. Specifically, the test consists of black-and-white works of art depicting people in various ambiguous circumstances. The first set of ten cards consists of pictures that are normal; the latter set of ten depicts more bizarre scenes. It is the task of the individual to create a story about each scene: to tell what is happening, what are the issues and how are they resolved. Murray believed that the person would project onto the cards unconscious revelations about his own life. Hence, the stories are analyzed for their manifest and, more importantly, latent content which contains hidden unconscious conflicts and themes.

The underlying theory of this test is that when a person observes behavior in a pictorial manner, he will interpret that behavior not only from the available clues but also from a perspective which reveals his own unique experiences in life. In "projecting" onto the cards his own unique experiences in life, we learn much about the individual's fears, motives, desires, and conflicts. For example, imagine you see a young boy, sitting at a table, contemplating a violin. You might say that the young boy is angry and mad at his parents for making him take violin lessons. He is staring at the instrument and thinking of a way to get out of his practice so that he can go and play with his friends. Or, you might say that the young boy is deep in thought, contemplating his forthcoming debut and performance at Symphony Hall. As you can see, these two stories are quite different and based upon the unique perspective or subjective interpretation of the person creating the story. Even today, the Thematic Apperception Test is used by psychotherapists, researchers and organizational psychologists.

---

[*] **Murray, Henry. (1938). Explorations in Personality.** *Explorations in Personality,* **531-545. London: Oxford University Press (US). In Hock, Roger R. (1995).** *Forty Studies That Changed Psychology: Explorations in the History of Psychological Research (2nd Ed).* **New Jersey: Prentice-Hall. Reprinted by permission.**

Theoretical Propositions

At the most basic level, the theory underlying the TAT, like that of the Rorschach test, is that people's behavior is driven by unconscious forces. Implicit in this notion is an acceptance of the principles of psychodynamic psychology developed originally by Freud. In this view, unconscious conflicts must be exposed for accurate diagnosis and successful treatment of psychological problems to take place. This was the purpose of Rorschach's inkblot test and it was also the goal of Murray's TAT.

Morgan and Murray wrote, "The purpose of this procedure is to stimulate literary creativity and thereby evoke fantasies that reveal covert and unconscious complexes" (p. 530). The way they conceived of this process was that a person would be shown ambiguous drawings of human behavior. In trying to explain the situation, the subject would become less self-conscious and less concerned about being observed by the therapist. This would, in turn, cause the person to become less defensive and reveal inner wishes, fears, and past experiences that might have been repressed. Murray also pointed out that part of the theoretical foundation for this test was that "a great deal of written fiction was the conscious or unconscious expression of the author's experiences or fantasies" (p. 531).

Method

In the test's original conceptualization, subjects were asked to guess the events leading up to the scene depicted in the drawing and what they thought the outcome of the scene would be. After testing this method, it was determined that a great deal more about the psychology of subjects could be obtained if they were simply asked to make up a story about the picture, rather than asked to guess the facts surrounding it.

The pictures themselves were developed to stimulate fantasies and the subjects about conflicts and important events in their own experiences. Therefore, it was decided that each picture should involve at least one person with whom the subject could easily identify. Through trial and error with several hundred pictures, a final set of 20 was chosen. Since the TAT is in common usage today, many believe that widespread publication of the pictures might compromise its validity. However, it is difficult to understand the test without being able to see the type of drawings chosen. Therefore, figure 1, is one of the original drawings that was under consideration but was not ultimately chosen as one of the final 20.

An early study of the TAT was conducted by Morgan and Murray and they reported in Murray's 1958: "The subjects for that study were men between the ages of 20 and 30. Each subject was seated in a comfortable chair facing away from the experimenter (as has been commonly practiced by psychotherapists when administering the TAT). These are the exact instructions given to each subject:

This is a test of your creative imagination. I shall show you a picture and I want you to make up a plot or a story for which it might be used as an illustration. What is the relation of the individuals in the picture? What happened to them? What are their present thoughts and feelings? What will be the outcome? Do your very best. Since I am asking you to indulge your literary imagination, you may make your story as long and as detailed as you wish (p. 532).

The experimenter handed the subject each picture in succession and took notes on what the subject said for each one. Each subject was given one hour. Due to the time limitations, most subjects only completed stories for about 15 of the 20 drawings.

A few days later the subjects returned and were interviewed about their stories in order to disguise the true purpose of the study; subjects were told that the purpose of the research was to compare their creative experiences with those of famous writers. Subjects were reminded of their responses to the pictures and were asked to explain what their sources for their stories were. They were also given a free-association test, in which they were to say the first thing that came to mind in response to words spoken by the experimenter. These exercises were designed to determine to what extent the stories the subjects made up about the drawings reflected their own personal experiences, conflicts, desires, and so on.

Figure 1. From Henry A. Murray, Thematic Apperception Test. Cambridge University Press. Copyright © 1943 by the President and Fellows of Harvard by Henry A. Murray. Reprinted by permission of the publishers.

Results and Discussion

Murray and Morgan reported two main findings from this early study of the TAT. The first was the discovery that the stories the subjects made up for the picture came from four sources: (1) books and movies, (2) real-life events involving a friend or a relative, (3) experiences in the subject's own life and (4) the subject's conscious or unconscious fantasies (see p. 533 of the original study).

The second and more important finding was that the subjects clearly projected their own personal, emotional and psychological existence into their stories. One such example reported by the authors was that most of the subjects who were students identified the person in one of the drawings as a student, but none of the non-student subjects did so. In another example the subject's father was a ship's carpenter, and the subject had strong desires to travel and see the world. This fantasy appeared in his interpretations of several of the drawings. For instance, when shown a drawing of two workers in conversation the subject's story was, "These two fellows are a pair of adventurers. They always manage to meet in out-of-the-way places. They are now in India. They have heard of a new revolution in South American and they are planning how they can get there...In the end they work their way there on a freighter" (p. 534). Murray reports that, without exception, every person who participated in the study injected aspects of their personalities into their stories.

To further illustrate how the TAT reflects personal characteristics, the authors report one subject in detail. "Virt" was a Russian Jew who had immigrated to the United States after terrible childhood experiences during World War I, including persecution, hunger, and separation from his mother. Picture number 13 of the TAT was given the following written description by Murray and Morgan: "On the floor against the couch is the huddled form of a boy whose head is bowed on his right arm. Beside him on the floor is an object which resembles a revolver" (p. 536). Virt's story about his drawing is as follows:

Some great trouble has occurred. Someone he loved has shot herself. Probably this is his mother. She may have done it out of poverty. He being fairly grown up sees the misery of it all and would like to shoot himself. But he is young and braces up after a while. For some time he lives in misery, the first few months thinking of death (p. 536).

It is interesting to compare this story with other, more recent stories made up about the same drawing.

A 35-year-old junior high school teacher: *"I think that this is someone who has been put in prison for something he did not do. He has denied that he committed any crime and has been fighting and fighting his case in the courts, but he has given up. Now he is completely exhausted, depressed, and hopeless. He made a fake gun to try to escape, but he knows this won't work either"* *(author's files).*

A 16-year-old high school student: *"The girl is playing hide-and-seek, probably with her brothers. She is counting from one to a hundred. She is sad and tired because she is never able to win and always has to be 'it.' It looks like the boys were playing some other game before because there's a toy gun here."(Author's files).*

You don't have to be a psychotherapist to make some predictions about the inner conflicts, motives, or desires that these three people might be projecting onto that one drawing. These examples also demonstrate the remarkably diverse responses that are possible on the TAT.

Murray and Morgan reported that, in addition to insights into unconscious conflicts, the TAT was useful in revealing specific hidden characteristics such as aggressive tendencies, creativity, and achievement motivation. Finally, the researchers measured each subject's level of optimism by rating the outcomes of their stories on a scale from -2 (very negative) to +2 (very positive). To find a subject's "optimism score," the ratings were totaled and divided by the number of stories. It was reported that the overall optimism or pessimism score for each subject coincided with other information obtained in the interviews.

Criticisms and Related Research

Although the TAT uses stimuli that are very different from Rorschach's inkblot test, it has been criticized on the same grounds of poor reliability and validity (see the reading on Rorschach's test for additional discussion of these issues). The most serious reliability problem for the TAT is that different clinicians offer differing interpretations of the same set of TAT responses. Some have suggested that therapists may unknowingly inject their own unconscious characteristics onto the subject's descriptions of the drawings. In other words, the interpretation of the TAT might be a projective test for the clinician who is administering it.

In terms of validity (that is, the extent to which the TAT truly measures what it is designed to measure), several types of criticisms have been cited frequently. If the test measures underlying psychological processes, then it should be able to distinguish between, say, normal people and people who are mentally ill, or between different types of psychological conditions. However, research has shown that it fails to make such distinctions. In a study by Eron (1950), the TAT was administered to two groups of male veterans. Some were students in college and others were patients in a psychiatric hospital. When the results of the TAT were analyzed, there were no significant differences found between the two groups or among psychiatric patients with different illnesses.

Other research has questioned the ability of the TAT to predict behavior. For example, if a person includes a great deal of violence in the stories and plots used to describe the drawings, this does not differentiate between aggression that merely exists in the subject's fantasies and the potential for real violent behavior.

For some people, it is possible to fantasize about aggression without ever expressing violent behavior, while for others; aggressive fantasy will predict actual violence. Since TAT responses do not indicate which category a particular person falls, the test is of little value in predicting aggressive tendencies (see Anastasi, 1982, pp. 587-88).

Another basic and very important criticism of the TAT (which could be made of the Rorschach inkblot technique as well) relates to whether the projective hypothesis itself is valid. The assumption underlying the TAT is that subjects' stories about the drawings reveal something about their stable, unconscious processes about *who they are.* There is scientific evidence to suggest, however, that responses to projective tests such as the Rorschach and TAT may depend upon temporary and situational factors. What this means is that if you are given the TAT on Monday, just after work, when you've had a big fight with your boss, and then again on Saturday, just after you've returned from a relaxing day at the beach, the stories you make up for the drawings might be completely different on the two occasions. Critics argue that, to the extent that the stories are different, the TAT has only tapped into your temporary state and not your "real" underlying self.

As a demonstration of this criticism, numerous studies have found variations in TAT performance relating to the following list of influences, hunger, lack of sleep, drug use, anxiety level, frustration, verbal ability, characteristics of the person administering the test, the attitude of the subject about the testing situation, and the subject's cognitive abilities. In light of these findings, Ann Anastasi, one of the leading authorities on psychological testing has written: "Many types of research have tended to cast doubt on the projective hypothesis. There is ample evidence that alternative explanations may account as well or better for the individual's responses to unstructured test stimuli" (Anastasi, 1982, p. 589)

Recent Applications

Recently, Murray's research and the TAT have been cited and incorporated in numerous studies for which assessment of personality characteristics is a factors (see the Conclusion section below for a discussion of the efficacy of this strategy). Forty-three such articles in professional psychology and related journals appeared in 1993 alone. One of these was a fascinating study that attempted to relate personality in childhood to a person's adult health status and life (Friedman, et. al., 1993). Using data from a 20-year longitudinal study conducted in the 1920s and '30s that included TAT assessments, the researchers claim to have found evidence that "childhood personality is related to health" (Friedman, et. al., 1993, p. 176). Examples of other recent studies employing Murray's concepts include the assessment of personality in relation to people's opinions about current controversial political topics (Reimann, et. al. 1993), and the use of TAT techniques in understanding the motivation behind suicide and suicide ideation (Shneidman, 1993).

Conclusion

One of the most remarkable aspects of projective tests such as the TAT and the Rorschach inkblot test is that in spite of a massive body of evidence condemning them as invalid, unreliable, and possibly based on faulty assumptions, they are to this day among the most frequently used psychological tests. The fact that clinicians continue to be enthusiastic about these tools while experimental psychologists grow increasingly wary is a key point of contention between these two groups. How can this contradiction be reconciled? The most commonly argued answer to this question is that the way the TAT and the Rorschach test are actually used in psychotherapy is not as tests at all, but rather as extensions of the usual interviews that occur between clinicians and their patients. It follows, then, that these tests are applied by therapists in very individual ways to open channels of communication with clients and enter psychological domains that might be hidden without the stories provided by the TAT. As one practicing psychotherapist explains, "I don't score my clients' responses on the TAT or use them for diagnosis, but the drawings are a wonderful and valuable vehicle for bringing to light troubled areas in a client's life. The identification and mutual awareness of these issues that flows from the TAT allows for more focused and effective therapy" (author's files).

Anastasi, A. (1982). *Psychological Testing (5ʰ Ed.).* New York: Macmillan.

Eron, I. (1950). A Normative Study of the Thematic Apperception Test. *Psychological Monographs,* 64 (whole number 315).

Friedman, H., Tucker, J., Tomlinson-Keasey, C., Schwartz, J., Wingard, D. & Criqui, M. (1993). Does Childhood Personality Predict Longevity? *Journal of Personality and Social Psychology,* 65, 176-85.

Shneidman, E. (1993). Some Controversies in Suicidology: Toward a Mentalistic Discipline, *Suicide and Life-Threatening Behavior,* 23, 292-98.

Chapter Nine
Cases and Archival Records In Humanism

"Holistic analysis of the total impressions yields the following characteristics of self-actualizing people for further clinical and experimental study: perception of reality, acceptance, spontaneity, problem centering, solitude, autonomy, fresh appreciation, peak experiences, human kinship, humility and respect, interpersonal relationships, ethics, means and ends, humor, creativity, resistance to enculturation, imperfections, values, and resolution of dichotomies."

Abraham Maslow

215

The Angry Adolescent
Carl R. Rogers, Ph.D.

Carl Rogers (1902-1987) is one of the most influential forces to American psychology. He is chiefly identified with a method of therapy which he originated and developed, influenced by the work of Otto Rank, one of the pioneer psychoanalysts who broke with Freud.

The therapy with which Rogers is identified is called non-directive or client-centered. He believes that the therapist must relate to the client (Rogers rarely refers to those coming for therapy as patients) not as a scientist to an object study, nor as a physician expecting to cure, but as one person deeply involved in the feelings of another. He further believes that the best reference point on which to understand the behavior of any individual is from the internal point of the individual himself.

Non-directive therapy has enjoyed wide popularity among academic psychologists because it is the one therapy which grew completely out of psychology and not out of medicine. It is probably the form of therapy most frequently taught in university graduate courses in counseling technique. Some believe that it is a comparatively easy technique to learn and that the treatment may be relatively brief. In its avoidance of suggestion or direction and in its emphasis on emotional ventilation and insight, non-directive therapy resembles psychoanalysis.

One of Rogers' greatest contributions in the areas of psychotherapy has been his initiation of and subsequent collaboration in a whole series of researches into the nature of the psychotherapeutic process and its results. Being a trained psychologist and working with trained psychologists, Rogers had the assistance of more individuals trained in research than most of the other psychoanalysts.

In this case, taken from Rogers' book but probably describing the work of a counselor other than Rogers, some of the methods of the non-directive counselor are indicated. The importance of this case is not so much in the technique, which is a little more active than Rogers' cases usually indicated, but in Rogers' emphasis on the development of insight. This case shows how the client develops her own insight into some of the causes of her difficulties.

---

* **Rogers, Carl. (1959). The Angry Adolescent. In Greenwald, Harold (Ed.),** *Great Cases in Psychoanalysis,* **209-216. New York: J. Aronson. Reprinted by permission.**

The development of insight often involves not only the recognition of the role which the individual is playing, but also the recognition of repressed impulses within the self. So long as the individual denies certain attitudes which he finds within himself, so long will he keep up compensatory attitudes of a defensive character. When he can face clearly, and can accept as a part of himself, these less praiseworthy feelings, the need for defensive reactions tends to disappear.

An excellent example of the development of this type of insight may be taken from the case of Cora, an adolescent girl of seventeen who was brought to the guidance clinic and to the children's court by her stepfather because of ungovernable behavior at home. The mother was an invalid, having spent periods in the hospital and a sanitarium. The stepfather had assumed much responsibility for Cora, and had also shown a peculiar attitude toward her, being jealous of her boy friends and behaving in ways which indicated a direct sex interest in the girl. As the friction in the home was extreme, Cora was placed in a foster home by the court, and after a short time the girl asked if she might again talk with the psychologist with whom she had had several contacts at the time she went to court. When she came in, she expressed a desire to talk about her family, and much of her conversation revolved around her stepfather. She told indignantly of the way in which he checked on her behavior, even while she was in the foster home, and how disturbed he seemed to be when he had any contact with her boy friend. The interview continues.

Finally *counselor* said, "Why do you think those things happen?" Cora said, "I think he does it for meanness. I can't understand why my mother doesn't stop him. Why does she always believe him?" Counselor said, "I have talked with your mother since you were here. Your mother has talked about this. She understands. Perhaps some day she'll explain it to you. Would you like to have me tell you what your mother and I talked about?" Cora expressed no interest in this, but went right on with the problem of her stepfather's behavior. "I think he just wants me home. I think he wants me to help with the work I think he's jealous. Several people have said it. The adviser at school said so, you remember I told you. I don't see why he should be jealous; what could he be jealous of? He hates to see me go out with a boy. I don't know how to explain it. I think he's not all there. Sometimes he is, and sometimes he isn't. He doesn't like any boys to take me out. He's jealous. I don't understand it. If he were a boy my age it would mean he wanted me just to go with him. But he's married to my mother. I don't understand it. A boy would come out and say it. He doesn't. He just acts that way. He acts as if he wanted to go with me. Why, that couldn't be true. He's married to my mother. That's hard to think of." She is very disturbed and silent for a long time; became very fussed and fidgeted.

Counselor: Talk about it some more."

Cora: I don't know what to say. It seems awfully unfair to my mother if that's it. After all, he married my mother. It wouldn't be fair to my mother, I haven't any feeling for him. I don't see why he should feel that way. I go crazy even if he touches me. He seems so devoted to my mother. I think he is. I realize it's been hard for him, my mother being in the hospital. If he must be like that, why pick on me? He might better go out with someone we didn't know, some woman we didn't know."

Counselor: "Why should he especially like you?"

Cora: "I don't think it's because I'm especially like my mother. People say I am. He says I am. I don't think I am. Maybe I am. There is something else to say. It makes me sort of horrified---my mother. The only reason would be that I remind him of my mother."

She talked about how wonderful her mother was. "He's married to my mother. I wouldn't feel that way. Why doesn't he say something? Why take it out on me? My mother's right there. Why doesn't he give her all his affection? Maybe it's because I'm younger, in better health, or something. I don't think it could be sex, because---unless"---- (there was a long pause) ----"I know he couldn't have any sex life with my mother. She's sick. I don't even like to talk about such things. What else is there to say?"

There was further conversation along this same line, devoted largely to discussion of the stepfather and his behavior. Two days later Cora came in for her next interview.

Cora looked very sober when she came in. "I'm still in a fog. I've thought and thought. It seems impossible. It's hard to believe, I can see the sense in it. It all adds up, and still I can't believe it. How could that be, when I see that it makes sense?"

Counselor explained to her something of how one could understand how a thing could be and still not emotionally accept it. Cora then said, "It's hard to believe that it's real. Nothing like that ever entered my head. I don't think about things like that anyway."

Counselor: "What is it that is hard to believe?"

Cora: "It's hard to believe, and yet I believe it. It's hard to believe that people would have feelings like that. He doesn't seem clean. When I think about it, I shudder. That was not included in my education. It ought to be for every girl, that there are such things. The idea that my stepfather would have such feelings. I'm not like my mother. I don't see why he should feel that way. I don't know how to say."

During the remainder of the interview she talked about family frictions, and about the fact that she did not think she would ever wish to go home. Cora missed the next two appointments which were given to her. It seems entirely reasonable to suppose that the painfulness of this increasing insight was the major factor in her failing to keep these appointments. Consequently, it was two weeks later that she came in for her next appointment.

Cora explained that she had made a mistake about the time of her appointment. "I didn't try to forget it. It was an accident. I've been thinking about what we talked about last time. It all makes sense, but I can't believe it."

Counselor said, "When you were here the last time, you were trying to answer the question of what had been you part in crating this situation." (No such statement is included in the counselor's account of the previous interview. If such a question was raised by the counselor, it no doubt accounts for Cora's failure to keep the appointments.)

Cora: "I don't know what it is. I can't think it out."

Counselor: "When your mother was in the hospital, your stepfather did things for you and gave you things and took you places. You were pleased, weren't you? How did you show it?"

Cora: "Oh, I'd jump up and down and be very gleeful. I might have hugged and kissed him. Sometimes I show my pleasure in that way. Sometimes I kissed him and made a great fuss."

Counselor: "Did you ever do something for someone else and have them show pleasure? How did you feel?" Cora thought for a few moments and then gave several examples of having done things for the foster mother. "I felt pretty good that she was pleased." She thought a long time. "I liked her maybe a little harder for a few minutes after that."

Counselor: "Go back again when you and your stepfather were together and your mother was in the hospital."

Cora talked about the things her stepfather had done for her, particularly taking her places. "He did those things then to please by mother, not for me. I was pleased and showed it. He was pleased because my mother was pleased. When she was pleased, he was more willing to do more for me. Then I got a feeling toward him, hero worship. No, I guess that isn't right. Something very different. Sometimes I thought he was very nice, and sometimes I didn't like him. I was also jealous that he had married my mother. I would be grateful to him, but then I would think it was my right that he should do things for me. No, it wasn't hero worship. I can't quite say what it was. He did things for me that pleased me. I guess he was a sort of Santa Claus. You get to expect and expect when people do things for you. Then the person gets kind of sick of it. Then you learn how to get little things. I guess that's what I did. I learned how to get things from him."

Counselor: "What did you do?"

Cora showed embarrassment paused a long time "Oh, I don't know. I have a lot of tricks. It wasn't hard to get him to go out. He didn't like to sit at home. I'd do a lot of things. When I wanted girls to go with me I'd pick the girls he liked to get him to take them along." She paused a long time and counselor waited, then said: "Anything else?"

Cora: "I suppose my voice was soft and persuasive and my face had a happy expression, the way I knew it would get him to do things." She talked about this for a little while, showing more and more embarrassment.

Counselor: "When you want a boy to take you some place, how do you get it?"

Cora: "I probably look sweet and defenseless." Then very quickly, "I'm not conscious of all this, but I guess I do know how to look that way, but it never works on my mother. I guess I learned how to do it particularly in thinking up ways to get things from my stepfather. I didn't consciously bring about this situation." She went back to discuss the idea that her stepfather liked her very much and identified her with her mother, again saying, "It makes sense, but I don't believe it."

Counselor: "Do you like this situation?"

There was a long pause. Cora flushed, fidget, and then hesitated, "No, but I do like my stepfather to pay attention to me." She was silent for a long time.

Though the counselor's approach in this situation seems too forceful and directive, the insights gained in this case are of considerable interest. First, Cora faces more clearly the fact of her stepfather's sexual interest in her, and the consequent reasons for his jealous behavior. Gradually, however, she comes to recognize that she has herself been encouraging his special interest in her, and that she has adopted various ways to cause him to continue this role of older "boy friend." It is of interest that as long as her insight is limited only to the stepfather's behavior, she speaks of him with disgust---"He doesn't seem clean." When she is able openly to recognize her own feelings in the situation, she no longer talks in this way, but faces her very ambivalent attitude toward him. In this last interview, a few moments following the excerpt quoted, the counselor asks, "How have you felt toward him?" and Cora replies, "I guess as a Santa Claus, and yet I hate him, but I do like him, too."

In a case of this sort, where counseling treatment has revealed the conflicts which are present, the symptomatic behavior of rebellion, sex delinquency, truancy, and the like becomes more understandable. Also the importance of genuine insight is emphasized. Until Cora was able to achieve a considerable degree of insight, all attempts at treatment were futile. With this insight, she was capable of assuming amore adult role, and aggressive behavior was less necessary as a substitute for her conflicts.

It is evident that the insight which was gained was first of all a clearer understanding of her relationship with her stepfather, but the more dynamic insight was her recognition of the tabooed feelings within herself, and the fact that she and the stepfather had each played a part in creating the situation.

Self-Actualizing People: A Study of Psychological Health [*]

Abraham H. Maslow

Abraham H. Maslow (1908-1970), the gifted initiator of a "healthy" psychology of personality, pursued his academic studies at City College of New York and the University of Wisconsin. Interestingly, the evolution of his Theory of Self-Actualization and famous Hierarchy of Needs had an unusual beginning. Maslow was trained as a behaviorist not a humanist, working and researching sexual dominance in monkeys. Given this background, you might question how it is that he became so famous of his humanistic theory. Several significant life experiences altered the course of Maslow's professional career. First, his close association with Gestalt theorist, Max Wertheimer, and Social Anthropologist, Ruth Benedict, led to his discovery that these two individuals were models of exceptional behavior. Through careful observation, he began to identify characteristics that defined their unique personalities. Eventually, he examined the historical archives and found that other individuals shared these same personality characteristics. Secondly, the birth of his daughter dramatically played a role in his transition from behaviorism to humanism. He claimed that anyone who experiences the miracle of birth cannot be a behaviorist. Finally, after witnessing a military parade during World War II and experiencing the evils and atrocities of war, he vowed to show the world that people were essentially good and healthy

Maslow's Third Force Movement or Humanistic psychology opposed orthodox behaviorism and psychoanalysis because they were too theoretically rigid and overly concerned with mental illness rather than psychological health. From a hierarchical perspective, he viewed the development of psychological health as a process in which a person progresses from the satisfaction of basic physiological needs to social needs, and to the highest of all needs called self-actualization. It is this process, the process of becoming everything that we are capable of becoming, that underlies his self-actualization model.

The study to be reported in this (essay) is unusual in various ways. It was not planned as an ordinary research, it was not a social venture but a private one; motivated by my own curiosity and pointed toward the solution of various personal moral, ethical, and scientific problems. I sought only to convince and to teach myself rather than to prove or to demonstrate to others.

Quite unexpectedly, however, these studies have proved to be so enlightening to me, and so laden with exciting implications, that it seems fair that some sort of report should be made to others in spite of its methodological shortcomings.

In addition, I consider the problem of psychological health to be so pressing that any suggestions, any bits of data, however moot, are endowed with great heuristic value. This kind of research is in principle so difficult---involving as it does a kind of lifting oneself by one's own norms---that if we were to wait for conventionally reliable data, we should have to wait forever. It seems that the necessary thing to do is not to fear mistakes, to plunge in, to do the best that one can, hoping to learn enough from blunders to correct them eventually. At present the only alternative is simply to refuse to work with the problem. Accordingly, for whatever use can be make of it, the following report is presented with the due apologies to those who insist on conventional reliability, validity, sampling, and the like.

The Study

Subjects and Methods

The subjects were selected from among personal acquaintances and friends, and from among public and historical figures. In addition, in a first research with young people, three thousand college students were screened, but yielded only one immediately usable subject and a dozen or two possible future subjects ("growing well").

I had to conclude that self-actualization of the sort I had found in my older subjects perhaps was not possible in our society for young, developing people.

Accordingly, in collaboration with E. Raskin and D. Freedman, a search was begun for a panel of *relatively* healthy college students. We arbitrarily decided to choose the healthiest 1 percent of the college population. This research, pursued over a two-year period as time permitted, had to be interrupted before completion, but it was, even so, very instructive at the clinical level.

It was also hoped that figures created by novelists or dramatists could be used for demonstration purposes, but none were found that were usable in our culture and our time (in itself a thought-provoking finding).

The first clinical definition, on the basis of which subjects were finally chosen or rejected, had a positive as well as a merely negative side. The negative criterion was an absence of neurosis, psychopathic personality, psychosis, or strong tendencies in these directions. Possibly psychosomatic illness called forth closer scrutiny and screening. Whenever possible, Rorschach tests were given, but turned out to be far more useful in revealing concealed psychopathology than in selecting healthy people. The positive criterion for selection was positive evidence of self-actualization (SA), as yet a difficult syndrome to describe accurately. For the purposes of this discussion, it may e loosely described as the full use and exploitation of talents, capacities, potentialities, and the like. Such people seem to be fulfilling themselves and to be doing the best that they are capable of doing, reminding us of Nietzsche's exhortation, "Become what thou art!" They are people who have developed or are developing to the full stature of which they are capable. These potentialities may be either idiosyncratic or species-wide.

This criterion implies also gratification, past or present, of the basic needs for safety, belongingness, love, respect, and self-respect, and of the cognitive needs for knowledge and for understanding, or in a few cases, conquests of these needs. This is to say that all subjects felt safe and unanxious, accepted, loved and loving, respect-worth and respected, and that they had worked out their philosophical, religious, or axiological bearings. It is still an open question as to whether this basic gratification is a sufficient or only a prerequisite condition of self-actualization.

The subjects have been divided into the following categories:

CASES Seven fairly sure and two highly probably contemporaries
    (Interviewed)
    Two fairly sure historical figures (Lincoln in his last years
    and Thomas Jefferson)
    Seven highly probably public and historical figures (Albert Einstein,
    Eleanor Roosevelt, Jane Addams, William James, Albert Schweitzer,
    Aldous Huxley, and Benedict de Spinoza).

PARTIAL CASES Five contemporaries who fairly certainly fall short
    somewhat but who can yet be used for study

Collection and Presentation of Data

Data here consist not so much in the usual gathering of specific and discrete facts as in the slow development of a global or holistic impression of the sort that we form of our friends and acquaintances. It was rarely possible to set up a situation, to ask pointed questions, or to do any testing with my older subjects (although this was possible and done with younger subjects). Contacts were fortuitous and of the ordinary social sort. Friends and relatives were questioned where this was possible.

Because of this and also because of the small number of subjects as well as the incompleteness of the data for many subjects, any quantitative presentation is impossible: only composite impressions can be offered for whatever they may be worth.

The Observations

Holistic analysis of the total impressions yields the following characteristics of self-actualizing people for further clinical and experimental study: perception of reality, acceptance, spontaneity, problem centering, solitude, autonomy, fresh appreciation, peak experiences, human kinship, humility and respect, interpersonal relationships, ethics, means and ends, humor, creativity, resistance to enculturation, imperfections, values, and resolution of dichotomies.

Perception of Reality

The first form in which this capacity was noticed was an unusual ability to detect the spurious, the fake, and the dishonest in personality, and in general to judge people correctly and efficiently. In an informal experiment with a group of college students, a clear tendency was discerned for the more secure (the more healthy) to judge their professors more accurately than did the less secure students, that is, high scorers I the S-I test (Maslow, 1952).

Acceptance

A good many personal qualities that can be perceived on the surface and that seem at first to be various and unconnected may be understood as manifestations or derivatives of a more fundamental single attitude, namely, of a relative lack of overriding guilt, or crippling shame, and of extreme or severe anxiety. This is in direct contrast with the neurotic person who in every instance may be described as crippled by guilt and/or shame and/or anxiety. Even the normal member of our culture feels unnecessarily guilty or ashamed about too many things and has anxiety n too many unnecessary situations. Our healthy individual as find it possible to accept themselves and their own nature without chagrin or complaint or, for that matter, even without thinking about the matter very much.

Spontaneity

Self-actualizing people can be described as relatively spontaneous in behavior and far more spontaneous than that in their inner life, thoughts, impulses, and so on. Their behavior is marked by simplicity and naturalness, and by lack of artificiality or straining for effect. This does not necessarily mean consistently unconventional behavior. If we were to take an actual count of the number of times that self-actualizing people behaved in an unconventional manner the tally would not be high. Their unconventionality is not superficial but essential or internal. It is their impulses, thought, and consciousness that are so unusually unconventional, spontaneous, and natural. Apparently recognizing that the world of people in which they live could not understand or accept this, and since they have no wish to hurt them or to fight with them over every triviality, they will go through the ceremonies and rituals of convention with a good-humored shrug and with the best possible grace. Thus I have seen a man accept an honor he laughed at and even despised in private, rather than make an issue of it and hurt the people who thought they were pleasing him.

Problem Centering

Our subjects are, in general, strongly focused on problems outside themselves. In current terminology they are problem centered rather than ego centered. They generally are not problems for themselves and are not generally much concerned about themselves (e.g., as contrasted with the ordinary introspectiveness that one finds in insecure people). These individuals customarily have some mission in life, some task to fulfill, some problem outside themselves which enlists much of their energies (Buhler & Massarik, 1968, Frankl, 1969).

Solitude

For all my subjects, it is true that they can be solitary without harm to themselves and without discomfort. Furthermore, it is true for almost all that they positively like solitude and privacy to a definitely greater degree than the average person.

Autonomy

One of the characteristics of self-actualizing people, which to a certain extent crosscuts much of what we have already described, is their relative independence of the physical and social environment. Since they are propelled by growth motivation rather than by deficiency motivation, self-actualizing people are not dependent for their main satisfactions on the real world, or other people or culture or means to ends or, in general, on extrinsic satisfactions. Rather they are dependent for their own development and continued growth on their own potentialities and latent resources. Just as the tree needs sunshine and water and food, so do most people need love, safety, and the other basic need gratifications that can come only from without. But once these external satisfiers are obtained, once these inner deficiencies, are satiated by outside satisfiers, the true problem of individual human development begins, name, self-actualization.

Fresh Appreciation

Self-actualizing people have the wonderful capacity to appreciate again and again, freshly and naively, the basic goods in life, with awe, pleasure, wonder, and even ecstasy, however stale these experiences may have become to others---what C. Wilson has called "newness" (1969). Thus, for such a person, any sunset may be as beautiful as the first one, any flower may be of breath-taking loveliness, even after a million flowers have been seen. The thousandth baby seen is just as miraculous a product as the first. A man remains as convinced of his luck in marriage 30 years after his marriage and is as surprised by his wife's beauty when she is 50 as he was 40 years before. For such people, even the casual workaday, moment-to-moment business of living can be thrilling, exciting, and ecstatic. These intense feelings do not come all the time, they come occasionally rather than usually, but at the most unexpected moments. The person may cross the river on the ferry ten times and at the eleventh crossing have a strong recurrence of the same feelings, reaction of beauty, and excitement as when riding the ferry for the first time (Eastman, 1928).

Peak Experiences

Those subjective expressions that have been called mystic experiences and described so well by William James (1958) are a fairly common experience for our subjects, though not for all. The strong emotions, described in the previous section sometimes get strong, chaotic, and widespread enough to be called mystic experiences. My interest and attention in this subject was first enlisted by several of my subjects who described their sexual orgasms in vaguely familiar terms, which later I remembered had been used by various writers to describe what they called the mystic experience. There were the same feelings of limitless horizons opening up to the vision, the feeling of being simultaneously more powerful and also more helpless than one ever was before, the feeling of great ecstasy and wonder and awe, the loss of placing in time and space with, finally, the conviction that something extremely important and valuable had happened, so that the subject is to some extent transformed and strengthened even in daily life by such experiences.

It is quite important to dissociate this experience from any theological or supernatural reference, even though for thousands or years, they have been linked. Because this experience is a natural experience, well within the jurisdiction of science, I call it the peak experience.

Human Kinship

Self-actualizing people have a deep feeling of identification, sympathy, and affection for human beings in general. They feel kinship and connection, as if all people were members of a single family. One's feelings towards siblings would be on the whole affectionate, even if they were foolish, weak, or even if they were sometimes nasty. They would still be more easily forgiven than strangers. Because of this, self-actualizing people have a genuine desire to help the human race.

Humility and Respect

All my subjects without exception may be said to be democratic people in the deepest possible sense. I say this on the basis of a previous analysis of authoritarian (Maslow, 1943) and democratic character structures; that is, too elaborate to present here, it is possible only to describe some aspects of this behavior in short space. These people have all the obvious or superficial democratic characteristics. They can be and are friendly with anyone of suitable character regardless of class, education, political belief, race, or color. As a matter of fact, it often seems as if they are not even aware of these differences, which are for the average person so obvious and so important.

Interpersonal Relationships

Self-actualizing people have deeper and more profound interpersonal relations than any other adults (although not necessarily deeper than those of children). They are capable of more fusion, greater love, more perfect identification, more obliteration of the ego boundaries than other people would consider possible. There are, however, certain special characteristics of these relationships. In the first place, it is my observation that the other members of these relationships are likely to be healthier and closer to self-actualization than the average, often much closer. There is high selectiveness here, considering the small proportion of such people in the general population.

Ethics

I have found none of my subjects to be chronically unsure about the difference between right and wrong in their actual living. Whether or not they could verbalize the matter, they rarely showed in their day-to-day living the chaos, the confusion, the inconsistency, or the conflict that are so common in the average person's ethical dealings. This may be phrased also in the following terms: these individuals are strongly ethical, they have definite moral standards, and they do right and do not do wrong. Needless to say, their notions of right and wrong and of good and evil are often not the conventional ones.

Humor

One very early finding that was quite easy to make, because it was common to all my subjects, was that their sense of humor is not of the ordinary types. They do not consider funny what the average person considers to be funny. Thus they do not laugh at hostile humor (making people laugh by hurting someone) or superiority humor (laughing at someone else's inferiority) or authority-rebellion humor (the unfunny, Oedipal, or smutty joke). Characteristically what they consider humor is more closely allied to philosophy than to anything else. It may also be called the humor of the real because it consists in large part in poking fun at human beings in general when they are foolish or forget their place in the universe, or try to be big when they are actually small. This can take the form of poking fun at themselves, but this is not done in any masochistic or clown-like way. Lincoln's humor can serve as a suitable example. Probably Lincoln never made a joke that hurt anybody else; it is also likely that many or even most of his jokes had something to say, had a function beyond just producing a laugh. They often seemed to be education in a more palatable form, akin to parables or fables.

Creativity

This is a universal characteristic of all the people studied or observed. There is no exception. Each one shows in one way or another a special kind of creativeness or originality or inventiveness that has certain peculiar characteristics. For one thing, it is different from the special talent creativeness of the Mozart type. We may as well face the fact that the so-called geniuses display ability that we do not understand. All we can say of them is that they seem to be specially endowed with a drive and a capacity that may have rather little relationship to the rest of the personality and with which, from all evidence, the individuals seem to be born. Such talent we have no concern with here since it does not rest upon psychic health or basic satisfaction. The creativeness of the self-actualized person seems rather to be kind to the naïve and universal creativeness of unspoiled children. It seems to be more a fundamental characteristic of common human nature---a potentially given to all human beings at birth. Most human beings lose this as they become enculturated, but some few individuals seem either to retain this fresh and naïve, direct way of looking at life, or if they have lost it, as most people do, they later in life recover it. Santanya called this the "second naivete," a very good name for it.

Imperfections

The ordinary mistake that is made by novelists, poets, and essayists about good human beings is to make them so good that they are caricatures, so that nobody would like to be like them. The individual's own wishes for perfection and guilt and shame about shortcomings are projected upon various kinds of people from whom average people demand much more than they themselves give. Thus teachers and ministers are sometimes conceived to be rather joyless people who have no mundane desires and who have no weaknesses. It is my belief that most of the novelists who have attempted to portray good (healthy) people did this sort of thing, making him into stuffed shirts or marionettes or unreal projections of unreal ideals, rather than into the robust, hearty, lusty individuals they really are. Our subjects show many of the lesser human ailings. They are too equipped with silly, wasteful, or thoughtless habits. They can be boring stubborn, irritating. They are by no means free from a rather superficial vanity, pride, partiality to their own productions, family, friends, and children. Temper outbursts are not rare.

Our subjects are occasionally capable of extraordinary and unexpected ruthlessness. It must be remembered that they are very strong people. This makes it possible for them to display a surgical coldness when this is called for, beyond the power of average people. The man who found that a long-trusted acquaintance was dishonest cut himself off from this friendship sharply and abruptly and without any observable pangs whatsoever. A woman who was married to someone she did not love, when she decided on divorce, did it with such decisiveness that looked almost like ruthlessness. Some of them recover so quickly from the death of people close to them as to seem heartless....

Values

A firm foundation for a value system is automatically furnished to self-actualizers by their philosophic acceptance of the nature of self, of human nature, of much of social life, and of nature and physical reality. These acceptance values account for a high percentage of the total of their individual value judgments from day to day. What they approve or, disapprove of, are loyal to, oppose or proposed what pleases them or displeases them can often be understood as surface derivations of this source trait of acceptance.

Chapter Ten
Research Studies in Behaviorism

"Experimental work has been done so far on only one child, Albert B. This infant was reared almost entirely from birth in a hospital environment; his mother was a wet nurse in the Harriet Lane Home for Invalid Children. Albert's life was normal: he was healthy from birth and one of the best developed youngsters ever brought to the hospital, weighing twenty-one pounds at nine months of age. He was on the whole stolid and unemotional. His stability was one of the principal reasons for using him as a subject in this test."

John B. Watson & Rosalie Rayner

Conditioned Emotional Reactions

John B. Watson and Rosalie Rayner

The origins of behaviorism as a major force in psychology may be traced to the laboratory research of the Russian physiologist, Ivan Pavlov. Intrigued by the findings of Pavlov and his classical conditioning model, John B. Watson set out to disprove Freudian theory and elevate behaviorism to the status of a scientific psychology. He believed that he could create a behavioral learning situation in his laboratory which applied Pavlov's stimulus-response associations to humans. The subject for his study was 11 month-old Little Albert B., who learned not only to fear a white rat but also other similar white furry objects

Watson (1878-1958), the founder of American behaviorism, and Rosalie Rayner, his assistant in the Little Albert experiment, collaborated and published the following selection in the Journal of Experimental Psychology in 1920. They eventually married. "Conditioned Emotional Reactions" provides a fascinating description of the details of this famous classical conditioning study and show how conditioning can modify behavior. Here, the two authors clearly describe the procedures they used and the results they obtained in their research. They demonstrated that human fears are learned.

In recent literature various speculations have been entered into concerning the possibility of conditioning various types of emotional response, but direct experimental evidence in support of such a view has been lacking. If the theory advanced by Watson and Morgan to the effect that in infancy the original emotional reaction patterns are few, consisting so far as observed of fear, rage and love, then there must be some simple method by means of which the range of stimuli which can call out these emotions and their compounds is greatly increased. Otherwise, complexity in adult responses could not be accounted for. These authors without adequate experimental evidence advanced the view that this range was increased by

* Watson, John B. and Rosalie Rayner. (1920). Conditioned Emotional Responses. *Journal of Experimental Psychology*, 3, 1-14. Public Domain.

means of conditioned reflex factors. It was suggested there that the early home life of the child furnishes a laboratory situation for establishing conditioned emotional responses. The present authors have recently put the whole matter to an experimental test.

Experimental work has been done so far on only one child, Albert B. This infant was reared almost from birth in a hospital environment; his mother was a wet nurse in the Harriet Lane Home for Invalid Children. Albert's life was normal; he was healthy from birth and one of the best developed youngsters ever brought to the hospital, weighing twenty-one pounds at nine months of age. He was on the whole stolid and unemotional. His stability was one of the principal reasons for using him as a subject in this test. We felt that we could do him relatively little harm by carrying out such experiments as those outlined below.

At approximately nine months of age we ran him through the emotional tests that have become a part of our regular routine in determining whether fear reactions can be called out by other stimuli than sharp noises and the sudden removal of support....In brief, the infant was confronted suddenly and for the first time successively with a white rat, a rabbit, a dog, a monkey, with masks with and without hair, cotton wool, burning newspapers, etc. A permanent record of Albert's reactions to these objects and situations has been preserved in a motion picture study. Manipulation was the most usual reaction called out. *At no time did this infant ever show fear in any situation.* These experimental records were confirmed by the casual observations of the mother and hospital attendants. No one had ever seen him in a state of fear and rage. The infant practically never cried.

Up to approximately nine months of age we had not tested him with loud sounds. The test to determine whether a fear reaction could be called out by a loud sound was made when he was eight months, twenty-six days of age. The sound that was made was by striking a hammer upon a suspended steel bar four feet in length and three-fourths of an inch in diameter. The laboratory notes are as follows:

> One of the two experimenters caused the child to turn its head and fixate her moving hand, the other, stationed back of the child, struck the steel bar a sharp blow. The child started violently, his breathing was checked and the arms were raised in a characteristic manner. On the second stimulation the same thing occurred, and in addition the lips began to pucker and tremble. On the third stimulation the child broke into a sudden crying fit. This is the first time an emotional situation in the laboratory has produced any fear or even crying in Albert.

We had expected just these results on account of our work with other infants brought up under similar conditions. It is worth while to call attention to the fact that removal of support (dropping and jerking the blanket upon which the infant was lying) was tried exhaustively upon this infant on the same occasion. It was not effective in producing the fear response. This stimulus is effective in younger children. At what age such stimuli lose their potency in producing fear is not known. Nor is it known whether less placid children ever lose their fear of them.

This probably depends upon the training the child gets. It is well known that children eagerly run to be tossed into the air and caught. On the other hand it is equally well known that in the adult fear responses are called out quite clearly by the sudden removal of support, if the individual is walking across a bridge, walking out upon a beam, etc. There is a wide field of study here which is aside from our present point.

The sound stimulus, thus, at nine months of age, gives us the means of testing several important factors. I. Can we condition fear of an animal, e.g., a white rat, by visually presenting it and simultaneously striking a steel bar? II. If such a conditioned emotional response can be established, will there be a transfer to other animals or other objects?

I. The establishment of conditional emotional responses. At first there was considerable hesitation upon our part in making the attempt to set up fear reactions experimentally. A certain responsibility attaches to such a procedure. We decided finally to make the attempt, comforting ourselves by the reflection that such attachments would arise anyway as soon as the child left the sheltered environment of the nursery for the rough and tumble of the home. We did not begin this work until Albert was eleven months, three days of age. Before attempting to set up a conditioned response we, as before, put him through all of the regular emotional tests. *Not the slightest sign of a fear response was obtained in any situation.*

The steps taken to condition emotional responses are shown in our laboratory notes.

11 Months 3 Days

1. White rat suddenly taken from the basket and presented to Albert. He began to reach for rat with left hand. Just as his hand touched the animal the bar was struck immediately behind his head. The infant jumped violently and fell forward, burying his face in the mattress. He did not cry, however.
2. Just as the right hand touched the rat the bar was again struck. Again the infant jumped violently, fell forward and begin to whimper.

In order not to disturb the child too seriously no further tests were given for one week.

11 Months 10 Days

1. Rat presented without sound. There was steady fixation but no tendency at first to reach for it. The rat was then placed nearer, whereupon tentative reaching movements began with the right hand. When the rat nosed the infant's left hand, the hand was immediately withdrawn. He started to reach for the head of the animal with the forefinger of the left hand, but withdrew it

suddenly before contact. It is thus seen that the two joint stimulations given the previous week were not without effect. He was tested with his blocks immediately afterwards to see if they shared in the process of conditioning. He began immediately to pick them up, dropping them, pounding them, etc. In the remainder of the tests the blocks were given frequently to quiet him and to test his general emotional state. They were always removed from sight when the process of conditioning was under way.

2. Joint stimulation with rat and sound. Started, then fell over immediately to right side. No crying.
3. Joint stimulation. Fell to right side and rested upon hands, with head turned away from rat. No crying.
4. Joint stimulation. Same reaction.
5. Rat suddenly presented alone. Puckered face, whimpered and withdrew body sharply to the left.
6. Joint stimulation. Fell over immediately to right side and began to whimper.
7. Joint stimulation. Started violently and cried, but did not fall over.
8. Rat alone. *The instant the rat was shown the baby began to cry. Almost instantly he turned sharply to the left, fell over on left side, raised himself on all fours and began to crawl away so rapidly that he was caught with difficulty before reaching the edge of the table.*

This was as convincing a case of a completely conditioned fear response as could have been theoretically pictured. In all seven joint stimulations were given to bring about the complete reaction. It is not likely had the sound been of greater intensity or of a more complex clang character that the number of joint stimulations might have been materially reduced. Experiments designed to define the nature of the sounds that will serve best as emotional stimuli are under way.

II. When a conditioned emotional response has been established for one object, is there a transfer? Five days later Albert was again brought back into the laboratory and tested as follows:

11 Months 15 Days

1. Tested first with blocks. He reached readily for them, playing with them a usual. This shows that there has been no general transfer to the room, table, blocks, etc.
2. Rat alone. Whimpered immediately, withdrew right hand and turned head and trunk away.
3. Blocks again offered. Played readily with them, smiling and gurgling.
4. Rat alone. Leaned over to the left side as far away from the rat as possible, then fell over, getting up on all fours and scurrying away

238

as rapidly as possible.

5. Blocks again offered. Reached immediately for them, smiling and laughing as before.

The above preliminary test shows that the conditioned response to the rat had carried over completely for the five days in which no tests were given. The question as to whether or not there is a transfer was next taken up.

6. Rabbit alone. The rabbit was suddenly placed on the mattress in front of him. The reaction was pronounced. Negative responses began at once. He leaned as far away from the animal as possible, whimpered, then burst into tears. When the rabbit was placed in contact with him, he buried his face in the mattress, then got up on all fours and crawled away, crying as he went. This was a most convincing test.

7. The blocks were next given him, after an interval. He played with them as before. It was observed by four people that he played far more energetically with them ever before. The blocks were raised high over his head and slammed down with a great deal of force.

8. Dog alone. The dog did not produce as violent a reaction as the rabbit. The moment fixation occurred the child shrank back and as the animal came nearer he attempted to get on all fours but did not cry at first. As soon as the dog passed out of his range of vision he became quiet. The dog was then made to approach the infant's head (he was lying down at the moment). Albert straightened up immediately, fell over to the opposite side and turned his head away He then began to cry.

9. The blocks were again presented. He began immediately to play with them.

10. Fur coat (seal). Withdrew immediately to the left side and began to fret. Coat put close to him on the left side, he turned immediately began to cry and tried to crawl on all fours.

11. Cotton wool. The wool was presented in a paper package. At the end of the cotton was not covered by the paper. It was placed first on his feet. He kicked it away but did not touch it with his hands. When his hand was laid on the wool he immediately withdrew it but did not show the shock that the animals or fur coat produced in him. He then began to play with the paper, avoiding contact with the wool itself. He finally, under the impulse of the manipulative instinct, lost some of his negativism to the wool.

12. Just in play W. put his head down to see if Albert would play with his hair. Albert was completely negative. Two other observers did the same thing. He began immediately to play with their hair. W. then brought the Santa Claus mask and presented it to Albert. He was again pronouncedly negative....

From the above results it would seem that emotional transfers do take place. Furthermore, it would seem that the number of transfers resulting from an experimentally produced conditioned emotional reaction may be very large. In our observations we had no means of testing the complete number of transfers which may have resulted.

Incidental Observations

(a) **Thumb sucking as a compensatory device for blocking fear and noxious stimuli.** During the course of these experiments....it was noticed that whenever Albert was on the verge of tears or emotionally upset generally he would continually thrust him thumb into his mouth. The moment the hand reached the mouth he became impervious to the stimuli producing fear. Again and again, while the motion pictures were being made at the end of the thirty-day rest period, we had to remove the thumb from his mouth before the conditioned response could be obtained. This method of blocking noxious and emotional stimuli (fear and rage) through erogenous stimulation seems to persist from birth onward.

(b) **Equal primacy of fear, love and possibly rage.** While in general the results of our experiment offer no particular points of conflict with Freudian concepts, one fact out of harmony with them should be emphasized. According to proper Freudians, sex (or in our terminology, love) is the principal emotion in which conditioned responses arise which later limit and distort personality. We wish to take sharp issue with this view on the basis of the experimental evidence we have gathered. Fear is as primal a factor as love in influencing personality. Fear does not gather its potency in any derived manner from love. It belongs to the original and inherited nature of man. Probably the same may be true of rage although at present we are not so sure of this.

It is probable that many of the phobias in psychopathology are true conditioned emotional reactions either of the direct or the transferred type. One may possibly have to believe that such persistence of early conditioned responses will be found only in persons who are constitutionally inferior. Our argument is meant to be constructive. Emotional disturbances in adults cannot be traced back to sex alone. They must be retraced along at least three collateral lines---to conditioned and transferred responses set up in infancy and early youth in all three of the fundamental human emotions.

Shaping and Maintaining Operant Behavior *

B. F. Skinner

Operant Conditioning is another theoretical model found in the field of behaviorism. It is based on the concept of reinforcement---an event that increases the probability that a given behavior will be repeated---which has profound implications for the acquisition of personality or behavior. As you know, the findings on reinforcement were initially discovered in the animal laboratory. These findings were then applied to the behavior of humans; for example, the classic Case of Little Albert

B.F. Skinner (1904-1990), a brilliant pioneer in operant conditioning, showed the power of reinforcement to the world. He is credited with developing a model that illustrates the significance of an individual's environment and consequences of his behavior. In the operant conditioning model, the equation for analysis is "a response is emitted by the organism, animal or human, and a stimulus results" in the form of reinforcement. Both positive and negative reinforcement always increase the probability that a given response will be repeated; punishment temporarily suppressed the behavior in questions and, as Skinner notes, is not as effective or powerful.

This article, "Shaping and Maintaining Operant Behavior," is taken from Chapter 6 of Skinner's Science and Human Behavior (MacMillan, 1953). In it, Skinner discusses his research of animals and builds a case for its application to human organisms. More specifically, he elaborates upon four intermittent schedules of reinforcement and illustrates how they are implemented in our everyday lives.

---

* Skinner, B F. ((1953). Shaping and Maintaining Operant Behavior. *Science and Human Behavior*, 91-93. Upper Saddle River, New Jersey: Prentice-Hall/Pearson Education. Reprinted by permission.

The Continuity of Behavior

Operant conditioning (a process in which reinforcement changes the frequency of a behavior) shapes behavior as a sculptor shapes a lump of clay. Although at some point the sculptor seems to have produced an entirely novel object, we can always follow the process back to the original undifferentiated lump, and we can make the successive stages by which we return to this condition as small as we wish. At no point does anything emerge which is very different from what preceded it. The final product seems to have a special unity or integrity of design, but we cannot find a point at which this suddenly appears. In the same sense, an operant (behavior generated by reinforcement consequences) is not something which appears full grown in the behavior of the organism. It is the result of a continuous shaping process.

The pigeon experiment demonstrates this clearly. "Raising the head" is not a discrete unit of behavior. It does not come, so to speak, in a separate package. We reinforce only slightly exceptional values of the behavior observed while the pigeon is standing or moving about. We succeed in shifting the whole range of heights at which the head is held, but there is nothing which can be accurately described as a new "response." A response such as turning the latch in a problem box appears to be a more discrete unit, but only because the continuity with other behavior is more difficult to observe. In the pigeon, the response of pecking at a spot on the wall of the experimental box seems to differ from stretching the neck because no other behavior of the pigeon resembles it. If in reinforcing such a response we simply wait for it to occur---and we may have to wait many hours or days or weeks---the whole unit appears to emerge in its final form and to be strengthened as such. There may be no appreciable behavior which we could describe as "almost pecking the spot."

The continuous connection between such an operant and the general behavior of the bird can nevertheless easily be demonstrated. It is the basis of a practical procedure for setting up a complex response. To get the pigeon to peck the spot as quickly as possible we proceed as follows: "We first give the bird food when it turns slightly in the direction of the spot from any part of the cage. This increases the frequency of such behavior. We then withhold reinforcement until a slight movement is made toward the spot. This again alters the general distribution of behavior without producing a new unit. We continue by reinforcing positions successively closer to the spot, then by reinforcing only when the head is moved slightly forward, and finally only when the beak actually makes contact with the spot. We may reach this final response in a remarkably short time. A hungry bird, well adapted to the situation and to the food tray, can usually be brought to respond in this way in two or three minutes.

The original probability of the response in its final form is very low; in some cases it may even be zero. In this way we can build complicated operants which would never appear in the repertoire of the organism otherwise. By reinforcing a series of successive approximations, we bring a rare response to a very high probability in a short time. This is an effective procedure because it recognizes and utilizes the continuous nature of a complex act. The total act of turning toward the spot from any point in the box, walking toward it, raising the head, and striking the spot may seem to be a functionally coherent unit of behavior; but it is constructed by a continual process of differential reinforcement from undifferentiated behavior, just as the sculptor shapes his figure from a lump of clay. When we wait for a single complete instance, we reinforce a similar sequence but far less effectively because the earlier steps are not optimally strengthened.

This account is inaccurate in one respect. We may detect a discontinuity between bringing the head close to the spot and pecking. The pecking movement usually emerges as an obviously preformed unit. There are two possible explanations. A mature pigeon will already have developed a well-defined pecking response which may emerge upon the present occasion. The history of this response might show a similar continuity if we could follow it. It is possible, however, that there is a genetic discontinuity, and that in a bird such as the pigeon the pecking response has a special strength and a special coherence as a form of species behavior. Vomiting and sneezing are human responses which probably have a similar genetic unity. Continuity with other behavior must be sought in the evolutionary process. But these genetic units are rare, at least in the vertebrates. The behavior, with which we are usually concerned, from either a theoretical or practical point of view, is continuously modified from a basic material which is largely undifferentiated.

Through the reinforcement of slightly exceptional instances of his behavior, a child learns to raise himself, to stand, to walk, to grasp objects, and to move them about. Later on, through the same process, he learns to talk, to sing, to dance, and to play games---in short, to exhibit the enormous repertoire characteristic of the normal adult. When we survey behavior in these later stages, we find it convenient to distinguish between various operants which differ from each other in topography and produce different consequences. In this way behavior is broken into parts to facilitate analysis. These parts are the units which we count and whose frequencies play an important role in arriving at the laws of behavior. They are the "acts" into which, in the vocabulary of the layman, behavior is divided. But if we are to account for many of its quantitative properties, the ultimately continuous nature of behavior must not be forgotten...

The Maintenance of Behavior

One reason the term "learning" is not equivalent to "operant conditioning" is that traditionally it has been confined to the process of learning *how to do something.* In trial-and-error learning, for example, the organism learns how to get out of a box or how to find its way through a maze. It is easy to see why the acquisition of behavior should be emphasized. Early devices for the study of learning did not reveal the basic process directly. The effect of operant reinforcement is most conspicuous when there is a gross change in behavior. Such a chance occurs when an organism learns how to make a response which it did not or could not make before. A more sensitive measure, however, enables us to deal with cases in which the acquisition of behavior is of minor importance.

Operant conditioning continues to be effective even when there is no further change which can be spoken of as acquisition or even as improvement in skill. Behavior continues to have consequences and these continue to be important. If consequences are not forthcoming, extinction occurs. When we come to consider the behavior of the organism in all the complexity of its everyday life, we need to be constantly alert to the prevailing reinforcements, which maintain its behavior. We may, indeed, have little interest in how that behavior was first acquired. Our concern is only with its present probability of occurrence, which can be understood only through an examination of current contingencies of reinforcement. This is an aspect of reinforcement which is scarcely ever dealt with in classical treatments of learning.

Intermittent Reinforcement

In general, behavior which acts upon the immediate physical environment is consistently reinforced. We orient ourselves toward objects and approach, reach for, and seize them with a stable repertoire of responses which have uniform consequences arising from the optical and mechanical properties of nature. It is possible, of course, to disturb the uniformity. In a "house of mirrors" in an amusement park, or in a room designed to supply misleading cues to the vertical, well-established responses may fail to have their usual effects. But the fact that such conditions are so unusual as to have commercial value testifies to the stability of the everyday world.

A large part of behavior, however, is reinforced only intermittently. A given consequence may depend upon a series of events which are not easily predicted. We do not always win at cards or dice, because the contingencies are so remotely determined that we call them "chance." We do not always find good ice or snow when we go skating or skiing. Contingencies which require the participation of people are especially likely to be uncertain. We do not always get a good meal in a particular restaurant because cooks are not always predictable. We do not always get an answer when we telephone a friend because the friend is not always at home.

We do not always get a pen by reaching into our pocket because we have not always put it there. The reinforcements characteristic of industry and education are almost always intermittent because it is not feasible to control behavior by reinforcing every response.

As might be expected, behavior which is reinforced only intermittently often shows an intermediate frequency of occurrence, but laboratory studies of various schedules have revealed some surprising complexities. Usually such behavior is remarkably stable and shows great resistance to extinction (Extinction is a decline in behavior frequency due to the withholding of reinforcement—Ed.). An experiment has already been mentioned in which more than 10,000 responses appeared in the extinction curve of a pigeon which had been reinforced on a special schedule. Nothing of the sort is ever obtained after continuous reinforcement. Since this is a technique for "getting more responses out of an organism" in return for a given number of reinforcements, it is widely used. Wages are paid in special ways and betting and gambling devices are designed to "pay off" on special schedules because of the relatively large return on the reinforcement in such a case. Approval, affection, and other personal favors are frequently intermittent, not only because the person supplying the reinforcement may behave in different ways at different times, but precisely because he may have found that such a schedule yields a more stable, persistent, and profitable return.

It is important to distinguish between schedules which are arranged by a system outside the organism and those which are controlled by the behavior itself. An example of the first is a schedule of reinforcement which is determined by a clock---as when we reinforce a pigeon every five minutes, allowing all intervening responses to go unreinforced. An example of the second is a schedule in which a response is reinforced after a certain number of responses have been emitted---as when we reinforce every fiftieth response the pigeon makes. The cases are similar in the sense that we reinforce intermittently in both, but subtle differences in the contingencies lead to very different results, often of great practical significance.

Interval reinforcement. If we reinforce behavior at regular intervals, an organism such as a rat or pigeon will adjust with a nearly constant rate of responding, determined by the frequency of reinforcement. If we reinforce it every minute, the animal responds rapidly; if every five minutes, much more slowly. A similar effect upon probability of response is characteristic of human behavior. How often we call a given number on the telephone will depend, other things being equal, upon how often we get an answer. If two agencies supply the same service, we are more likely to call the one which answers more often. We are less likely to see friends or acquaintances with whom we only occasionally have a good time, and we are less likely to write to a correspondent who seldom answers. The experimental results are precise enough to suggest that in general the organism gives back a certain number of responses for each response reinforced. We shall see, however, that the results of schedules of reinforcement are not always reducible to a simple equating of input with output.

Since behavior which appears under interval reinforcement is especially stable, it is useful in studying other variables and conditions. The size or amount of each reinforcement affects the rate---more responses appearing in return for a larger reinforcement. Different kinds of reinforcers also yield different rates, and these may be used to rank reinforcers in the order of their effectiveness. The rate varies with the immediacy of the reinforcement: a slight delay between response and the receipt of the reinforce means a lower over-all rate. Other variables which have bee studied under interval reinforcement will be discussed in later chapters. They include the degree of deprivation and the presence or absence of certain emotional circumstances.

Optimal schedules of reinforcement are often of great practical importance. They are often discussed in connection with other variables which affect the rate. Reinforcing a man with fifty dollars at one time may not be so effective as reinforcing him with five dollars at ten different times during the same period. This is especially the case with primitive people where conditioned reinforcers have not been established to bridge the temporal span between a response and its ultimate consequence. There are also many subtle interactions between schedules of reinforcement and levels of motivation, immediacy of reinforcement, and so on.

If behavior continues to be reinforced at fixed intervals, another process intervenes. Since responses are never reinforced just after reinforcement, a change…eventually takes place in which the rate of responding is low for a short time after each reinforcement. The rate rises again when an interval of time has elapsed which the organism presumably cannot distinguish from the interval at which it is reinforced. These changes in rate are not characteristic of the effect of wages in industry, which would otherwise appear to be an example of a fixed-interval schedule. The discrepancy is explained by the fact that other reinforcing systems are used to maintain a given level of work.…Docking a man for time absent guarantees his presence each day by establishing a time-card entry as a conditioned reinforcer. The aversive reinforcement supplied by a supervisor or boss is, however, the principal supplement to a fixed-interval wage.

A low probability of response just after reinforcement is eliminated with what is called *variable-interval* reinforcement. Instead of reinforcing a response every five minutes, for example, we reinforce every five minutes *on the average,* where the intervening interval may be as short as a few seconds or as long as, say, ten minutes. Reinforcement occasionally occurs just after the organism has been reinforced, and the organism therefore continues to respond at that time. Its performance under such a schedule is remarkably stable and uniform. Pigeons reinforced with food with a variable interval averaging five minutes between reinforcements have been observed to respond for as long as fifteen hours at a rate of from two to three responses per second without pausing longer than fifteen or twenty seconds during the whole period. It is usually very difficult to extinguish a response after such a schedule. Many sorts of social and personal reinforcement are supplied on what is essentially a variable-interval basis, and extraordinarily persistent behavior is sometimes set up.

Ratio reinforcement. An entirely different result is obtained when the schedule of reinforcement depends upon the behavior of the organism itself---when, for example, we reinforce every fiftieth response. This is reinforcement at a "fixed ratio"---the ratio of reinforced to unreinforced responses. It is a common schedule in education, where the student is reinforced for completing a project or a paper or some other specific amount of work. It is essentially the basis of professional pay and of selling on commission. In industry it is known as piecework pay. It is a system of reinforcement which naturally recommends itself to employers because the cost of the labor required to produce a given result can be calculated in advance.

Fixed-ratio reinforcement generates a very high rate of response provided the ratio is not too high. This should follow from the input-output relation alone. Any slight increase in rate increases the frequency of reinforcement with the result that the rate should rise still further. If no other factor intervened, the rte should reach the highest possible value. A limiting factor, which makes itself felt in industry, is simple fatigue. The high rate of responding and the long hours of work generated by this schedule can be dangerous to health. This is the main reason why piecework pay is usually strenuously opposed by organized labor.

Another objection to this type of schedule is based upon the possibility that as the rate rises, the reinforcing agency will move to a larger ratio. In the laboratory, after first reinforcing every tenth response and then every fiftieth, we may find it possible to reinforce only every hundredth, although we could not have used this ratio in the beginning. In industry, the employee whose productivity has increased as the result of piecework schedule may receive so large a weekly wage that the employer feels justified in increasing the number of units of work required for a given unit of pay.

Under ratios of reinforcement which can be sustained, the behavior eventually shows a very low probability just after reinforcement, as it does in the case of fixed-interval reinforcement. The effect is marked under high fixed ratios because the organism always has "a long way to go" before the next reinforcement. Wherever a piecework schedule is used---in industry, education, salesmanship, or the professions---low morale or low interest is most often observed just after a unit of work has been completed. When responding begins, the situation is improved by each response and the more the organism responds, the better the chances of reinforcement become. The result is a smooth gradient of acceleration as the organism responds more and more rapidly. The condition eventually prevailing under high fixed-ratio reinforcement is not an efficient over-all mode of responding. It makes relatively poor use of the available time, and the higher rates of responding may be especially fatiguing.

The laboratory study of ratio reinforcement has shown that for a given organism and a given measure of reinforcement there is a limiting ratio beyond which behavior cannot be sustained. The result of exceeding this ratio is an extreme degree of extinction of the sort which we call abulia. Long periods of inactivity begin to appear between separate ratio runs. This is not physical fatigue, as we may easily show by shifting to another schedule. It is often called "mental" fatigue, but this designation adds nothing to the observed fact that beyond a certain high ratio of reinforcement the organism simply has no behavior available. In both the laboratory study of ratio reinforcement and its practical application in everyday life, the first signs of strain imposed by too high a ratio are seen in these breaks. Before a pigeon stops altogether---in complete "abulia"---it will often not respond for a long time after reinforcement. In the same way, the student who has finished a term paper, perhaps in a burst of speed at the end of the gradient, finds it difficult to start work on a new assignment.

Exhaustion can occur under ratio reinforcement because there is no self-regulating mechanism. In interval reinforcement, on the other hand, any tendency toward extinction is opposed by the fact that when the rate declines, the next reinforcement is received in return for fewer responses. The variable-interval schedule is also self-protecting; an organism will stabilize its behavior at a given rate under any length of interval.

We get rid of the pauses after reinforcement on a fixed-ratio schedule by adopting essentially the same practice as in variable-interval reinforcement: we simply vary the ratios over a considerate range around some mean value. Successive responses may be reinforced or many hundred of unreinforced responses may intervene. The probability of reinforcement at any moment remains essentially constant and the organism adjusts by holding to a constant rate. This "variable-ratio reinforcement" is much more powerful than a fixed-ratio schedule with the same mean number of responses. A pigeon may respond as rapidly as five times per second and maintain this rate for many hours.

The efficacy of such schedules in generating high rates has long been known to the proprietors of gambling establishments. Slot machines, roulette wheels, dice cages, horse races, and so on pay off on a schedule of variable-ratio reinforcement. Each device has its own auxiliary reinforcements, but the schedule is the important characteristic. Winning depends upon placing a bet and in the long run upon the number of bets placed, but no particular payoff can be predicted. The ratio is varied by any one of several "random" systems. The pathological gambler exemplifies the result. Like the pigeon with its five responses per second for many hours, he is the victim of an unpredictable contingency of reinforcement. The long-term net gain or loss is almost irrelevant in accounting for the effectiveness of this schedule.

Imitation of Film-mediated Aggressive Models [*]

Albert Bandura, Dorothea Ross, & Sheila A. Ross

For many decades, psychologists have examined and analyzed aggression, violence and crime from various theoretical perspectives.   More recently, there has been a great debate over the role of observation and imitation in such behavior.   In fact, a whole array of professionals (psychologists, sociologists, criminologists, learning specialists and even politicians) are concerned with the media and its relationship to the rising levels of destructive behaviors evidenced in America today. They question whether individuals, especially children, imitate the behaviors they observe on their television sets, computer games or movies?

One prominent social learning theorist, Albert Bandura (1925-present), and his colleagues have conducted numerous studies investigating the question posed by our leaders.   His research suggests that there is, indeed, a relationship between observation and imitation.   In this selection, "Imitation of Film-mediated Aggressive Models," Bandura and his colleagues present their study on aggression imitation.   It clearly shows that filmed aggression can facilitate aggression in children. The implications of this research are significant in light of the recent upsurge of violence in our schools, streets and communities.

[*] **Bandura, A., Ross, D. and S. Ross. (1963). Imitation of Film-Mediated Aggressive Models.** *Journal of Abnormal and Social Psychology,* **66, 3-11, American Psychological Association (APA). Reprinted by permission.**

In a test of the hypothesis that exposure of children to film-mediated aggressive models would increase the probability of S's (Subjects—i.e., children) aggression to subsequent frustration, 1 group of experimental Ss observed real-life aggressive models, a 2nd group observed these same models portraying aggression on film, while a 3rd group viewed a film depicting an aggressive cartoon character. Following the exposure treatment, Ss were mildly frustrated and tested for the amount of imitative and non-imitative aggression in a different experimental setting. The overall results provide evidence for both the facilitating and the modeling influence of film-mediated aggressive stimulation. In addition, the findings reveal that the effects of such exposure are to some extent a function of the sex of the model, sex of the child, and the reality cues of the model...

A recent incident (San Francisco Chronicle, 1961) in which a boy was seriously knifed during a re-enactment of a switchblade knife fight the boys had seen the previous evening on a televised rerun of the James Dean movie, *Rebel Without a Cause,* is a dramatic illustration of the possible imitative influence of film stimulation. Indeed, anecdotal data suggest that portrayal of aggression through a pictorial media may be more influential in shaping the form aggression will take when a person is instigated on later occasions, than in altering the level of instigation to aggression.

In an earlier experiment (Bandura & Huston, 1961), it was shown that children readily imitated aggressive behavior exhibited by a model in the presence of a model. A succeeding investigation (Bandura, Ross, & Ross, 1961), demonstrated that children exposed to aggressive models generalized aggressive responses to a new setting in which the model was absent. The present study sought to determine the extent to which film-mediated aggressive models may serve as an important source of imitative behavior.

Aggressive models can be ordered on a reality-fictional stimulus dimension with real-life models located at the reality end of the continuum, nonhuman cartoon characters at the fictional end, and films portraying human models occupying an intermediate position. It was predicted, on the basis of saliency and similarity of cues, that the more remote the model was from reality, the weaker would be the tendency for subjects to imitate the behavior of the model....

To the extent that observation of adults displaying aggression conveys a certain degree of permissiveness for aggressive behavior, it may be assumed that such exposure not only facilitates the learning of new aggressive responses but also weakens competing inhibitory responses in subjects and thereby increases the probability of occurrence of previously learned patterns of aggression. It was predicted, therefore, that subjects who observed aggressive models would display significantly more aggression when subsequently frustrated than subjects who were equally frustrated but who had no prior exposure to models exhibiting aggression. The subjects were 48 boys and 48 girls enrolled in the Stanford University Nursery School. They ranged in age from 35 to 60 months, with a mean age of 52 months.

Two adults, a male and a female, served in the role of models both in the real-life and the human film-aggression condition, and one female experimenter conducted the study for all 96 children.

General Procedure

Subjects were divided into three experimental groups and one control group of 24 subjects each. One group of experimental subjects observed real-life aggressive models, a second group observed these same models portraying aggression on film, while a third group viewed a film depicting an aggressive cartoon character. The experimental groups were further subdivided into male and female subjects so that half the subjects in the two conditions involving human models were exposed to same-sex models, while the remaining subjects viewed models of the opposite sex.

Following the exposure experience, subjects were tested for the amount of imitative and non-imitative aggression in a different experimental setting in the absence of the model.

The control group subjects had no exposure to the aggressive models and were tested only in the generalization situation.

Subjects in the experimental and control groups were matched individually on the basis of ratings of their aggressive behavior in social interactions in the nursery school. The experimenter and a nursery school teacher rated the subjects on four five-point rating scales which measured the extent to which subjects displayed physical aggression, verbal aggression, aggression toward inanimate objects, and aggression inhibition. The latter scale, which dealt with the subjects' tendency to inhibit aggressive reactions in the face of high instigation, provided the measure of aggression anxiety. Seventy-one percent of the subjects were rated independently by both judges so as to permit an assessment of interrater agreement. The reliability of the composite aggression score, estimated by means of the Pearson product-moment correlation, was .80.

Experimental Conditions

Subjects in the Real-Life Aggressive condition were brought individually by the experimenter to the experimental room and the model, who was in the hallway outside the room, was invited by the experimenter to come and join in the game. The subject was then escorted to one corner of the room and seated at a small table which contained potato prints, multicolor picture stickers, and colored paper. After demonstrating how the subject could design pictures with the materials provided, the experimenter escorted the model to the opposite corner of the room which contained a small table and chair, a tinker toy set, a mallet, and a 5-foot inflated Bobo doll. The experimenter explained that this was the model's play area and after the model was seated, the experimenter left the experimental room.

The model began the session by assembling the tinker toys but after approximately a minute had elapsed, the model turned to the Bobo doll and spent the remainder of the period aggressing toward it with highly novel responses which are unlikely to be performed by children independently of the observation of the model's behavior. Thus, in addition to punching the Bobo doll, the model exhibited the following distinctive aggressive acts which were to be scored as *imitative responses:*

The model sat on the Bobo doll and punched it repeatedly in the nose.

The model then raised the Bobo doll and pummeled it on the head with a mallet.

Following the mallet aggression, the model tossed the doll up in the air aggressively and kicked it about the room. This sequence of physically aggressive acts was repeated approximately three times, interspersed with verbally aggressive responses such as, "Sock him in the nose...," "Hit him down...," "Throw him in the air...," "Kick him...," and "Pow."

Subjects in the Human Film-Aggression condition were brought by the experimenter to the semi-darkened experimental room, introduced to the picture materials, and informed that while the subjects worked on potato prints, a movie would be shown on a screen, positioned approximately 6 feet from the subject's table. The movie projector was located in a distant corner of the room and was screened from the subject's view by large wooden panels.

The color movie and a tape recording of the sound track was begun by a male projectionist as soon as the experimenter left the experimental room and was shown for a duration of 10 minutes. The models in the film presentations were the same adult males and females who participated in the Real-Life condition of the experiment. Similarly, the aggressive behavior they portrayed in the film was identical with their real-life performances.

For subjects in the Cartoon Film-Aggression condition, after seating the subject at the table with the picture construction material, the experimenter walked over to a television console approximately 3 feet in front of the subject's table, remarked, "I guess I'll turn on the color TV," and ostensibly tuned in a cartoon program. The experimenter then left the experimental room. The cartoon was shown on a glass lens screen in the television set by means of a rear projection arrangement screened from the subject's view by large panels.

In both film conditions, at the conclusion of the movie the experimenter entered the room and then escorted the subject to the test room.

Aggression Instigation

In order to differentiate clearly the exposure and test situations subjects were tested for the amount of imitative learning in a different experimental room which was set off from the main nursery school building.

The degree to which a child has learned aggressive patterns of behavior through imitation becomes most evident when the child is instigated to aggression on later occasions. Thus, for example, the effects of viewing the movie, *Rebel Without a Cause,* were not evident until the boys were instigated to aggression the following day, at which time they re-enacted the televised switchblade knife fight in considerable detail. For this reason, the children in the experiment, both those in the control group, and those who were exposed to the aggressive models, were mildly frustrated before they were brought to the test room.

Following the exposure experience, the experimenter brought the subject to a anteroom which contained a varied array of highly attractive toys. The experimenter explained that the toys were for the subject to play with, but, as soon as the subject became sufficiently involved with the play material, the experimenter remarked that these were her very best toys, that she did not let just anyone play with them, and that she had decided to reserve these toys for some other children. However, the subject could play with any of the toys in the next room. The experimenter and the subject then entered the adjoining experimental room.

Test for Delayed Imitation

The experimental room contained a variety of toys, some of which could be used in imitative or non-imitative aggression, and others which tended to elicit predominantly non-aggressive forms of behaviors. The aggressive toys included a 3-foot Bobo doll, a mallet and peg board, two dart guns, and a tether ball with a face painted on it which hung from the ceiling. The non-aggressive toys, on the other hand, included a tea set, crayons and coloring paper, a ball, two dolls, three bears, cars and trucks, and plastic farm animals.

The subject spent 20 minutes in the experimental room during which time his behavior was rated in terms of predetermined response categories by judges who observed the session through a one-way mirror in an adjoining observation room. The 20-minute session was divided in 5-second intervals by means of an electric interval timer, thus yielding a total number of 240 response units for each subject.

RESULTS

The mean imitative and non-imitative aggression scores for subjects in the various experimental and control groups are presented in Table 1.

Since the distribution of scores departed from normality and the assumption of homogeneity of variance could not be made for most of the measures, the Friedman two-way analysis of variance by ranks was employed for testing the significance of the obtained differences.

TABLE 1

Mean Aggression Scores for Subgroups of Experimental and Control Subjects

				Experimental groups		
Response category	Real–life aggressive		Human	Film aggressive	Cartoon film aggressive	Control group
	F Model	M Model	F Model	M Model		
Total aggression						
Girls	65.8	57.3	87.0	79.5	80.9	36.4
Boys	76.8	131.8	114.5	85.0	117.2	72.2
Imitative aggression						
Girls	19.2	9.2	10.0	8.0	7.8	1.8
Boys	18.4	38.4	34.3	13.3	16.2	3.9
Mallet aggression						
Girls	17.2	18.7	49.2	19.5	36.8	13.1
Boys	15.5	28.8	20.5	16.3	12.5	13.5
Sits on Bobo doll *						
Girls	10.4	5.6	10.3	4.5	15.3	3.3
Boys	1.3	0.7	7.7	0.0	5.6	0.6
Nonimitative aggression						
Girls	27.6	24.9	24.0	34.3	27.5	17.8
Boys	35.5	48.6	46.8	31.8	71.8	40.4
Aggressive gun play						
Girls	1.8	4.5	3.8	17.6	8.8	3.7
Boys	7.3	15.9	12.8	23.7	16.6	14.3

* This response category was not included in the total aggression score.

Total Aggression

The mean total aggression scores for subjects in the real-life, human film, cartoon film, and the control groups are 83, 92, 99, and 54 respectively. The results of the analysis of variance performed on these scores reveal that the main effect of treatment conditions is significant ($Xr2 = p < .05$), confirming the prediction that exposure of subjects to aggressive models increases the probability that subjects will respond aggressively when instigated on later occasions. Further analysis of pairs of scores by means of the Wilcoxin matched-pairs signed-ranks test show that subjects who viewed the real-life models and the film-mediated models do not differ from each other in total aggressiveness but all three experimental groups expressed significantly more aggressive behavior than the control subjects.

In order to determine the influence of sex of model and sex of child on the expression of imitative and non-imitative aggression, the data from the experimental groups were combined and the significance of the differences between groups was assessed by t tests for uncorrelated means. In statistical comparisons involving relatively skewed distributions of scores the Mann-Whitney U test was employed.

Sex of subjects had a highly significant effect on both the learning and the performance of aggression. Boys, in relation to girls, exhibited significantly more total aggression ($t = 2.69$, $p < .01$), more imitative aggression ($t = 2.82$, $p < .005$), more aggressive gun play ($z = 3.38$, $p < .001$), and more non-imitative aggressive behavior ($t = 2.98$, $p < .005$). Girls, on the other hand, were more inclined than boys to sit on the Bobo doll but refrained from punching it ($z = 3.47$, $p < .001$).

The analyses also disclosed some influences of the sex of the model. Subjects exposed to the male model, as compared to the female model, expressed significantly more aggressive gun plan ($z = 2.83$, $p < .0059$. The most marked differences in aggressive gun play ($U = 9.5$, $p < .001$), however, were found between girls exposed to the female model ($M = 2.9$) and males who observed the male model ($M = 19.8$). Although the overall model difference in partially imitative behavior, "Sits on Bobo," was not significant, Sex x Model subgroup comparisons yielded some interesting results. Boys who observed the aggressive female model, for example, were more likely to sit on the Bobo doll without punching it than boys who viewed the male model ($U = 33$, $p < .05$). Girls reproduced the non-aggressive component of the male model's aggressive pattern of behavior (i.e., sat on the doll without punching it) with considerably higher frequency than did boys who observed the same model ($U = 21.5$, $p < .02$). The highest incidence of partially imitative responses was yielded by the group of girls who viewed the aggressive female model ($M = 10.4$), and the lowest values by the boys who were exposed to the male model ($M = 0.3$). This difference was significant beyond the .05 significant level. These findings, along with the sex of the child and sex of model differences reported in the preceding sections, provide further support for the view that the influence of models in promoting social learning is determined, in part, by the sex appropriateness of the model's behavior (Bandura, et. al., 1961).

DISCUSSION

The results of the present study provide strong evidence that exposure to filmed aggression heightens aggressive reactions in children. Subjects who viewed the aggressive human and cartoon models on film exhibited nearly twice as much aggression than did subjects in the control group who were not exposed to the aggressive film content.

Filmed aggression, not only facilitated the expression of aggression, but also effectively shaped the form of the subjects' aggressive behavior. The finding that children modeled their behavior to some extent after the film characters suggests that pictorial mass media, particularly television, may serve as an important source of social behavior. In fact, a possible generalization of responses originally learned in the television situation to the experimental film may account for the significantly greater amount of aggressive gun play displayed by subjects in the film condition as compared to subjects in the real-life and control groups. It is unfortunate that the qualitative features of the gun behavior were not scored since subjects in the film condition, unlike those in the other two groups, developed interesting elaborations in gun play (for example, stalking the imaginary opponent, quick drawing, and rapid firing), characteristic of the Western gun fighter.

References

1. Bandura, A., & Huston, Aletha, C. Identification as a process of incidental learning. *Journal of Abnormal and Social Psychology,* 1961, 63, 311-318.
2. Bandura, A., Ross, Dorothea, & Ross, Sheila A. Transmission of aggression through imitation of aggressive models. *Journal of Abnormal and Social Psychology*, 1961, 63, 575-582.
3. San Francisco Chronicle. "James Dean" knifing in South City. *San Francisco Chronicle,* March 1, 1961, p. 6.

Part Two

Case Histories, Research Studies and Psychotherapies

Key Questions

1. In your opinion, what are the assets and liabilities of using the case history method in the field of personality psychology? Elaborate.

2. Historically speaking, Freud himself said that the creation of psychoanalysis began with Josef Breuer's Case of Anna O. In what way(s) did her problem contribute to the establishment of the psychoanalytic school of thought?

3. What psychological insights did you gain from reading Reuben Fine's famous Freudian case histories? In what way(s) are these cases similar or dissimilar?

4. In what way is the case history of the Russian aristocrat, the Wolf Man, unique in the field of personality psychology? What did you learn about the personality of Sigmund Freud as a result of reading the Wolf Man's recollections?

5. Do you believe that the case histories by Carl Jung, Alfred Adler and Harry Stack Sullivan reflect their revisionist ideas and concepts? Why? What are their contributions to the field of personality?

6. How can personal correspondence such as Allport's *Letters from Jenny,* be effectively used to assess an individual's personality? Would you be inclined to rely upon qualitative rather than quantitative data in your evaluation of a person?

7. Do you concur with Henry Murray that "projective techniques" such as the Thematic Apperception Test (TAT) or Rorschach Test are useful in obtaining relevant information of about personality and a person's psychological problems and conflicts? Elaborate.

8. What are some of the nondirective or client-centered methods of psychotherapy used by Carl Rogers in his case, The Angry Adolescent?

9. Abraham Maslow is credited with presenting and adding a theory of psychological health to the field of personality psychology. In what way did he establish this theory and how did he come to identify individuals as self-actualized persons?

10. According to the behaviorists, "we are what we do!" How do the studies of John B. Watson and Rosalie Rayner, B. F. Skinner and Albert Bandura and colleagues reflect and substantiate this behavioral tenet? Do you agree with their theories?

Part Two

Case Histories, Research Studies and Psychotherapies

Suggested Readings

Allport, G. W. (1965). *Letters from Jenny.* New York: Harcourt, Brace & World.

Corsini, R. (1991). *Five Therapies and One Client.* Itasca, IL: F. E. Peacock Publishers, Inc.

Erikson, E. H. (1967). **Cross-Cultural and Psycho-Historical Analyses.** In R. Evans *Dialogue with Erik Erikson.* New York: Harper & Row.

Eysenck, H. J. ((1995). **How Valid is the Psychoticism Scale? A Comment on the Van Kampen Critique.** *European Journal of Personality, 9,* 103-108.

Gardiner, M. (Ed.,) (1971). *The Wolf Man: The Double Story of Freud's Most Famous Case.* New York: Basic Books, Inc.

Greenwald, H. (Ed.,) (1959). *Great Cases in Psychoanalysis.* New York: Balantine Books.

Fine, R. (1973). *The Development of Freud's Thought.* New York: Jason Aronson.

Freeman, L. (1972). *The Story of Anna O.* New York: Walker & Company.

Houts, A. C. & W. C. Follette. (1992). **Philosophical and Theoretical Issues in Behavior Therapy.** *Behavior Therapy, 23,* 145-149.

Murray, H. A. (1936). **Facts Which Support the Concept of Need or Drive.** *The Journal of Psychology, 3,* 27-42.

259

Murray, H. A. (1943). *The Thematic Apperception Test: Manual.* Cambridge, MA: Harvard University Press.

Murray, H. A. (1951). Uses of the Thematic Apperception Test. *American Journal Of Psychiatry,* 107, 577-581.

Murray, H. A. (1962). *Explorations in Personality.* New York: Science Editions.

Rogers, C. R. (1942). *Counseling and Psychotherapy.* Boston, MA: Houghton Mifflin.

Rogers, C. R. (1965). *Client-Centered Therapy.* Boston, MA: Houghton Mifflin.

Rogers, C. R. (1975). Empathic: An Unappreciated Way of Being. *Counseling Psychologist,* 5, 2-10.

Rogers, C. R. (1979). The Foundations of the Person-Centered Approach. *Education,* 100, 98-107.

Skinner, B F. (1956). A Case History in Scientific Method. *American Psychologist,* 11, 221-233.

Wedding, D. & R. Corsini (Eds.,) (1995). *Case Studies in Psychotherapy.* Itasca, IL: F. E. Peacock Publishers.

Wolpe, J. (1961). The Systematic Desensitization Treatment of Neuroses. *The Journal Of Nervous and Mental Diseases,* 132, 180-203.

Part Three

Personality Exercises and Applications

Part Three
Exercises and Applications in Personality

Now that you have been exposed to a number of theoretical foundations and models, research methodologies, and psychotherapies associated with the major paradigms of personality psychology, it is important for you to determine how useful they are in your life. In order to make this determination, you are invited to engage in a process of assessment; that is, to evaluate your unique personality or aspects thereof by completing a variety of inventories, compiling your results, and interpreting your findings from these five major perspectives.

In Chapter Eleven, you may wish to assess your current theoretical orientation with respect to all of the major schools of thought by completing Potkay and Allen's *Personal Personality Theory* questionnaire. It might be interesting to take this test again at the end of the semester and determine whether your theoretical position has changed as a result of participating in this course. Bolt's *Self-Rating Inventory* enables you to rate yourself along a number of personality dimensions.

The assessment exercises in Chapter Twelve focus on applications of Freudian and Eriksonian theory. To evaluate your position on psychoanalysis, you may complete Miserandino's *Beliefs about Freudian Principles* or Merrens and Brannigan's *Personality Assessment* which measures the anal characteristics of frugality, orderliness, and obstinacy. If you are more inclined towards Erikson's Eight Stages of Life and his underlying focus of identity formation, you may wish to complete Osche and Plug's *A Sense of Personal Identity Scale.*

Exercises in Chapter Thirteen reflect various theoretical tenets emanating from the revisionist schools of thought, neo-analysis. If you are interested in measuring your level of anxiety, you may wish to take Schlenker and Leary's *Social Anxiety Test.* Parrot's *Early Recollections Exercise*, based on Adler's Individual Psychology, enables you to assess your style of life and determine how your early memories contributed to it.

Kring, Smith, and Neale's *Emotional Expressivity Scale* measures your position along the optimism-pessimism continuum and determine what you need to do in order to possess a more optimistic view of life.

Dispositional conceptualizations are presented in the exercises listed in Chapter Fourteen. Buss and Plomin's *Temperament Survey* measures temperament based on the personality dispositions of emotionality, activity, and sociability. If you interested in knowing the level of your achievement motivation, you may wish to take Helmreich and Spence's *Achievement Motivation* Test and determine its relationship to your work, mastery, and competitiveness. Social desirability, response sets and styles are issues of concern to psychologists who rely upon personality inventories and tests. If you are interested in gaining first hand experience with these issues, you may take Crowne and Marlowe's *Response Tendencies Test* to determine your social desirability tendency.

Chapter Fifteen exercises highlight the humanistic theme of self-actualization. By completing Jones and Crandall's *Self-Actualization Inventory* and Polyson's *Peak Experience Exercise*, you will be able to determine your position along Maslow's hierarchy of needs and more fully appreciate the peak experiences you have already experienced in life. Merrens and Brannigan's *Q-Sort Technique* represents a method used by Rogers to measure his clients' self congruence or incongruence. You may wish to assess whether your real and ideal self concepts are in a state of harmony or congruence or, on the other hand, in a state of disharmony or incongruence.

Our final group of applications exercises, presented in Chapter Sixteen, illustrates the principles of behaviorism. Merrens and Brannigan's *Observing and Recording a Personality Behavior* affords you the opportunity to participate in an observational study of your own behavior. If you are interested in determining your assertiveness, you may assess your level by completing Rathus' *Assertiveness Exercise* and compare your score to established norms. Finally, Scheier and Carver's *Life Orientation Test* provides insight into how you perceive your future and measures optimism, coping and health.

In conclusion, it is my hope that you have gained some invaluable insight and knowledge from examining the various schools of personality thought, their methods of investigation, and their applications to contemporary life.

Chapter Eleven

Studying Personality

A Personal Personality Theory

C. R. Potkay and B. P. Allen

Instructions: For each of the following statements, circle the number that corresponds most closely to your point of view.

1. Human behavior results primarily from *heredity,* what has been genetically transmitted by parents, or from *environment,* the external circumstances and experiences that shape a person after conception has occurred.

1   2   3   4   5   6   7

heredity _____ *environment*

2. An important part of every person is a *self,* some central aspect of personality referred to as "I" or "me," or there really is *no self* in personality.

1   2   3   4   5   6   7

self _____ *no self*

3. Personality is relatively *unchanging,* with each person showing the same behavior throughout a lifetime, or personality is relatively *changing,* with each person showing different behavior throughout a lifetime.

1   2   3   4   5   6   7

unchanging _____ *changing*

* Potkay, C. R. and Allen, B.P. (1986). A Personal Personality Theory. *Personality Theory, Research, and Application,* 1-4. Monterey, CA: Brooks/Cole. Reprinted by permission of (author) Potkay, Charles.

4. The most important influences on behavior are *past* events, what has previously occurred to a person, or *future* events, what a person seeks to bring about by striving to meet certain goals.

	1	2	3	4	5	6	7	
past								*future*

5. The most important characteristics about people are *general* ones, those commonly shared by many people, or *unique* ones, those that make each person different from every other person.

	1	2	3	4	5	6	7	
general								*unique*

6. People are motivated to cooperate with others mainly because they are *self centered*, expecting to receive some personal gain, or mainly they are *altruistic*, seeking to work with others only for the benefit of doing things with and for others.

	1	2	3	4	5	6	7	
self-centered								*altruistic*

7. People learn best when they motivated by *reward* involving pleasure, or by *punishment,* involving pain.

	1	2	3	4	5	6	7	
reward								*punishment*

8. The main reason you behave as you do (for example, attend college) is because of conscious *personal* decisions to do so or because *social* factors outside your control leave you little real choice in the matter.

	1	2	3	4	5	6	7	
personal								*social*

9. Human nature is essentially *constructive,* with people showing positive personal growth and a desire to help others fulfill their potentials, or *destructive,* with people showing behavior that is ultimately self-defeating and a desire to keep others from improving themselves.

	1	2	3	4	5	6	7	
constructive								*destructive*

10. Human beings have *no purpose* or reason for their existence other than what they experience on a day-to-day basis, or human beings have some *purpose* for living that is outside themselves.

	1	2	3	4	5	6	7	
no purpose								*purpose*

The questionnaire you have just completed was developed by Potkay and Allen (1986) to illustrate that we all have theories of personality. It is a good idea to review your own conceptions prior to investigating the field in depth. You can compare your responses to the ideas of major personality theorists, as organized by Potkay and Allen.

Theorists' Assumptions About Personality

1. **Human behavior results primarily from** *heredity,* **what has been genetically transmitted by parents, or from** *environment,* **the external circumstances and experiences that shape a person after conception has occurred.**

	1	2	3	4	5	6	7	

heredity _____ *environment*

Eysenck, Cattell	Skinner, Watson, Rotter
Sheldon, Freud, Jung	Bandura, Rogers

2. **An important part of every person is a** *self,* **some central aspect of personality referred to as "I" or "me," or there really is** *no self* **in personality.**

	1	2	3	4	5	6	7	

self _____ *no self*

Rogers, Maslow, Erikson	Watson, Skinner, Rotter,
Horney, Jung	Mischel

3. Personality is relatively *unchanging,* with each person showing the same behavior throughout a lifetime, or personality is relatively *changing,* with each person showing different behavior throughout a lifetime.

1   2   3   4   5   6   7

*unchanging*_____ *changing*
        Freud, Eysenck, Cattell   Rogers, Mischel

4. The most important influences on behavior are *past* events, what has previously occurred to a person, or *future* events, what a person seeks to bring about by striving to meet certain goals.

1   2   3   4   5   6   7

past _____ *future*
    Freud, Jung, Fromm   Adler, Rogers, Maslow
                                   Rotter

5. The most important characteristics about people are *general* ones, those commonly shared by many people, or *unique* ones, those that make each person different from every other person.

1   2   3   4   5   6   7

general _____ *unique*
  Watson, Skinner, Eysenck   Adler, Rogers, Bandura
  Fromm   Rotter

6. People are motivated to cooperate with others mainly because they are *self centered*, expecting to receive some personal gain, or mainly they are *altruistic*, seeking to work with others only for the benefit of doing things with and for others.

1   2   3   4   5   6   7

*self-centered*_____ *altruistic*
    Freud, Jung   Adler, Fromm, Maslow
                             Rogers, Bandura

7. People learn best when they motivated by *reward* involving pleasure, or by *punishment,* involving pain.

	1	2	3	4	5	6	7	
reward								*punishment*

Skinner, Bandura, Freud   Watson
Maslow

8. The main reason you behave as you do (for example, attend college) is because of conscious *personal* decisions to do so or because *social* factors outside your control leave you little real choice in the matter.

	1	2	3	4	5	6	7	
personal								*social*

Rogers, Maslow, Fromm   Skinner, Bandura, Mischel

9. Human nature is essentially *constructive,* with people showing positive personal growth and a desire to help others fulfill their potentials, or *destructive,* with people showing behavior that is ultimately self-defeating and a desire to keep others from improving themselves.

	1	2	3	4	5	6	7	
constructive								*destructive*

Adler, Rogers, Maslow   Freud

10. Human beings have *no purpose* or reason for their existence other than what they experience on a day-to-day basis, or human beings have some *purpose* for living that is outside themselves.

	1	2	3	4	5	6	7	
no purpose								*purpose*

Skinner, Watson   Adler, Fromm, Horney
Bandura, Mischel   Rogers, Maslow, Jung

Self-Ratings *

M. Bolt

Instructions: Compared with other college students of the same class level and sex as yourself, how would you rate yourself on the following characteristics? Using the following scale in marking your responses:

1 = **Considerably Well Below Average**
2 = **Well Below Average**
3 = **Below Average**
4 = **Slightly Below Average**
5 = **Average**
6 = **Slightly Above Average**
7 = **Above Average**
8 = **Well Above Average**
9 = **Considerably Well Above Average**

_____ 1. leadership ability

_____ 2. athletic ability

_____ 3. ability to get along with others

_____ 4. tolerance

_____ 5. energy level

_____ 6. helpfulness

_____ 7. responsibility

_____ 8. creativeness

_____ 9. patience

_____ 10. trustworthiness

_____ 11. sincerity

_____ 12. thoughtfulness

_____ 13. cooperativeness

_____ 14. reasonableness

_____ 15. intelligence

---

* **Bolt, M. (1993). Self Ratings Inventory. Instructor's Manual to Myers'(1993)** *Social Psychology* **(4th Ed.),** *p. 97.* **New York: McGraw-Hill. Reprinted by permission.**

After completing the Self-Rating questionnaire, calculate your mean score by adding up all 15 items and dividing by 15. Previous demonstrations by the author indicate that almost all students will have mean ratings above the average of 5.0. This self-serving bias, termed the better than average phenomenon, suggests that almost all of us see ourselves as better than average. Myers (1993) suggests the following explanations for this self-serving bias: (1) we like to present a good image to others and ourselves; (2) we assume more responsibility for our successes than our failures and tend to blame occasional failures on circumstances rather than on ourselves; and (3) we are strongly motivated to maintain, enhance, and preserve ourselves.

Score =

Interpretation:

Reference

Myers, D. G. (1993). *Social Psychology (4th Ed.).* New York: McGraw-Hill.

Chapter Twelve
Psychoanalytic Perspective

Beliefs About Freudian Principles

Matthew Merrens & Gary Brannigan

Adapted from Miserandino, M. (1994). Freudian Principles in Everyday Life. *Teaching of Psychology*, 21, (2), 93-95 Scale.

Instructions: The following exercise is designed to assess people's beliefs about their everyday behaviors. Before reading further, complete the following questionnaire.

Respond to each statement by circling one of the following responses: Strongly Disagree (SD), Disagree (D), Neutral (N), Agree (A), or Strongly Agree (SA).

1. Events that occurred during childhood have no effect on one's personality in adulthood.   SD   (D)   N   A   SA

2. Sexual adjustment is easy for most people.   SD   (D)   N   A   SA

3. Culture and society have evolved as ways to curb human beings' natural aggressiveness.   SD   D   N   (A)   SA

4. Little boys should not become too attached to their mothers.   SD   D   N   (A)   SA

5. It is possible to deliberately "forget" something too painful to remember.   (SD)   D   N   A   (SA)

6. People who chronically smoke, eat, or chew gum have some deep psychological problems.   SD   (D)   N   A   SA

7. Competitive people are no more aggressive than noncompetitive people.   SD   D   (N)   A   SA

---

* Miserandino, M. (1994). Beliefs about Freudian Principles. *Teaching of Psychology*, 21, (2), 93-95. Lawrence Erlbaum and Associates, Inc. Reprinted by permission.

8. Fathers should remain somewhat aloof to their daughters.   SD   (D)   N   A   SA

9. Toilet training is natural and not traumatic for most children.   SD   D   N   (A)   SA

10. The phallus is a symbol of power.   SD   D   N   (A)   SA

11. A man who dates a woman old enough to be his mother has problems.   SD   (D)   N   A   SA

12. There are some women who are best described as being "castrating bitches."   SD   D   (N)   A   SA

13. Dreams merely replay events that occurred during the day and have no deep meaning.   (SD)   D   N   A   SA

14. There is something wrong with a woman who dates a man old enough to be her father.   SD   (D)   N   A   SA

15. A student who wants to postpone an exam by saying "My grandmother lied…er, I mean died," should probably be allowed the postponement.   SD   D   N   (A)   SA

SCORING

Each response receives a score of 1 through 5.

ιI ι2   ㉓

Items 3, 4, 5, 6, 8, 10, 11, 12 and 14 are scored as follows: Strongly Disagree = 1, Disagree = 2, Neutral = 3, Agree = 4, and Strongly Agree 5.

Items 1, 2, 7, 9, 13 and 15 are scored in the reverse direction: Strongly Disagree = 5, Disagree = 4, Neutral = 3, Agree = 2, and Strongly Agree = 1.   ㉕

1. Total your scores across the 15 items. High scores (Maximum score = 75) indicate agreement with the Freudian position, and low scores (Minimum score = 15) indicate disagreement with this position.

    SCORE =   43

2. Calculate a mean and standard deviation for the class.

    MEAN =
    SD =

3. How would you interpret the overall agreement/disagreement with Freud's position?

4. Next, calculate means and standard deviations for each of the 15 items separately.

	MEAN	SD		MEAN	SD
1.			9.		
2.			10.		
3.			11.		
4.			12.		
5.			13.		
6.			14.		
7.			15.		
8.					

5. Which items seem to elicit the most agreement? Disagreement? Why?

Personality Assessment
W. B. Davidson[*]

Adapted from Davidson.W.B. (1987). Undergraduate Lab Project in Personality Assessment. Measurement of Anal Character. *Teaching of Psychology*, 14 (2), 101-103. Scale from Kline, P. (1968). Obsessional Traits, Obsessional Symptoms and Anal Eroticism. *British Journal of Medical Psychology*, 41, 299-305.

As Davidson (1987) noted, personality constructs can be difficult to grasp at more than a rudimentary level. Consequently, graphic illustrations of these constructs in people's daily lifestyles can be especially enlightening.

This exercise will give you firsthand, personal experience with a personality scale based on one of Freud's constructs. More information will be provided once you complete the following scale.

Instructions: Respond to each statement by circling one of the following responses: Strongly Disagree (SD), Disagree (D), Neutral (N), Agree (A), or Strongly Agree (SA). Then follow the directions provided at the end of the scale.

1. I keep careful accounts of the money I spend. SD (D) N A SA

2. I like to think out my own methods rather than use other people's. SD D N (A) SA

3. I find more pleasure in doing things than in planning them. SD D N (A) SA

4. There's nothing more infuriating than people who don't keep appointments. SD (D) N A SA

5. I like to see something solid and substantial for my money. SD D N A (SA)

---

[*] Davidson, W. (1968). Measurement of Anal Characters. *Teaching in Psychology*, 14, (2), 101-103, Lawrence Erlbaum and Associates, Inc. Reprinted by permission.

6. I easily change my mind once I've made a decision.

SD   D   (N)   A   SA

7. Only a fool with his/her money does not think of the years ahead.

SD   (D)   N   A   SA

8. I can usually put my hand on anything I want in my room.

SD   (D)   N   A   SA

9. Waste not, want not; every child should have this imprinted on his/her mind.

SD   (D)   N   (A)   SA

10. I continue doing something even when I really know I'm not employing the best method.

SD   D   N   (A)   SA

11. It is sheepish to follow the dictates of style and fashion.

SD   D   N   (A)   SA

12. I have a special place for important documents.

SD   D   N   (A)   SA

SCORING

Each response receives a score of 1 through 5.

13   18   31

Items 1, 2, 4, 5, 7, 8, 9, 10, 11, and 12 are scored as follows: Strongly

Disagree = 1, Disagree = 2, Neutral = 3, Agree = 4, and Strongly Agree 5.

Items 3 and 6 are scored in the reverse direction: Strongly Disagree = 5,

Disagree = 4, Neutral = 3, Agree = 2, and Strongly Agree = 1.   0 5

Total your scores across the 12 items. High scores (Maximum score = 60)
indicate anal retentive tendencies that are characterized by three traits: frugality,
orderliness, and obstinacy/individuality.

SCORE =   57 36

INTERPRETATION

The following table will show how you compare with other college students.

SCORE	PERCENTILE
55	99
52	95
48	90
44	80
42	70
41	60
39	50
37	40
34	30
32	20
31	10
29	5
28	1

1. How well (or poorly) did this scale assess your personality with respect to the three traits mentioned?

2. In what ways might anal retentive traits benefit us in our daily lives?

3. In what ways might they hinder us in our daily lives?

A Sense of Personal Identity [*]
R. Ochse & C. Plug

According to Erik Erikson, most teenagers and young adults struggle to form a sense of personal identity. As with other stages of development, how well you resolve this crisis sets the pattern for future personality development and adjustment. Ochse and Plug (1986) developed a scale to measure the extent to which adults have already successful paved through each of Erikson's eight stages of development. The items for the identity formation versus role confusions stage are presented below. You can take this part of the test yourself by indicating how often each of these statements applies to you, using the following four point scale:

1 = Never Applies To Me
2 = Only occasionally or Seldom Applies To Me
3 = Fairly Often Applies To Me
4 = Very Often Applies To Me

1. I wonder what sort of person I really am.

2. People seem to change their opinions of me.

3. I feel certain about what I should do with my life.

4. I feel uncertain as to whether something is morally right or wrong.

5. Most people seem to agree about what sort of person I am.

6. I feel my way of life suits me.

[*] Ochse, R. and Plug, C. (1986). A Sense of Personal Identity. *Journal of Personality and Social Psychology*, 50, 1240-1252. American Psychological Association (APA). Reprinted by permission.

7. My worth is recognized by others.

8. I feel freer to be my real self when I am away from those who know me very well.

9. I feel that what I am doing in life is not really worthwhile.

10. I feel I fit in well in the community in which I live.

11. I feel proud to be the sort of person I am.

12. People seem to see me very differently from the way I see myself.

13. I feel left out.

14. People seem to disapprove of me.

15. I change my ideas about what I want from life.

16. I am unsure as to how people feel about me.

17. My feelings about myself change.

18. I feel I am putting on an act or doing something for effect.

19. I feel proud to be a member of the society in which I live.

SCORING

To obtain your score, first reverse the values you assigned to items 1, 2, 4, 8, 9, 12, 13, 14, 15, 16, 17, and 18. That is, for these items, change an answer of 1 to 4, 2 to 3, 3 to 2, and 4 to 1. The values for the remaining items stay the same. Then add all the values for all 19 items.

Ochse and Plug (1986) found average scores for the scale between 56 and 58 when they administered it to South African citizens between the ages of 15 and 60. The standard deviation for this score was between seven and eight, indicated that the majority of people obtain scores that fall within seven or eight points of these average scores. Scores considerably higher than this indicate a particularly well developed sense of identity, whereas significantly lower scores suggest the test taken is still progressing through the identity development stage.

Chapter Thirteen
Neo-analytic Perspective

Early Recollections *

L. Parrott

Based on Parrott, L. (1992). Earliest Recollections and Birth Order: Two Adlerian Exercises. *Teaching of Psychology, 19,* 40-42.

*B*efore reading further, write out a detailed account of your earliest memory.

Consider the following questions (Parrott, 1992, p. 41) in examining your early recollections.

a. **Who is present in your early recollections?**

* Merrens, Matthew and Brannigan, Gary. (1992). Early Recollections. *Teaching of Psychology,* 19, 40-42, Lawrence Erlbaum and Associates, Inc. Reprinted by permission.

b. How are different people portrayed (basic thoughts and feelings)?

c. What is the world like (e.g., friendly, hostile, depressing, exciting)?

d. What is your role or behavior?

e. What is the outcome of your behavior?

f. What is your primary social attitude (i.e., I or we)?

g. What is your dominant emotion (e.g., happy, worried, fearful, proud, guilty)?

h. What is your primary motive (e.g., to help, to gain attention, to exert power)?

i. What are the underlying themes?

Adler (1959) considered early recollections "the most trustworthy way of exploring personality"(p. 92) "because they often encapsulate a person's life theme or script" (Parrott, 1992, p. 40). As Parrott (1992) noted, in contrast to "Freud's belief that the past determines the future, Adler believed that the present determines the past" (p. 40). More specifically, Adler (1958) noted:

> There are no "chance memories." Out of the incalculable number of impressions which meet an individual, he must choose to remember only those which he feels, however darkly, to have a bearing on his situation (p. 73).

Therefore, "if people live their lives believing that others are always trying to humiliate them, the memories they are likely to recall will be interpreted as humiliating experiences" (Parrott, 1992, p. 41).

Your response to the questions above should shed some light on your life-style---that is, your view of yourself, your role in life, and the world in general.

REFERENCES

Adler, A. (1958). *What Life Should Mean To You.* New York: Capricorn.

Adler, A. (1959). *The Practice and Theory of Individual Psychology.* Totowa, NJ: Littlefield Adams.

Parrott, L. (1992). Earliest Recollections and Birth Order: Two Adlerian Exercises. *Teaching of Psychology*, 19, 40-42.

Chapter Fourteen

Dispositional Perspective

Hostility

E. Dolnick

Gauging your hostility quotient isn't as simple as measuring blood pressure or cholesterol. But the following 12 questions---supplied by Redford Williams, Director of Behavioral Research at Duke University and the author of Anger Kills---could indicate whether a hostile temperament is getting the best of you. Circle yes or no for each of the questions.

Y **N** 1. Have you ever been so angry at someone that you've thrown things or slammed the door?

Y **N** 2. Do you tend to remember irritating incidents and get mad all over again?

Y **N** 3. Do little annoyances have a way of adding up during the day, leaving you frustrated and impatient?

Y **N** 4. Stuck in a long line at the express checkout in the grocery store, do you often count to see if anyone ahead of you has more than ten items?

Y **N** 5. If the person who cuts your hair trims off more than you wanted, do you fume about it for days afterward?

Y **N** 6. When someone cuts you off in traffic, do you flash your lights or honk your horn?

Y **N** 7. Over the past few years, have you dropped any close friends because they just didn't live up to your expectations?

Y **N** 8. Do you find yourself getting annoyed at little things your spouse does that get under your skin?

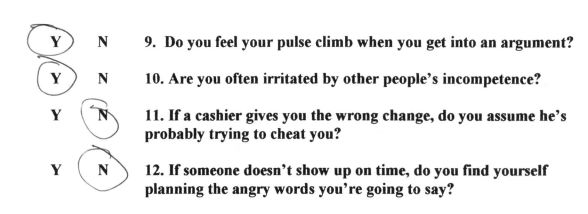

Y N 9. Do you feel your pulse climb when you get into an argument?

Y N 10. Are you often irritated by other people's incompetence?

Y **N** 11. If a cashier gives you the wrong change, do you assume he's probably trying to cheat you?

Y **N** 12. If someone doesn't show up on time, do you find yourself planning the angry words you're going to say?

Men, Women and Anger[∞]

We All Get Angry

According to a number of studies, women and men tend to get angry equally often (about six or seven times a week), equally intense; and for more or less the same reasons. Tests designed to reveal aggressive feelings, hidden anger, or hostility turned toward inward haven't discovered any sex differences at all.

Men Explode, Women Mostly Seethe

Some angry women do shout and pound their fists, of course---just as some men do. But in general, studies show, women and men have very different styles when it comes to getting angry. Women are more likely to express anger by crying, for example, or to keep their anger under wraps. "Women have cornered the market on the seething, unspoken fury that is always threatening to explode," says Anne Campbell, a psychologist at England's Durham University. Women are also more likely to express their anger in private. They might get angry at a boss or coworker, but chances are they'll wait until they're alone or with a spouse or close friend to show their anger.

In Women, An Angry Outburst, Then Regret

Surveys show that anger itself means different things to men than it does to women. Men's anger tends to be uncomplicated by restraint and guilt, says Campbell. It is straightforwardly about winning and losing. Women are more

[∞] Dolnick, E. (1995), July/August). Hotheads and Heart Attacks. *Health*, pp. 58-64. Reprinted from Health, Copyright © 1995, with permission.

likely to feel embarrassed when they show anger, equating it with a loss of control, she says. Women are also more likely than men to believe their anger is out of proportion to the events that cause it. "After an outburst," she says, "women tell themselves, 'Whoa! Get a grip.' Men say, 'That ought to show him.'" According to one study, the more furious a woman gets, the longer it takes her to get over the episode. That's not true for men---at least not to the same degree.

The way women and men view crying is different, too. According to Campbell and other researchers, men often see women's crying as a sign of remorse or contrition---or as a tactic used to win a fight. Women are more likely to view crying as a sign of frustration or rage---a way to release tension. According to one study, 78 percent of women who cried during fights did so out of frustration.

So what does all this mean for women's risk of heart disease? Researchers say that whether anger is expressed through clenched teeth or raised voices, in public or private, it appears to wreak the same havoc on the heart.

Evolutionary Perspectives Questionnaire[∞]

B. Weiner

Complete the following questions before reading further about this exercise.

1. You are on a boat that overturns. It contains your 5-year-old and your 1-year-old children (of the same sex). The boat sinks and you can save only one. Whom do you choose to save? Circle one.

    5-year-old   1-year-old

2. That same boat (you are slow to learn lessons) contains your 40-year-old and 20-year-old children (both of the same sex). Neither can swim. As the boat sinks, whom do you choose to save? Circle one.

    40-year-old   **20-year-old**

3. You and your spouse are the proud parents of a new child. The grandparents are ecstatic. Who do you think will be kinder to the child? Circle one.

    The mother of the mother   **The mother of the father**

4. Who will mourn at the death of a child? Circle the answer in each pair.

    a. father   **mother**
    b. **parents of the father**   parents of the mother
    c. **younger parents**   **older parents**

5. Which will elicit more grief? Circle the answer in each pair.

       a. death of a son   death of a daughter
       b. death of an unhealthy child   death of a healthy child

The questionnaire you completed will allow you to become familiar with the major concepts of evolutionary psychology, a new and important method of viewing personality. Evolutionary thinking suggests that humans are basically motivated to extend their own genetic makeup. Basically, our genes influence us to behave in a manner that facilitates our chance of surviving and reproducing. The following analysis is based on Weiner's (1992) presentation.

Analyzing The Evolutionary Perspective Questionnaire

Questions #1 and #2: Most respondents will select the 5-year old (#1) and the 20-year old (#2) for their answers. The evolutionary reasoning for this is that children are more likely to die between 1 and 5, and the 5-year-olds are more likely to live and reproduce. Selecting an older child in #1 will lead to a better chance of continuation of the gene pool. Using the same reasoning, a 20-year-old would be a better candidate for reproduction than a 40-year-old and therefore would in the same way perpetuate the gene pool.

Question #3: Men cannot be sure that women have positively given birth to their offspring, whereas women are always sure that the baby they bear is theirs. The woman's parents (baby's maternal grandparents) therefore are sure that they are contributing 25% of the child's genetic endowment. The man's parents (baby's paternal grandparents) cannot be certain that they have contributed any genetic material to the child and therefore may be less ecstatic and kinder.

Question #4: Evolutionary views predict that the greater the genetic investment, the greater will be the joy and the greater will be the grief should the child die. Therefore, those individuals with the greater genetic ties will feel the most significant loss (mother, parents of mother and older parents). Older parents are selected over younger because they are less likely to have more offspring.

Question #5: The death of a healthy son will yield the greatest grief. Why is this so from an evolutionary perspective?

Chapter Fifteen
Humanistic Perspective

Peak Experience [∞]

J. Polyson

By describing and analyzing a meaningful personal event in your life, this exercise will help you to understand Maslow's concept of the peak experience. In the space below, describe a peak experience you have had. To quote from Maslow's book *Toward A Psychology of Being*, "think of the most wonderful experience of your life: the happiest moments, ecstatic moments, moments of rapture" (1962, p. 67)

[∞] Adapted from Polyson, J. (1985). Students' Peak Experiences: A Written Exercise. *Teaching of Psychology* 12 (4), 211-213. Lawrence Erlbaum and Associates, Inc. Reprinted by permission.

Peak Experience

After completing your essay, respond to the following questions:

1. Where were you at the time of this peak experience?

2. What were you doing?

3. How did you feel during this experience?

4. How did you feel after the experience?

5. What did the experience mean for you?

6. What does the experience mean to you now?

Reference

Maslow, A. H. (1962). *Toward A Psychology of Being.* New York: Van Nostrand.

Q-Sort[∞]

Matthew Merrens & Gary Brannigan

This exercise is designed to give you experience with the Q-Sort Technique—a major assessment device used by humanistic psychologists. While the actual procedure is more comprehensive, this modified version will give you an opportunity to experience the Q-Sort. In this exercise, you will first sort the 25 statement cards according to your perception of your "actual" self. You will then re-sort the statement cards according to your perception of your "ideal" self. After each sort, you will record the rank-order placement of each statement card so that you will be able to make a comparison in the form of a correlation. The correlation will yield information about the relationship between your actual and ideal self-perceptions.

Procedure

1. Cut out the 25 statement cards and the nine category cards on the following pages.

2. Arrange the nine category cards in a line ranging from #1 to #9 on a table. In each of the two "sorts" that you will be doing, you are required to place a specific number of statements in each of the nine categories. The following distribution will tell you how many of the 25 statement cards must be placed in each of the nine categories:

Category	No. of Statements	Rank No.
1 Most Characteristic	1	1
2 Very Characteristic	2	2.5
3 Moderately Characteristic	3	5
4 Mildly Characteristic	4	8.5
5 Neutral	5	13
6 Mildly Uncharacteristic	4	17.5
7 Moderately Uncharacteristic	3	21
8 Very Uncharacteristic	2	23.5
9 Most uncharacteristic	1	25

[∞] Merrens, M. and Brannigan, G . (1998). Q-Sort. *Experiences in Personality, 179-185.* New York: John Wiley & Sons, Inc. Reprinted by permission.

3. First sort (Actual Self)---sort the 25 statement cards into the nine categories according to how you feel these statements characterize your Actual Self. After you complete the sorting, transfer the rank number associated with each category to the Data Sheet. For example, if you put "independent" in Category 4, you would enter "8.5" on the Data Sheet in the Actual Self Rank column next to "Independent."

4. Second sort (Ideal Self)---sort the 25 statement cards into the nine categories according to how you feel these statements characterize your Ideal Self. After you complete the sorting, transfer the rank number associated with each category to the Data Sheet. For example, if your put "Assertive" in Category 8, you would enter "23.5" on the Data Sheet in the Ideal Self Rank column next to "Assertive."

5. Actual-Ideal Correlation---steps (a) to (f) will guide you through the calculation of a rank-order correlation (rho) that will compare your ratings of actual and ideal self. The actual formula that the calculation is based on:

$$rho = 1 - \frac{6 \sum D^2}{N (N^2 - 1)}$$

D = absolute difference between actual and ideal self ratings.

N = number of ranked pairs, in this case, 25.

a. Obtain the absolute difference between actual and ideal ranking for each self characteristic by subtracting the smaller rank from the larger rank. This is the Absolute Rank Difference score. Do this for all 25 self characteristics.
b. Square each Absolute Rank Difference Score and sum up all 25 squared differences.
c. Multiply the sum of the differences by 6.
d. Take the outcome of step c and divide it by 15,600.
e. Subtract the outcome of step d from +1.00.
f. The number you obtained in step 3 will be the rho between your actual and ideal self. The number must lie between -1.00 and +1.00. If it doesn't, you made an arithmetic error.

   Correlation =

Interpretation of Correlation

A positive correlation indicates a similarity (i.e., congruence) between actual and ideal self, whereas a negative correlation indicates a dissimilarity (i.e., incongruence), respectively.   The following graphic display illustrates this interpretation.

-1.00...0...+1.00

| High | Moderate | Mild | Mild | Moderate | High |
| Dissimilarity | Dissimilarity | Dissimilarity | Similarity | Similarity | Similarity |

Another approach to interpretation is to review the particular shifts in placement of statement cards between actual and ideal self ratings. Shifts of specific statement card ratings tell you a great deal about how individual self characteristics are viewed. For example, what characteristics would you ideally like to have as part of your self that are currently not characteristic?

Q-Sort Data Sheet

Self Characteristic	Actual Self Rank	Ideal Self Rank	Absolute Rank Difference	Difference Squared
Independent				
Assertive				
Sociable				
Studious				
Confident				
Helpful				
Open-minded				
Careful about Appearance				
Insightful				
High personal Standards				
Goal-oriented				
Adventurous				
Energetic				
Happy				
Responsible				
Tolerant of Others				
Exercise Regularly				
Wide interests				
Eat Right				
Even-tempered				
Creative				
Competent				
Organized				
A Leader				
Enjoy leisure				

Category 1	Category 2	Category 3
Most Characteristic	**Very Characteristic**	**Moderately Characteristic**
1 statement	2 statements	3 statements
Category 4	**Category 5**	**Category 6**
Mildly Characteristic	**Neutral**	**Mildly Uncharacteristic**
4 statements	5 statements	4 statements
Category 7	**Category 8**	**Category 9**
Moderately Uncharacteristic	**Very Uncharacteristic**	**Most Uncharacteristic**
3 statements	2 statements	1 statement

A Leader	Enjoy Leisure Time	Helpful	Confident
Studious	Organized	Competent	Insightful
Open-Minded	Assertive	Creative	Independent
Careful About Appearance	Even-Tempered	Sociable	High Personal Standards
Tolerant of Others	Adventurous	Eat Right	Wide Interests
Responsible	Exercise Regularly	Happy	Energetic
Goal-Oriented			

Chapter Sixteen
Behavioral Perspective

Observing And Recording A Personal Behavior[∞]

Matthew Merrens & Gary Brannigan

The best way to appreciate and understand the behavioral perspective is to engage actively in the process of recording and analyzing a segment of your own behavior. The initial step will be for you to choose a behavior that you engage in on a regular basis. The following is a list of some behaviors that students have selected in the past:

Smoking	*Fears*	*Eating*	*Smiling*
Studying	*Exercise*	*Arguing*	*Using Profanities*
Nail Biting	*Socializing*	*Sleep*	*Hair Twirling*
Telephoning	*Looking in Mirror*		

This list is meant to give you an idea of some possibilities. Don't think of it as the definitive list for you to choose from. The list suggests some ideas to help you select a behavior that you want to observe and record. It is often interesting to record a behavior that you might want to modify (e.g., increase or decrease the frequency of occurrence). A project that is important to you will be more fun and ultimately yield more useful information. Remember to pick a behavior that occurs with sufficient frequency so that you have something to record. (Do not pick how many times a day you run a 1-minute mile (likely to be never) or how many times you move your thumb (likely to be too frequent).

[∞] **Merrens, M. and Brannigan, G . (1998). Observing and Recording A Personal Behavior.** *Experiences in Personality, 157-160.* **New York: John Wiley & Sons, Inc. Reprinted by permission.**

Guidelines

1. Make sure the behavior you are observing and recording is clearly specified so that you don't have to make decisions about whether it has occurred. Clear up all doubts about the characteristics of the response before you start recording.

2. While recording your behavior look for the situations in which the behavior occurs and what happens once you initiate the behavior. Behaviors often do not occur in a random manner, and they often have consequences that are significant. For example, some people smoke while driving or studying but not while eating or watching TV. Some smokers experience coughing or nausea after smoking. Recognizing the context in which behaviors occur and the consequences of the behaviors give us useful information for analysis and behavior change.

3. There are two basic ways of recording behavior: (a) counting the frequency of the occurrence of the behavior, and (b) recording the time duration of the behavior. If you are interested in your smoking behavior, you could count the number of cigarettes you smoke per day (frequency) or the amount of time, in minutes and seconds, you engage in smoking. With some behaviors a frequency counting system is easier to employ (e.g., smoking), while with other behaviors, duration may be more desirable (e.g., running, swimming). Whatever system you use, be sure it adequately reflects the behavior you are interested in. A student who was interested in her telephone usage set up a system in which she recorded the number of phone calls she made each day. The results indicated that she made one or two phone calls a day, which did not seem to be a problem. On closer inspection, the results revealed that she mostly talked to her boyfriend, who attended another college, and that each phone call lasted 1 to 2 hours. The student should have used a duration measure, recording the amount of time engaged in talking on the phone behavior. By doing so, the data would have better reflected her behavior. Her behavior should not have been the frequency of phone calling but rather the time spent on the phone.

4. It is important to record behavior as it occurs without delay. Don't attempt to remember the data and record them later. A good system is to carry a file card with you and keep records up to date by recording the frequency or time durations immediately. Be strict and count all occurrences, even if you are surprised, elated, or annoyed by the data. Don't use other people to help you recognize or record your behaviors. It is important for you to be alert and focus on the target behavior you have identified. It is important not to intervene or modify your behavior intentionally during this recording project. Sometimes people discover unexpectedly high or low rates of behavior in a study like this and immediately attempt to intervene. For

example, if a student who believes he is studying 3 hours per night discovered by careful recording that he is actually studying only 40 minutes per night, he might want to make some behavioral changes. Indeed, recording one's behavior may serve not only as a method of analysis but also as a treatment. Once you have discovered the actual rate of certain behaviors, you may immediately want to intervene to increase or decrease their occurrence. For this project, try to restrain yourself from making personal changes and complete the recording period without modifying your actions.

5. At the end of each day, transfer your daily data to a permanent record that you keep at home. This lessens the danger of losing all the data if you misplace the daily record card. You should record your behavior for (7) to 10 consecutive days. This will allow you to observe the effect of days of the week, particularly the weekend, on your data. It is a long enough period of time to allow you to get a sense of the typical rates of the behavior. The period of recording in behavioral interventions is referred to as the *baseline*. It is the period that reflects typical behaviors and the period against which behavioral interventions and treatments are compared.

6. It is also useful to graph the data so that you can get a visual picture of your recorded behavior. The following graph is a sample of what you might use for this exercise. Use the X and Y axes on the next page to display your data.

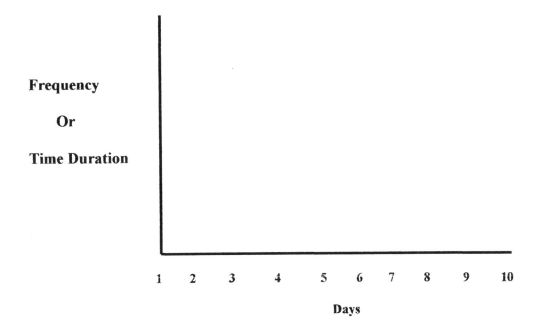

323

Your Behavior Recording

Target Behavior: _____

Specific Behavior Recorded: _____

Method of Recording: _____

Data:

      Day 1. _____

      Day 2. _____

      Day 3. _____

      Day 4. _____

      Day 5. _____

      Day 6. _____

      Day 7. _____

      Day 8. _____

      Day 9. _____

      Day 10. _____

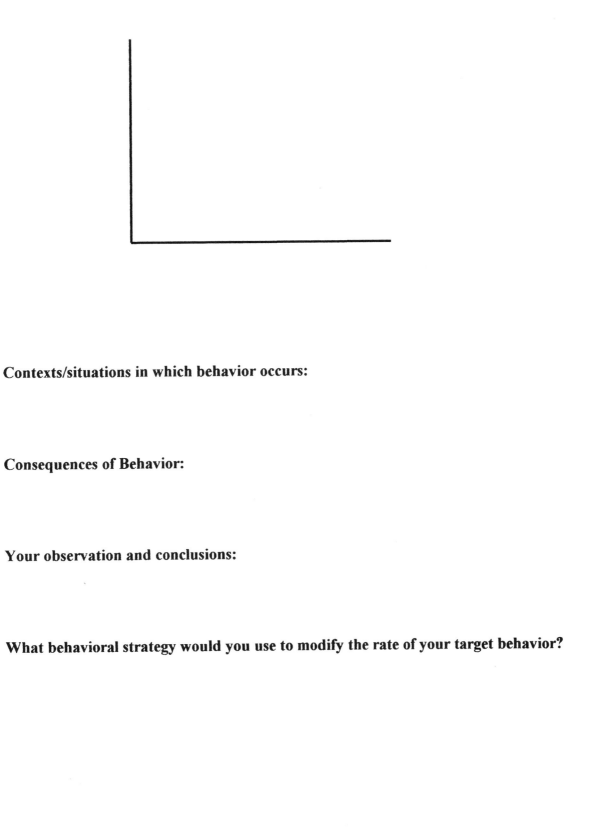

Contexts/situations in which behavior occurs:

Consequences of Behavior:

Your observation and conclusions:

What behavioral strategy would you use to modify the rate of your target behavior?

Assertiveness [∞]

S. D. Rathus

Assertive behavior has been investigated by behaviorists for many years. A significant number of people find it difficult to act in an assertive manner and often resort to passive behaviors. For example, it is appropriate to state complaints when you feel they are justified rather than to accept poor service or a mediocre product. Although assertiveness is not passivity, it is also not aggressive behavior. Behavior therapists have been successful in treating nonassertive behavior through a variety of strategies. This exercise will assess your level of assertiveness and give you a chance to compare your score to established norms.

Directions: Indicate how well each item describes you by using this code:

3 = Very Much Like Me	-1 = Slightly Unlike Me
2 = Rather Like Me	-2 = Rather Unlike Me
1 = Slightly Like Me	-3 = Very Much Unlike Me

___ 1. **Most people seem to be more aggressive and assertive than I am.** *

___ 2. **I have hesitated to make or accept dates because of "shyness."** *

___ 3. **When the food served at a restaurant is not done to my satisfaction, I complain about it to the waiter or waitress.**

___ 4. **I am careful to avoid hurting other people's feelings, even when I feel that I have been injured.** *

∞ **Rathus, S.D. (1973). A 30-Item Schedule for Assessing Assertive Behavior.** *Behavior Therapy, 4, 399-400.* **Copyright © 1973 by the Association for the Advancement of Behavior Therapy. Reprinted by permission of the publisher and author.**

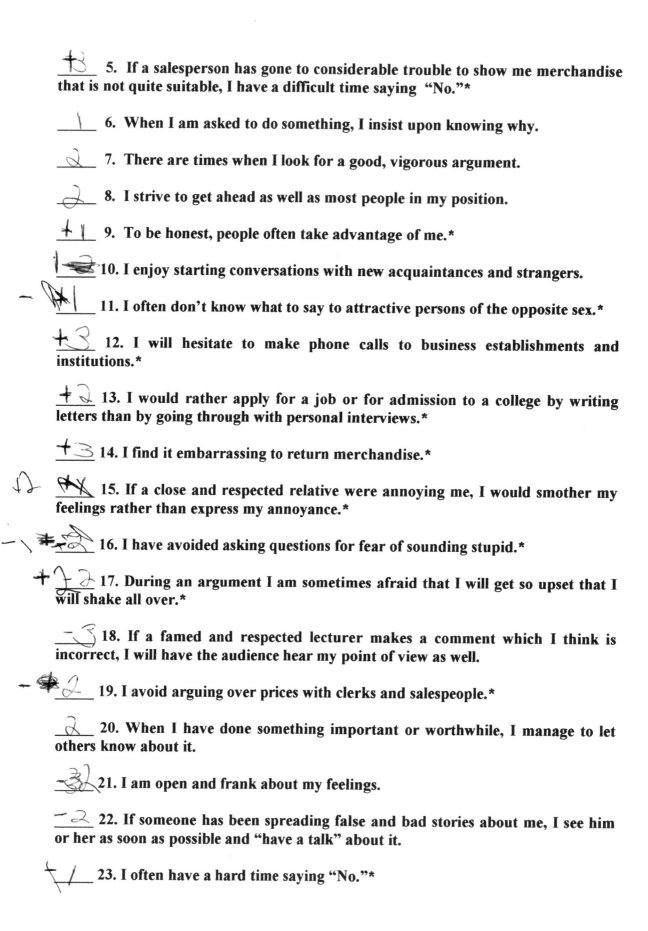

_+3_ 5. If a salesperson has gone to considerable trouble to show me merchandise that is not quite suitable, I have a difficult time saying "No."*

_1_ 6. When I am asked to do something, I insist upon knowing why.

_2_ 7. There are times when I look for a good, vigorous argument.

_2_ 8. I strive to get ahead as well as most people in my position.

_+1_ 9. To be honest, people often take advantage of me.*

_10. I enjoy starting conversations with new acquaintances and strangers.

_11. I often don't know what to say to attractive persons of the opposite sex.*

_+3_ 12. I will hesitate to make phone calls to business establishments and institutions.*

_+2_ 13. I would rather apply for a job or for admission to a college by writing letters than by going through with personal interviews.*

_+3_ 14. I find it embarrassing to return merchandise.*

_15. If a close and respected relative were annoying me, I would smother my feelings rather than express my annoyance.*

_16. I have avoided asking questions for fear of sounding stupid.*

_17. During an argument I am sometimes afraid that I will get so upset that I will shake all over.*

_-3_ 18. If a famed and respected lecturer makes a comment which I think is incorrect, I will have the audience hear my point of view as well.

_19. I avoid arguing over prices with clerks and salespeople.*

_2_ 20. When I have done something important or worthwhile, I manage to let others know about it.

_21. I am open and frank about my feelings.

_-2_ 22. If someone has been spreading false and bad stories about me, I see him or her as soon as possible and "have a talk" about it.

_23. I often have a hard time saying "No."*

328

24. I tend to bottle up my emotions rather than make a scene.*

25. I complain about poor service in a restaurant and elsewhere.

26. When I am given a compliment, I sometimes just don't know what to say.*

27. If a couple near me in a theatre or at a lecture were conversing rather loudly, I would ask them to be quiet or to take their conversation elsewhere.

28. Anyone attempting to push ahead of me in a line is in for a good battle.

29. I am quick to express an opinion.

30. There are times when I just can't say anything.*

Scoring[∞]

Tabulate your score as follows. For those items followed by an asterisk (*), change the signs (plus to minus, minus to plus). For example, if the response to an asterisked item was 2, place a minus sign (-) before the two. If the response to an asterisked (*) item was -3, change the minus sign to a plus sign (+) by adding a vertical stroke. Then add up the scores of the 30 items. Scores on the assertiveness schedule can vary from +90 to -90.

Score =

Interpretation

The following table will show you how your score compares to those of 764 college women and 637 men from 35 campuses across the United States. For example, if you are a woman and your score was 26, it exceeds that of 80 percent of the women in the sample. A score or 15 for a male exceeds that of 55-60 percent of the men in the sample.

Women's Scores	Percentile	Men's Scores
55	99	65
48	97	54
45	95	48
37	90	40
31	85	33
26	80	30
23	75	26

[∞] Nevid, J., S. & Rathus, S.D. (1978). Multivariate and Normative Data Pertaining to the RAS with a College Population.. *Behavior Therapy, 9, 675.* Copyright © 1978 by the Association for the Advancement of Behavior Therapy. Reprinted by permission of the publisher and author.

Women's Scores Cont.	Percentile	Men's Scores
19	70	24
17	65	19
14	60	17
11	55	15
8	50	11
6	45	8
2	40	6
-1	35	3
-4	30	1
-8	25	-3
-13	20	-7
-17	15	-11
-24	10	-15
-34	5	-24
-39	3	-30
-48	1	-41

Life Orientation Test[∞]

Scheier & Carver

_____

Indicate the extent to which you agree with each of the following statements using the following response scale:

Key:
0 = Strongly Disagree
1 = Disagree
2 = Neutral
3 = Agree
4 = Strongly Agree

Place the appropriate number in the blank before each item.

1. In uncertain times, I usually expect the best.

2. It's easy for me to relax.

3. If something can go wrong for me, it will.

4. I always look on the bright side of things.

5. I'm always optimistic about my future.

6. I enjoy my friends a lot.

7. It's important for me to keep busy.

[∞] Scheier, M. & Carver, C. (1985). Optimism, Coping, and Health: Assessment and Implications of Generalized Outcome Expectancies. *Health Psychology, 4, 219-220.* Reprinted by permission from American Psychological Association (APA).

8. I hardly ever expect things to go my way.

9. Things never work out the way I want them to.

10. I don't get upset too easily.

11. I'm a believer in the idea that "every cloud has a silver lining."

12. I rarely count on good things happening to me.

Scoring

The Life Orientation Test, which you just completed, was developed by Scheier and Carver (1985) to measure how favorably or unfavorably one sees the future. In essence, it is an assessment of optimism/pessimism. To obtain your score on this measure, follow these steps:

1.   For questions 3, 8, 9 and 12, reverse the ratings you assigned (a score of 0 becomes 4, a score of 1 becomes a 3, a score of 2 remains the same, a score of 3 becomes a 1, and a score of 4 becomes a 0).

2.   Questions 2, 6, 7, and 10 do not count. They are referred to as filler questions and are used to disguise the true nature of the test.

3.   Sum up your scores on questions 1, 3, 4, 5, 8, 9, 11 and 12.

   Score =

4. Because there are eight scorable items with ratings from 0 to 4, it is possible to obtain a final score of 0 to 32. Research has indicated that the mean score is close to 21.

Interpretation

Scheier and Carver's (1993) article describes the research on optimism and strongly suggests the benefits of this orientation in a number of areas of adaptation. Optimists tend to cope more effectively in stressful situations, they are more focused in attempting to deal with problems, they tend to learn from negative experiences, and they plan to deal with bad times through direct actions. In terms of health and physical adjustment, optimists do better in surgery and in postoperative recovery.

Furthermore, optimism is negatively correlated with postpartum depression. In terms of adjustment, students who are optimistic make better adjustments to college life than their pessimistic peers.

Reference

Scheier, M., & Carver, C. (1993). On the Power of Positive Thinking: The Benefits of Being Optimistic. *Current Directions in Psychological Science, 2,* 26-30.

Part Three

Applications and Exercises in Personality

Key Questions

1. In your opinion, what are some of the advantages and disadvantages of participating in personality research that requires you to respond to self-report inventories, questionnaires, interviews and projective techniques?

2. Were you surprised with the results of your response to Potkay and Allen's **Personal Personality Theory Questionnaire**? Do you agree with your theoretical orientation(s)? In what way(s) might your theoretical orientation change after completing a course in personality psychology?

3. Do you agree that your in-depth examination of Sigmund Freud's theory might have unconsciously influenced your responses to Miserandino's personality inventory, **Beliefs About Freudian Principles**? If so, in what way(s)?

4. What are your initial impressions of Davidson's **Personality Assessment** questionnaire? Do you believe that this instrument measures Freud's anal retentive personality characterized by frugality, orderliness, and obstinacy/individuality?

5. Administer Ochse and Plug's **A Sense of Personality Identity** inventory to several individuals and compile some statistics on their achievement of Erikson's sense of identity versus role confusion? Were you surprised by your findings? If so, in what way(s)?

6. Do you believe that test-taking responses such as social desirability or response acquiescence might influence an individual's response to Schlenker and Leary's **Social Anxiety Scale?** Why?

7. From a dispositional perspective, do the surveys listed in chapter fourteen accurately measure temperament, achievement motivation, and response tendency?

8. After taking Merrens and Brannigan's **Q-Sort Technique**, did you determine your self concept to be in a state of congruence or incongruence? If incongruent, how might you bridge the gap between the real and ideal self?

9. What does "self-actualization" mean to you? How do the results of your self-actualization performance on Jones and Crandall's **Self-Actualization** inventory compare with the norms of other college students?

10. Identify some other behaviors that you might observe using Merrens and Brannigan's **Personal Behavior Record.**

Part Three

Applications and Exercises in Personality

Suggested Readings

Bullock, W. A . & K. Gilliland. (1993). Eysenck's Arousal Theory of Introversion-Extroversion: A Converging Investigation. *Journal of Personality and Social Psychology*, 64, 113-123.

Cartwright, D. DeBruin, J., & S. Berg. (1991). Some Scales for Assessing Personality Based on Carl Rogers' Theory: Further Evidence of Validity. *Personality and Individual Differences,* 12, 151-156.

Cote, J. E. & C. G. Levine. (1994). An Empirical Test of Erikson's Theory of Ego Identity Formation. *Youth and Society,* 20, 388-415.

Cramer, P. (1987, December). The Development of Defense Mechanisms. *Journal Of Personality,* 55 (4), 597-614.

Dolnick, E. (1995, July/August). Hotheads and Heart Attacks. *Health,* pp. 58-64.

Domino, G. & D. D. Affonso. (1990). A Personality Measure of Erikson's Life Stages: The Inventory of Social Balance. *Journal of Personality Assessment,* 54, 576-588.

Merrens, M. R. & G. G. Brannigan. (1998). *Experiences in Personality.* New York: John Wiley & Sons .

Myers, I. (1962). *The Myers-Briggs Type Indicator.* Princeton, NJ: Educational Testing Service.

Parrott, L. (1992). Earliest Recollections and Birth Order: Two Adlerian Exercises. *Teaching of Psychology,* 19, 40-42.

Weiner, B. (1992). Evolutional Perspectives Questionnaire. *Human Motivation: Metaphors, Theories and Research.* Thousand Oaks, CA: Sage Press.